THE ROUGH RIDERS

Theodore Roosevelt
THE ROUGH
RIDERS

Caleb Carr
SERIES EDITOR

Introduction by Edmund Morris

THE MODERN LIBRARY

NEW YORK

Modern Library Paperback Edition

Biographical note copyright © 1996 by Random House, Inc.
Introduction © 1999 by Edmund Morris
Series Introduction © 1999 by Caleb Carr

LIBRARY OF CONGRESS CATALOGING-IN-PUBLICATION DATA
Roosevelt, Theodore, 1858–1919.
The Rough Riders / by Theodore Roosevelt. — Modern Library
paperback ed.
p.   cm.
Originally published: New York: C. Scribner's, 1899.
ISBN 0-375-75476-8
1. United States. Army. Volunteer Cavalry, 1st—History.
2. Spanish-American War, 1898—Regimental histories.   3. Roosevelt,
Theodore, 1858–1919.   4. Spanish-American War, 1898—Personal narratives.
I. Title.
E725.45 1st.R64   1999
973.8'94—dc21   99-25584

Modern Library website address: www.modernlibrary.com

Printed in the United States of America

BVG 01

THEODORE ROOSEVELT

Theodore Roosevelt—the naturalist, writer, historian, soldier, and politician who became twenty-sixth president of the United States—was born in New York City on October 27, 1858, into a distinguished family. He was the second of four children of Theodore Roosevelt, Sr., a wealthy philanthropist of Dutch descent, and the former Martha ("Mittie") Bulloch, an aristocratic Southern belle. An endlessly inquisitive young man, he was especially interested in natural history, which became the focus of his first published works, *Summer Birds of the Adirondacks* (1877) and *Notes on Some of the Birds of Oyster Bay* (1879). Upon graduating Phi Beta Kappa from Harvard in 1880 Roosevelt briefly studied law. The next year he was elected to the New York State Assembly on the Republican ticket and soon made a name for himself as a historian with *The Naval War of 1812* (1882).

Following the death of his wife, Alice, in childbirth in 1884, Roosevelt sought change and headed west to ranch lands he had acquired in the Dakota Territory. The young outdoorsman chronicled his years in the Bad Lands in *Hunting Trips of a Ranchman* (1885), the first volume in the nature trilogy that eventually included *Ranch Life and the Hunting-Trail* (1888) and *The Wilderness*

Hunter (1893). After failing to win the New York City mayoral election in 1886 as a self-styled "Cowboy Candidate," Roosevelt married childhood sweetheart Edith Kermit Carow and retired for a time to Sagamore Hill, his estate at Oyster Bay, Long Island. He wrote *Gouveneur Morris* (1888), a biography of the revolutionary-era statesman intended as a companion to the political memoir *Life of Thomas Hart Benton* (1887) and conceived the masterful four-volume history *The Winning of the West* (1889–1896).

Roosevelt returned to public life in 1889. Appointed Civil Service Commissioner he spent the next six years in Washington energetically pushing for reform of the government system, all the while propelling himself into the national spotlight. In 1895 he accepted a position as member, and later president, of the Board of Police Commissioners of New York City. Known as "a man you can't cajole, can't frighten, can't buy," Roosevelt continued to enjoy growing prestige nationwide, and within two years he was named assistant secretary of the navy under President William McKinley. Resigning this office in May 1898 at the outbreak of the Spanish-American War, Roosevelt helped organize and train the "Rough Riders," a regiment of the First U.S. Volunteer Cavalry whose legendary exploits he recorded in *The Rough Riders* (1899). A popular hero upon returning from Cuba, Roosevelt was elected governor of New York in November 1898, and two years later he became vice president of the United States in the second administration of William McKinley.

The assassination of President McKinley in September 1901 placed Roosevelt in the White House, and he was elected president in 1904. For the remainder of the decade he embodied the boundless confidence of the nation as it entered the American Century. He promised a square deal for the workingman, brought about trust-busting reforms aimed at regulating big business, and instituted modern-day environmental measures. The first American leader to play an important role in world affairs, Roosevelt guided construction of the Panama Canal, advocated a "big stick" policy to enforce the Monroe Doctrine, and sought to keep the Open Door course in China. In 1906 he was awarded the Nobel Peace Prize for resolving the Russo-Japanese War.

After leaving office in 1909 he took an almost yearlong hunting trip to Africa and described his adventures in *African Game Trails* (1910). In 1912 he made a bid for reelection on the progressive Bull Moose ticket but lost to Woodrow Wilson, who became a bitter enemy. Afterward he completed *Theodore Roosevelt: An Autobiography* (1913) and *Through the Brazilian Wilderness* (1914), an account of his explorations in South America. With the outbreak of World War I, Roosevelt became an outspoken advocate of United States military preparedness in books such as *America and the World War* (1915). His last work, *The Great Adventure*, appeared in 1918. Still entertaining the idea of running again for office, Theodore Roosevelt died in his sleep at Sagamore Hill on January 6, 1919.

Introduction to the Modern Library War Series

Caleb Carr

The term "military history" has always been a bit of a problem for me, as it has, I suspect, for many other students of the discipline. The uninitiated seem to have a prejudicial belief that those who study war are an exceedingly odd lot: men (few women enter the field) who at best have never outgrown boyhood and at worst are somewhat alienated, perhaps even dangerous, characters. Of course, much of this general attitude was formed during the sixties and early seventies (my own high school and college years), when an interest in the details of human conflict was one of the most socially ostracizing qualities a person could have. That tarnish has never quite disappeared: In our own day the popular belief that military historians are somehow, well, *off,* endures in many circles.

By way of counterargument let me claim that enthusiasts of military history are often among the most committed and well-read people one might hope to encounter. Rarely does an important work of military history go out of print; and those who know war well can usually hold their own in discussions of political and social history, as well. The reason for this is simple: The history of war represents fully half the tale of mankind's social interactions, and one cannot understand war without understanding its political and social underpinnings. (Conversely, one cannot understand political history or cultural development without understanding war.) Add to this the fact that military history very often involves tales of high adventure—peopled by extreme and fascinating characters and told by some of the best writers ever to take up a pen—and you have the actual secret of why the subject has remained so popular over the ages.

The new Modern Library War Series has been designed to both introduce the uninitiated to this, the real nature of military history, and to reacquaint the initiated with important works that they may have either forgotten or overlooked. For the sake of coherence, we have chosen to focus our four initial offerings on American military history specifically, in order to show how the study of war illuminates so many other aspects of a particular people's experience and character. Francis Parkman's *Montcalm and Wolfe*, for example, not only shows how very much about the psychology of pre-Revolutionary leaders one must understand in order to grasp the conflict known in North America as the French and Indian War, but is also the work of one of the great American prose stylists of the nineteenth century. Ulysses S. Grant's *Personal Memoirs* (which owe more than a little to the editorial efforts of one of Grant's champions, Mark Twain) contrast the remarkable humility of their author with the overwhelmingly dramatic circumstances into which Fate flung him, and that he struggled so hard—in the end, successfully—to master. Theodore Roosevelt's *The Naval War of 1812*, too long neglected, was the first work to reveal the prodigious intellect, irrepressible character, and remarkably entertaining style of this future president, who (his father having spent most of the family fortune on charities) consistently made a good part of his income through writing. And finally we have *A Soldier's Story*, the memoirs of Omar Bradley, "the G.I. General," who, surrounded by a sea of prima donnas during World War II, never stopped quietly learning his trade, until he became, during the conquest of Germany in 1945, arguably the most progressive and important senior American commander in the European theater.

To read any or all of these books is to see that military history is neither an obscure nor a peculiar subject, but one critical to any understanding of the development of human civilization. That warfare itself is violent is true and unfortunate; that it has been a central method through which every nation in the world has established and maintained its independence, however, makes it a critical field of study. The fact that the personalities and stories involved in war are often so compelling is simply a bonus—but it is the kind of bonus that few academic disciplines can boast.

INTRODUCTION

by Edmund Morris

"All men who feel any power of joy in battle," runs the most memorable sentence in Theodore Roosevelt's *The Rough Riders,* "know what it is like when the wolf rises in the heart."

Through most of his forty years he had managed to control this prowling aggression (so at odds, in youth, with his frail and sickly body). Big game hunting and a variety of strenuous sports, from boxing and rowing to woodland treks and mountaineering, relieved most of the physical pressure, while politics and writing served as outlets for his need to wage ideological warfare. He boasted that he was primarily a "literary feller," but an analysis of the books he wrote before 1898 shows that every one of them dealt with ways to establish mastery, whether it be war itself (*The Naval War of 1812*), the "manly chase" (*Hunting Trips of a Ranchman*), or expansionism and moral ferocity (*Thomas Hart Benton, The Winning of the West*).

Even in the hypermasculine, social-Darwinian context of the late nineteenth century, Roosevelt's prose was notable for its violence, especially against men whom he considered not red-blooded enough, such as "the filthy little atheist" Thomas Paine and Henry James, "that little emasculated mass of inanities."

James, at least, could give as good as he got, calling TR "the mere monstrous embodiment of unprecedented and resounding Noise," not to mention "a dangerous and ominous jingo."

The last phrase reflected the fears of many Americans, as the new century loomed, that a clique of young imperialists—Roosevelt prominently included—was determined to make the United States a colonial power. These plotters had been inspired by the annexation of Hawaii in 1894 to look for other islands that would perfect the nation's defenses, provide new markets for its burgeoning production, and confirm its supremacy in the Western Hemisphere. No prize glowed more alluringly in their eyes than "the Pearl of the Antilles," Cuba.

Richest colony in the world, lush with sugarcane and fragrant with tobacco, it lay just a skiff's ride south of Key West, offering the U.S. Navy a necklace of magnificent harbors from which to command the Caribbean and Gulf of Mexico. Geographically, economically, strategically, it was as much an adjunct of the American continent as Spain was of Europe. And in 1895, the moment came when Cubans themselves were ready to throw off Spanish rule, if the *norteamericanos* would only assist.

—

On February 24 of that year, a long-fomented rebellion broke out in the eastern part of the island, to the wild excitement of Civil Service Commissioner Theodore Roosevelt. The rebellion spread and strengthened despite brutally repressive measures by Spanish authorities, who did not hesitate to scorch the countryside and crowd most of the rural population into "reconcentration" camps. A steady flow of arms and money was funneled to the *insurrectos* from revolutionary headquarters in New York (where, coincidentally, Roosevelt was now Police Commissioner), but the United States government did not become involved until early 1896, when Congress passed a resolution in overwhelming support of *Cuba Libre*.

President Grover Cleveland and his Republican successor William McKinley stood as bulwarks against the rising tide of popular hostility toward Spain. They both felt, as responsible commanders in chief, that they had no right to interfere in the sovereign affairs of another state—unless and until American interests were threatened. When Theodore Roosevelt joined the McKinley administration as Assistant Secretary of the Navy on April 19, 1897, American war fever had temporarily abated, and the *insurrectos* fought on with diminishing chances of success.

Not until January 1898 did McKinley authorize the first show of naval might in Cuban waters. Riots by Spanish loyalists in Havana put the lives and property of American citizens at risk, so the battleship *Maine* was ordered south on a "friendly" visit of indefinite duration. She was by no means the biggest or most lethal weapon in the U.S. arsenal, but nevertheless amounted to 6,683 tons of armored steel, packing seventeen big guns and a heavy cargo of torpedoes. She dropped anchor in Havana harbor on the twenty-fifth.

—

Meanwhile American popular newspapers had been waging a constant propaganda campaign against the "butchers" and "devastators" who ruled Cuba. The effect of this "yellow press" agitation upon William McKinley—a principled and peaceable man—has been much exaggerated. Like all business-minded conservatives, he feared any disruption in the political status quo. He also had strong moral reservations about foreign military adventure, and felt that his fiery young appointee in the Navy Department was too warhungry by half. Roosevelt was already agitating for a commission, or the promise of a commission, as "a major or lieutenant colonel in one of the National Guard regiments," in the event of any American invasion of Cuba.

This hotheadedness did not alarm McKinley so much as TR's relentless efforts, within the department, to concentrate the deployment of U.S. warships for possible blockade duty off Cuba and the Philippines, and to have them all fueled, rearmed, and ready for instant action. "When war comes," Roosevelt wrote to Navy Secretary John D. Long, "*it should come finally on our initiative, and after we have had time to prepare.*"

Long, and on occasion the President himself, had to remind TR that such an initiative was highly unlikely. A new, liberally inclined government was now installed in Madrid, and many of the previous regime's cruelest disciplinarians had been recalled from Cuba.

Reconcentrado camps were being abolished or reduced in size, while terrorist incidents around the island continued to decline.

What happened at 9:40 P.M. in Havana harbor on February 15, 1898, was one of those freak concatenations of physical, political, and temporal factors that precipitate fate and change history. The *Maine* blew up with such violence that 254 men died instantly, as blackened bits of steel shrapnel flew in all directions and the entire bay seemed to incandesce. To this day the cause of the explosion (which claimed another eight fatalities in its aftermath) is a matter of conjecture. A U.S. naval court of inquiry concluded that the *Maine* was destroyed by a submarine bomb, placed by persons unknown. The most modern reassessment of available evidence, by Rear Admiral Hyman G. Rickover in 1976, theorized that a likely source was "heat from a fire in the coal bunker adjacent to the 6-inch reserve magazine."

Whatever the truth, there was no doubt in the American popular mind next morning that Spain was responsible, and that Spain must pay. TR forgot his ancient scruple that "in forty-nine cases out of a hundred, *vox populi* is likely to be the voice of a fool," and girded his loins for battle. "The *Maine* was sunk by an act of dirty treachery on the part of the Spaniards *I* believe." In consequence, they must be expelled from the Western Hemisphere, not to mention the Far East. Waiting only for one of Secretary Long's frequent absences from the Navy Department, Roosevelt fired off a peremptory cable to Admiral Dewey in the far Pacific.

ORDER THE SQUADRON, EXCEPT THE MONOCACY, TO HONG KONG. KEEP FULL OF COAL. IN THE EVENT OF A DECLARATION WAR SPAIN, YOUR DUTY WILL BE TO SEE THAT THE SPANISH SQUADRON DOES NOT LEAVE THE ASIATIC COAST, AND THEN OFFENSIVE OPERATIONS IN THE PHILIPPINE ISLANDS.

Dewey later characterized this message as "the first step" toward America's long and painful experiment with colonization in the Philippines. As President in 1901, TR would have to deal with an insurrective nightmare there that made his "splendid little war" in Cuba seem but nostalgic memory.

President McKinley tried with increasing anguish to quell the war fever rising nationwide and in Congress. But he proved eventually powerless, and on April 11, he asked for legislative authority to use the U.S. military as a peacekeeping force in Cuba. Congress responded by sending him an act of war effective April 21. Two days later Secretary of War Russell A. Alger offered Theodore Roosevelt command of the first of three volunteer regiments "to be composed exclusively of frontiersmen possessing exclusive qualifications as horsemen and marksmen."

———

More than ten years before, TR had dreamed of leading a troop of "harum-scarum roughriders" into war. But now, with surprising levelheadedness, he declined the honor. He told Alger that his limited experience as a captain in the New York National Guard did not qualify him for regimental command—at least, not until he had served a month or so in the field. He therefore accepted the lieutenant-colonelcy of the First U.S. Volunteer Cavalry, commanded by a professional soldier, Colonel Leonard Wood. On May 12, he left for the regimental muster camp in San Antonio, Texas.

John D. Long was both relieved and sorry to see him go. "A man of unbounded energy and force," the Secretary wrote in his diary. "He thinks he is following his highest ideal, whereas, in fact, as without exception every one of his friends advises him, he is acting like a fool. And yet, how absurd this will all sound if, by some turn of fate, he should accomplish some great thing and strike a very high mark."

Six months later, as a war hero and newly elected governor of New York State, TR began to dictate the following book. It tells the story of how he indeed accomplished a "great thing," having victoriously commanded the Rough Riders in battle, and purged his bloodlust at the crest of San Juan Hill. In doing so, he by no means waited for others to advertise his achievement. Modern-day readers of *The Rough Riders* will notice, as did contemporary critics, that Roosevelt has a fondness for the personal pronoun that borders on the erotic. (It was rumored that typesetters of the first edition had to send out for an extra supply of the letter "I.") But there is something engaging about the boyishness of his vanity, the force and clarity of his prose, and the acts of bravery he truthfully narrates.

Whether or not TR deserved the Medal of Honor for leading that famous charge up San Juan Hill (actually Kettle Hill, an eminence in the San Juan Heights) is a matter almost as vexed as the mystery of the *Maine*. He himself, of course, was under no doubt whatsoever, and the frenzy with which he campaigned (unsuccessfully) to get it afterwards is one of the few blots on his exemplary public record. At the time this volume goes to press, President Clinton is deciding whether to award him the medal posthumously, over the objections of the Secretary of the Army. More than a century after his "crowded hour," Theodore Roosevelt is still courting official controversy.

Perhaps the final word should rest with that wisest and funniest of all American dialect satirists, Peter Finlay Dunne's "Mr. Dooley." In 1899 Dunne published a review of *The Rough Riders* which made such sublime fun of its egocentric style that even TR was amused. (The two men became fast friends as a result, and when Roosevelt became President he used to recite it to White House dinner guests, with his hand on Dunne's shoulder.) Here is an opening sample. "Mr. Dooley" is addressing his friend "Mr. Hennessy" in a Chicago saloon:

> Well, sir,... I jus' got hold iv a book, Hinnissy, that suits me up the th' handle, a gran' book, th' grandest iver seen.... 'Tis "Th' Biography iv a Hero be Wan who Knows." 'Tis "Th' Darin' Exploits iv a Brave Man be an Actual Eye Witness." 'Tis "Th' Account in th' Desthruction iv Spanish Power in th' Ant Hills," as it fell fr'm th' lips of Tiddy Rosenfelt an' was took down be his own hands. Ye see 'twas this way, Hinnissy, as I r-read th' book. Whin Tiddy was blowed up in th' harbor iv Havana, he instantly con-cluded they must be war. He debated th' question long an' earnestly an' fin'lly passed a jint resolution declarin' war.... But there was no wan to carry it on. What shud he do? I will lave th' janial author tell th' story in his own wurruds.

And so will I.

CONTENTS

ILLUSTRATIONS

Roosevelt at San Antonio

Soldiers waiting for the train to Port Tampa

Rough Riders' camp at Tampa

Port Tampa dock on the Day of Sailing of the Transports

Twenty-third Infantry in the trenches

Troops crossing Rio San Juan

Troops forming for march

First Division field hospital

Rough Riders bringing in the wounded

Sergeant Hamilton Fish

View from the San Juan trenches

Surgeon attending to the wounded

Funeral for Rough Rider

Rough Riders cheering the surrender of Santiago

Camp at Montauk

Roosevelt at Montauk

ON BEHALF OF THE ROUGH RIDERS
I DEDICATE THIS BOOK
TO THE OFFICERS AND MEN OF THE
FIVE REGULAR REGIMENTS
WHICH TOGETHER WITH MINE MADE UP THE
CAVALRY DIVISION AT SANTIAGO

THEODORE ROOSEVELT

EXECUTIVE MANSION
ALBANY, N.Y., MAY 1, 1899

Hark! I hear the tramp of thousands,
And of armed men the hum;
Lo! a nation's hosts have gathered
Round the quick-alarming drum—
Saying, "Come,
Freemen, come!
Ere your heritage be wasted," said the quick-alarming drum.

"Let me of my heart take counsel:
War is not of Life the sum;
Who shall stay and reap the harvest
When the autumn days shall come?"
But the drum
Echoed, "Come!
Death shall reap the braver harvest," said the solemn-sounding drum.

"But when won the coming battle,
What of profit springs therefrom?
What if conquest, subjugation,
Even greater ills become?"
But the drum
Answered, "Come!
You must do the sum to prove it," said the Yankee-answering drum.

—BRET HARTE

THE ROUGH RIDERS

RAISING THE REGIMENT

During the year preceding the outbreak of the Spanish War I was Assistant Secretary of the Navy. While my party was in opposition, I had preached, with all the fervor and zeal I possessed, our duty to intervene in Cuba, and to take this opportunity of driving the Spaniard from the Western World. Now that my party had come to power, I felt it incumbent on me, by word and deed, to do all I could to secure the carrying out of the policy in which I so heartily believed; and from the beginning I had determined that, if a war came, somehow or other, I was going to the front.

Meanwhile, there was any amount of work at hand in getting ready the navy, and to this I devoted myself.

Naturally, when one is intensely interested in a certain cause, the tendency is to associate particularly with those who take the same view. A large number of my friends felt very differently from the way I felt, and looked upon the possibility of war with sincere horror. But I found plenty of sympathizers, especially in the navy, the army, and the Senate Committee on Foreign Affairs. Commodore Dewey, Captain Evans, Captain Brownson, Captain Davis—with these and the various other naval officers on duty at Washington I used to hold long consultations, during which we went over and over, not only every question of naval administration, but specifically everything necessary to do in order to put the navy in trim to strike quick and hard if, as we believed would be the case, we went to war with Spain. Sending an ample quantity of ammunition to the Asiatic squadron and providing it with coal; getting the battle-ships and the armored cruisers on the Atlantic into one squadron, both to train them in manœuvring together, and to have them ready to sail against either the Cuban or the Spanish coasts; gathering the torpedo-boats into a flotilla for practice; securing ample target exercise, so conducted as to raise the standard of our marksmanship; gathering in the small ships from European and South American waters; settling on the number and kind of craft needed as auxiliary cruisers—every one of these points was threshed over in conversations with officers who were present in Washington, or in correspondence with officers who, like Captain Mahan, were absent.

As for the Senators, of course Senator Lodge and I felt precisely alike; for to fight in such a cause and with such an enemy was merely to carry out the doctrines we had both of us preached for many years. Senator Davis, Senator Proctor, Senator Foraker, Senator Chandler, Senator Morgan, Senator Frye, and a number of others also took just the right ground; and I saw a great deal of them, as well as of many members of the House, particularly those from the West, where the feeling for war was strongest.

Naval officers came and went, and Senators were only in the city while the Senate was in session; but there was one friend who was steadily in Washington. This was an army surgeon, Dr. Leonard Wood. I only met him after I entered the navy department, but we soon found that we had kindred tastes and kindred principles. He had served in General Miles's inconceivably harassing campaigns against the Apaches, where he had displayed such courage that he won that most coveted of distinctions—the Medal of Honor; such extraordinary physical strength and endurance that he grew to be recognized as one of the two or three white men who could stand fatigue and hardship as well as an Apache; and such judgment that toward the close of the campaigns he was given, though a surgeon, the actual command of more than one expedition against the bands of renegade Indians. Like so many of the gallant fighters with whom it was later my good fortune to serve, he combined, in a very high degree, the qualities of entire manliness with entire uprightness and cleanliness of character. It was a pleasure to deal with a man of high ideals, who scorned everything mean and base, and who also possessed those robust and hardy qualities of body and mind, for the lack of which no merely negative virtue can ever atone. He was by nature a soldier of the highest type, and, like most natural soldiers, he was, of course, born with a keen longing for adventure; and, though an excellent doctor, what he really desired was the chance to lead men in some kind of hazard. To every possibility of such adventure he paid quick attention. For instance, he had a great desire to get me to go with him on an expedition into the Klondike in mid-winter, at the time when it was thought that a relief party would have to be sent there to help the starving miners.

In the summer he and I took long walks together through the beautiful broken country surrounding Washington. In winter we sometimes varied these walks by kicking a foot-ball in an empty lot, or, on the rare occasions when there was enough snow, by trying a couple of sets of skis or snow-skates, which had been sent me from Canada.

But always on our way out to and back from these walks and sport, there was one topic to which, in our talking, we returned, and that was the possible war with Spain. We both felt very strongly that such a war would be as righteous as it would be advantageous to the honor and the interests of the nation; and after the blowing up of the Maine, we felt that it was inevitable. We then at once began to try to see that we had our share in it. The President and my own chief, Secretary Long, were very firm against my going, but they said that if I was bent upon going they would help me. Wood was the medical adviser of both the President and the Secretary of War, and could count upon their friendship. So we started with the odds in our favor.

At first we had great difficulty in knowing exactly what to try for. We could go on the staff of any one of several Generals, but we much preferred to go in the line. Wood hoped he might get a commission in his native State of Massachusetts; but in Massachusetts, as in every other State, it proved there were ten men who wanted to go to the war for every chance to go. Then we thought we might get positions as field-officers under an old friend of mine, Colonel—now General—Francis V. Greene, of New York, the Colonel of the Seventy-first; but again there were no vacancies.

Our doubts were resolved when Congress authorized the raising of three cavalry regiments from among the wild riders and riflemen of the Rockies and the Great Plains. During Wood's service in the Southwest he had commanded not only regulars and Indian scouts, but also white frontiersmen. In the Northwest I had spent much of my time, for many years, either on my ranch or in long hunting trips, and had lived and worked for months together with the cow-boy and the mountain hunter, faring in every way precisely as they did.

Secretary Alger offered me the command of one of these regiments. If I had taken it, being entirely inexperienced in military work, I should not have known how to get it equipped most rapidly, for I should have spent valuable weeks in learning its needs, with the result that I should have missed the Santiago campaign, and might not even have had the consolation prize of going to Porto Rico. Fortunately, I was wise enough to tell the Secretary that while I believed I could learn to command the regiment in a month, yet that it was just this very month which I could not afford to spare, and that therefore I would be quite content to go as Lieutenant-Colonel, if he would make Wood Colonel.

This was entirely satisfactory to both the President and Secretary, and, accordingly, Wood and I were speedily commissioned as Colonel and Lieutenant-Colonel of the First United States Volunteer Cavalry. This was the official title of the regiment, but for some reason or other the public promptly christened us the "Rough Riders." At first we fought against the use of the term, but to no purpose; and when finally the Generals of Division and Brigade began to write in formal communications about our regiment as the "Rough Riders," we adopted the term ourselves.

The mustering-places for the regiment were appointed in New Mexico, Arizona, Oklahoma, and Indian Territory. The difficulty in organizing was not in selecting, but in rejecting men. Within a day or two after it was announced that we were to raise the regiment, we were literally deluged with applications from every quarter of the Union. Without the slightest trouble, so far as men went, we could have raised a brigade or even a division. The difficulty lay in arming, equipping, mounting, and disciplining the men we selected. Hundreds of regiments were being called into existence by the National Government, and each regiment was sure to have innumerable wants to be satisfied. To a man who knew the ground as Wood did, and who was entirely aware of our national unpreparedness, it was evident that the ordnance and quartermaster's bureaus could not meet, for some time to come, one-tenth of the demands that would be made upon them; and it was all-important to get in first with our demands. Thanks to his knowledge of the situation and promptness, we immediately put in our requisitions for the articles indispensable for the equipment of the regiment; and then, by ceaseless worrying of excellent bureaucrats, who had no idea how to do things quickly or how to meet an emergency, we succeeded in getting our rifles, cartridges, revolvers, clothing, shelter-tents, and horse gear just in time to enable us to go on the Santiago expedition. Some of the State troops, who were already organized as National Guards, were, of course, ready, after a fashion, when the war broke out; but no other regiment which had our work to do was able to do it in anything like as quick time, and therefore no other volunteer regiment saw anything like the fighting which we did.

Wood thoroughly realized what the Ordnance Department failed to realize, namely the inestimable advantage of smokeless powder; and, moreover, he was bent upon our having the weapons of the regulars, for this meant that we would be brigaded with them, and it was evident that they would do the bulk of the fighting if the war were short. Accordingly, by acting with the utmost vigor and promptness, he succeeded in getting our regiment armed with the Krag-Jorgensen carbine used by the regular cavalry.

It was impossible to take any of the numerous companies which were proffered to us from the various States. The only organized bodies we were at liberty to accept were those from the four Territories. But owing to the fact that the number of men originally allotted to us, 780, was speedily raised to 1,000, we were given a chance to accept quite a number of eager volunteers who did not come from the Territories, but who possessed precisely the same temper that distinguished our Southwestern recruits, and whose presence materially benefited the regiment.

We drew recruits from Harvard, Yale, Princeton, and many another college; from clubs like the Somerset, of Boston, and Knickerbocker, of New York; and from among the men who belonged neither to club nor to college, but in whose veins the blood stirred with the same impulse which once sent the Vikings over sea. Four of the policemen who had served under me, while I was President of the New York Police Board, insisted on coming—two of them to die, the other two to return unhurt after honorable and dangerous service. It seemed to me that almost every friend I had in every State had some one acquaintance who was bound to go with the Rough Riders, and for whom I had to make a place. Thomas Nelson Page, General Fitzhugh Lee, Congressman Odell of New York, Senator Morgan; for each of these, and for many others, I eventually consented to accept some one or two recruits, of course only after a most rigid examination into their physical capacity, and after they had shown that they knew how to ride and shoot. I may add that in no case was I disappointed in the men thus taken.

Harvard being my own college, I had such a swarm of applications from it that I could not take one in ten. What particularly pleased me, not only in the Harvard but the Yale and Princeton men, and, indeed, in these recruits from the older States generally, was that they did not ask for commissions. With hardly an exception they entered upon their duties as troopers in the spirit which they held to the end, merely endeavoring to show that no work could be too hard, too disagreeable, or too dangerous for them to perform, and neither asking nor receiving any reward in the way of promotion or consideration. The Harvard contingent was practically raised by Guy Murchie, of Maine. He saw all the fighting and did his duty with the utmost gallantry, and then left the service as he had entered it, a trooper, entirely satisfied to have done his duty—and no man did it better. So it was with Dudley Dean, perhaps the best quarterback who ever played on a Harvard Eleven; and so with Bob Wrenn, a quarterback whose feats rivalled those of Dean's, and who, in addition, was the champion tennis player of America, and had, on two different years, saved this championship from going to an Englishman. So it was with Yale men like Waller, the high jumper, and Garrison and Girard; and with Princeton men like Devereux and Channing, the foot-ball players; with Larned, the tennis player; with Craig Wadsworth, the steeple-chase rider; with Joe Stevens, the crack polo player; with Hamilton Fish, the ex-captain of the Columbia crew, and with scores of others whose names are quite as worthy of mention as any of those I have given. Indeed, they all sought entry into the ranks of the Rough Riders as eagerly as if it meant something widely different from hard work, rough fare, and the possibility of death; and the reason why they turned out to be such good soldiers lay largely in the fact that they were men who had thoroughly counted the cost before entering, and who went into the regiment because they believed that this offered their best chance for seeing hard and dangerous service. Mason Mitchell, of New York, who had been a chief of scouts in the Riel Rebellion, travelled all the way to San Antonio to enlist; and others came there from distances as great.

Some of them made appeals to me which I could not possibly resist. Woodbury Kane had been a close friend of mine at Harvard. During the eighteen years that had passed since my graduation I had seen very little of him, though, being always interested in sport, I occasionally met him on the hunting field, had seen him on the deck of the Defender when she vanquished the Valkyrie, and knew the part he had played on the Navajoe, when, in her most important race, that otherwise unlucky yacht vanquished her opponent, the Prince of Wales's Britannia. When the war was on, Kane felt it his duty to fight for his country. He did not seek any position of distinction. All he desired was the chance to do whatever work he was put to do well, and to get to the front; and he enlisted as a trooper. When I went down to the camp at San Antonio he was on kitchen duty, and was cooking and washing dishes for one of the New Mexican troops; and he was doing it so well that I had no further doubt as to how he would get on.

My friend of many hunts and ranch partner, Robert Munro Ferguson, of Scotland, who had been on Lord Aberdeen's staff as a Lieutenant but a year before, likewise could not keep out of the regiment. He, too, appealed to me in terms which I could not withstand, and came in like Kane to do his full duty as a trooper, and like Kane to win his commission by the way he thus did his duty.

I felt many qualms at first in allowing men of this stamp to come in, for I could not be certain that they had counted the cost, and was afraid they would find it very hard to serve—not for a few days, but for months—in the ranks, while I, their former intimate associate, was a field-officer; but they insisted that they knew their minds, and the events showed that they did. We enlisted about fifty of them from Virginia, Maryland, and the Northeastern States, at Washington. Before allowing them to be sworn in, I gathered them together and explained that if they went in they must be prepared not merely to fight, but to perform the weary, monotonous labor incident to the ordinary routine of a soldier's life; that they must be ready to face fever exactly as they were to face bullets; that they were to obey unquestioningly, and to do their duty as readily if called upon to garrison a fort as if sent to the front. I warned them that work that was merely irksome and disagreeable must be faced as readily as work that was dangerous, and that no complaint of any kind must be made; and I told them that they were entirely at liberty not to go, but that after they had once signed there could then be no backing out.

Not a man of them backed out; not one of them failed to do his whole duty.

These men formed but a small fraction of the whole. They went down to San Antonio, where the regiment was to gather and where Wood preceded me, while I spent a week in Washington hurrying up the different bureaus and telegraphing my various railroad friends, so as to insure our getting the carbines, saddles, and uniforms that we needed from the various armories and storehouses. Then I went down to San Antonio myself, where I found the men from New Mexico, Arizona, and Oklahoma already gathered, while those from Indian Territory came in soon after my arrival.

These were the men who made up the bulk of the regiment, and gave it its peculiar character. They came from the Four Territories which yet remained within the boundaries of the United States; that is, from the lands that have been most recently won over to white civilization, and in which the conditions of life are nearest those that obtained on the frontier when there still was a frontier. They were a splendid set of men, these Southwesterners—tall and sinewy, with resolute, weather-beaten faces, and eyes that looked a man straight in the face without flinching. They included in their ranks men of every occupation; but the three types were those of the cow-boy, the hunter, and the mining prospector—the man who wandered hither and thither, killing game for a living, and spending his life in the quest for metal wealth.

In all the world there could be no better material for soldiers than that afforded by these grim hunters of the mountains, these wild rough riders of the plains. They were accustomed to handling wild and savage horses; they were accustomed to following the chase with the rifle, both for sport and as a means of livelihood. Varied though their occupations had been, almost all had, at one time or another, herded cattle and hunted big game. They were hardened to life in the open, and to shifting for themselves under adverse circumstances. They were used, for all their lawless freedom, to the rough discipline of the round-up and the mining company. Some of them came from the small frontier towns; but most were from the wilderness, having left their lonely hunters' cabins and shifting cow-camps to seek new and more stirring adventures beyond the sea.

They had their natural leaders—the men who had shown they could master other men, and could more than hold their own in the eager driving life of the new settlements.

The Captains and Lieutenants were sometimes men who had campaigned in the regular army against Apache, Ute, and Cheyenne, and who, on completing their term of service, had shown their energy by settling in the new communities and growing up to be men of mark. In other cases they were sheriffs, marshals, deputy-sheriffs and deputy-marshals—men who had fought Indians, and still more often had waged relentless war upon the bands of white desperadoes. There was Bucky O'Neill, of Arizona, Captain of Troop A, the Mayor of Prescott, a famous sheriff throughout the West for his feats of victorious warfare against the Apache, no less than against the white road-agents and man-killers. His father had fought in Meagher's Brigade in the Civil War; and he was himself a born soldier, a born leader of men. He was a wild, reckless fellow, soft spoken, and of dauntless courage and boundless ambition; he was stanchly loyal to his friends, and cared for his men in every way. There was Captain Llewellen, of New Mexico, a good citizen, a political leader, and one of the most noted peace-officers of the country; he had been shot four times in pitched fights with red marauders and white outlaws. There was Lieutenant Ballard, who had broken up the Black Jack gang of ill-omened notoriety, and his Captain, Curry, another New Mexican sheriff of fame. The officers from the Indian Territory had almost all served as marshals and deputy-marshals; and in the Indian Territory, service as a deputy-marshal meant capacity to fight stand-up battles with the gangs of outlaws.

Three of our higher officers had been in the regular army. One was Major Alexander Brodie, from Arizona, afterward Lieutenant-Colonel, who had lived for twenty years in the Territory, and had become a thorough Westerner without sinking the West Pointer—a soldier by taste as well as training, whose men worshipped him and would follow him anywhere, as they would Bucky O'Neill or any other of their favorites. Brodie was running a big mining business; but when the Maine was blown up, he abandoned everything and telegraphed right and left to bid his friends get ready for the fight he saw impending.

Then there was Micah Jenkins, the Captain of Troop K, a gentle and courteous South Carolinian, on whom danger acted like wine. In action he was a perfect game-cock, and he won his majority for gallantry in battle.

Finally, there was Allyn Capron, who was, on the whole, the best soldier in the regiment. In fact, I think he was the ideal of what an American regular army officer should be. He was the fifth in descent from father to son who had served in the army of the United States, and in body and mind alike he was fitted to play his part to perfection. Tall and lithe, a remarkable boxer and walker, a first-class rider and shot, with yellow hair and piercing blue eyes, he looked what he was, the archetype of the fighting man. He had under him one of the two companies from the Indian Territory; and he so soon impressed himself upon the wild spirit of his followers, that he got them ahead in discipline faster than any other troop in the regiment, while at the same time taking care of their bodily wants. His ceaseless effort was so to train them, care for them, and inspire them as to bring their fighting efficiency to the highest possible pitch. He required instant obedience, and tolerated not the slightest evasion of duty; but his mastery of his art was so thorough and his performance of his own duty so rigid that he won at once not merely their admiration, but that soldierly affection so readily given by the man in the ranks to the superior who cares for his men and leads them fearlessly in battle.

All—Easterners and Westerners, Northerners and Southerners, officers and men, cow-boys and college graduates, wherever they came from, and whatever their social position—possessed in common the traits of hardihood and a thirst for adventure. They were to a man born adventurers, in the old sense of the word.

The men in the ranks were mostly young; yet some were past their first youth. These had taken part in the killing of the great buffalo herds, and had fought Indians when the tribes were still on the war-path. The younger ones, too, had led rough lives; and the lines in their faces told of many a hardship endured, and many a danger silently faced with grim, unconscious philosophy. Some were originally from the East, and had seen strange adventures in different kinds of life, from sailing round the Horn to mining in

Alaska. Others had been born and bred in the West, and had never seen a larger town than Santa Fé or a bigger body of water than the Pecos in flood. Some of them went by their own name; some had changed their names; and yet others possessed but half a name, colored by some adjective, like Cherokee Bill, Happy Jack of Arizona, Smoky Moore, the bronco-buster, so named because cowboys often call vicious horses "smoky" horses, and Rattlesnake Pete, who had lived among the Moquis and taken part in the snake-dances. Some were professional gamblers, and, on the other hand, no less than four were or had been Baptist or Methodist clergymen—and proved first-class fighters, too, by the way. Some were men whose lives in the past had not been free from the taint of those fierce kinds of crime into which the lawless spirits who dwell on the border-land between civilization and savagery so readily drift. A far larger number had served at different times in those bodies of armed men with which the growing civilization of the border finally puts down its savagery.

There was one characteristic and distinctive contingent which could have appeared only in such a regiment as ours. From the Indian Territory there came a number of Indians—Cherokees, Chickasaws, Choctaws, and Creeks. Only a few were of pure blood. The others shaded off until they were absolutely indistinguishable from their white comrades; with whom, it may be mentioned, they all lived on terms of complete equality.

Not all of the Indians were from the Indian Territory. One of the gamest fighters and best soldiers in the regiment was Pollock, a full-blooded Pawnee. He had been educated, like most of the other Indians, at one of those admirable Indian schools which have added so much to the total of the small credit account with which the White race balances the very unpleasant debit account of its dealings with the Red. Pollock was a silent, solitary fellow—an excellent pen-man, much given to drawing pictures. When we got down to Santiago he developed into the regimental clerk. I never suspected him of having a sense of humor until one day, at the end of our stay in Cuba, as he was sitting in the Adjutant's tent working over the returns, there turned up a trooper of the First who had been acting as barber. Eying him with immovable face Pollock asked, in a guttural voice, "Do you cut hair?" The man answered "Yes"; and Pollock continued, "Then you'd better cut mine," muttering, in an explanatory soliloquy, "Don't want to wear my hair long like a wild Indian when I'm in civilized warfare."

Another Indian came from Texas. He was a brakeman on the Southern Pacific, and wrote telling me he was an American Indian, and that he wanted to enlist. His name was Colbert, which at once attracted my attention; for I was familiar with the history of the Cherokees and Chickasaws during the eighteenth century, when they lived east of the Mississippi. Early in that century various traders, chiefly Scotchmen, settled among them, and the half-breed descendants of one named Colbert became the most noted chiefs of the Chickasaws. I summoned the applicant before me, and found that he was an excellent man, and, as I had supposed, a descendant of the old Chickasaw chiefs.

He brought into the regiment, by the way, his "partner," a white man. The two had been inseparable companions for some years, and continued so in the regiment. Every man who has lived in the West knows that, vindictive though the hatred between the white man and the Indian is when they stand against one another in what may be called their tribal relations, yet that men of Indian blood, when adopted into white communities, are usually treated precisely like anyone else.

Colbert was not the only Indian whose name I recognized. There was a Cherokee named Adair, who, upon inquiry, I found to be descended from the man who, a century and a half ago, wrote a ponderous folio, to this day of great interest, about the Cherokees, with whom he had spent the best years of his life as a trader and agent.

I don't know that I ever came across a man with a really sweeter nature than another Cherokee named Holderman. He was an excellent soldier, and for a long time acted as cook for the headquarters mess. He was a half-breed, and came of a soldier stock on both sides and through both races. He explained to me once why he had come to the war; that it was because his people always had fought when there was a war, and he could not feel happy to stay at home when the flag was going into battle.

Two of the young Cherokee recruits came to me with a most kindly letter from one of the ladies who had been teaching in the academy from which they were about to graduate. She and I had known one another in connection with Governmental and philanthropic work on the reservations, and she wrote to commend the two boys to my attention. One was on the Academy foot-ball team and the other in the glee-club. Both were fine young fellows. The foot-ball player now lies buried with the other dead who fell in the fight at San Juan. The singer was brought to death's door by fever, but recovered and came back to his home.

There were other Indians of much wilder type, but their wildness was precisely like that of the cow-boys with whom they were associated. One or two of them needed rough discipline; and they got it, too. Like the rest of the regiment, they were splendid riders. I remember one man, whose character left much to be desired in some respects, but whose horsemanship was unexceptionable. He was mounted on an exceedingly bad bronco, which would bolt out of the ranks at drill. He broke it of this habit by the simple expedient of giving it two tremendous twists, first to one side and then to the other, as it bolted, with the result that, invariably, at the second bound its legs crossed and over it went with a smash, the rider taking the somersault with unmoved equanimity.

The life histories of some of the men who joined our regiment would make many volumes of thrilling adventure.

We drew a great many recruits from Texas; and from nowhere did we get a higher average, for many of them had served in that famous body of frontier fighters, the Texas Rangers. Of course, these rangers needed no teaching. They were already trained to obey and to take responsibility. They were splendid shots, horsemen, and trailers. They were accustomed to living in the open, to enduring great fatigue and hardship, and to encountering all kinds of danger.

Many of the Arizona and New Mexico men had taken part in warfare with the Apaches, those terrible Indians of the waterless

Southwestern mountains—the most bloodthirsty and the wildest of all the red men of America, and the most formidable in their own dreadful style of warfare. Of course, a man who had kept his nerve and held his own, year after year, while living where each day and night contained the threat of hidden death from a foe whose goings and comings were unseen, was not apt to lose courage when confronted with any other enemy. An experience in following in the trail of an enemy who might flee at one stretch through fifty miles of death-like desert was a good school out of which to come with profound indifference for the ordinary hardships of campaigning.

As a rule, the men were more apt, however, to have had experience in warring against white desperadoes and law-breakers than against Indians. Some of our best recruits came from Colorado. One, a very large, hawk-eyed man, Benjamin Franklin Daniels, had been Marshal of Dodge City when that pleasing town was probably the toughest abode of civilized man to be found anywhere on the continent. In the course of the exercise of his rather lurid functions as peace-officer he had lost half of one ear—"bitten off," it was explained to me. Naturally, he viewed the dangers of battle with philosophic calm. Such a man was, in reality, a veteran even in his first fight, and was a tower of strength to the recruits in his part of the line. With him there came into the regiment a deputy marshal from Cripple Creek named Sherman Bell. Bell had a hernia, but he was so excellent a man that we decided to take him. I do not think I ever saw greater resolution than Bell displayed throughout the campaign. In Cuba the great exertions which he was forced to make, again and again opened the hernia, and the surgeons insisted that he must return to the United States; but he simply would not go.

Then there was little McGinty, the bronco-buster from Oklahoma, who never had walked a hundred yards if by any possibility he could ride. When McGinty was reproved for his absolute inability to keep step on the drill-ground, he responded that he was pretty sure he could keep step on horseback. McGinty's short legs caused him much trouble on the marches, but we had no braver or better man in the fights.

One old friend of mine had come from far northern Idaho to join the regiment at San Antonio. He was a hunter, named Fred Herrig, an Alsatian by birth. A dozen years before he and I had hunted mountain sheep and deer when laying in the winter stock of meat for my ranch on the Little Missouri, sometimes in the bright fall weather, sometimes in the Arctic bitterness of the early Northern winter. He was the most loyal and simple-hearted of men, and he had come to join his old "boss" and comrade in the bigger hunting which we were to carry on through the tropic mid-summer.

The temptation is great to go on enumerating man after man who stood pre-eminent, whether as a killer of game, a tamer of horses, or a queller of disorder among his people, or who, mayhap, stood out with a more evil prominence as himself a dangerous man—one given to the taking of life on small provocation, or one who was ready to earn his living outside the law if the occasion demanded it. There was tall Proffit, the sharp-shooter, from North Carolina—sinewy, saturnine, fearless; Smith, the bear-hunter from Wyoming, and McCann, the Arizona book-keeper, who had begun life as a buffalo-hunter. There was Crockett, the Georgian, who had been an Internal Revenue officer, and had waged perilous war on the rifle-bearing "moonshiners." There were Darnell and Wood of New Mexico, who could literally ride any horses alive. There were Goodwin, and Buck Taylor, and Armstrong the ranger, crack shots with rifle or revolver. There was many a skilled packer who had led and guarded his trains of laden mules through the Indian-haunted country surrounding some out-post of civilization. There were men who had won fame as Rocky Mountain stage-drivers, or who had spent endless days in guiding the slow wagon-trains across the grassy plains. There were miners who knew every camp from the Yukon to Leadville, and cow-punchers in whose memories were stored the brands carried by the herds from Chihuahua to Assiniboia. There were men who had roped wild steers in the mesquite brush of the Nueces, and who, year in and year out, had driven the trail herds northward over desolate wastes and across the fords of shrunken rivers to the fattening grounds of the Powder and the Yellowstone. They were hardened to the scorching heat and bitter cold of the dry plains and pine-clad mountains. They were accustomed to sleep in the open, while the picketed horses grazed beside them near some shallow, reedy pool. They had wandered hither and thither across the vast desolation of the wilderness, alone or with comrades. They had cowered in the shelter of cut banks from the icy blast of the norther, and far out on the midsummer prairies they had known the luxury of lying in the shade of the wagon during the noonday rest. They had lived in brush lean-tos for weeks at a time, or with only the wagon-sheet as an occasional house. They had fared hard when exploring the unknown; they had fared well on the round-up; and they had known the plenty of the log ranch-houses, where the tables were spread with smoked venison and calf-ribs and milk and bread, and vegetables from the garden-patch.

Such were the men we had as recruits: soldiers ready made, as far as concerned their capacity as individual fighters. What was necessary was to teach them to act together, and to obey orders. Our special task was to make them ready for action in the shortest possible time. We were bound to see fighting, and therefore to be with the first expedition that left the United States; for we could not tell how long the war would last.

I had been quite prepared for trouble when it came to enforcing discipline, but I was agreeably disappointed. There were plenty of hard characters who might by themselves have given trouble, and with one or two of whom we did have to take rough measures; but the bulk of the men thoroughly understood that without discipline they would be merely a valueless mob, and they set themselves hard at work to learn the new duties. Of course, such a regiment, in spite of, or indeed I might almost say because of, the characteristics which made the individual men so exceptionally formidable as soldiers, could very readily have been spoiled. Any weakness in the commander would have ruined it. On the other hand, to treat it from the stand-point of the martinet and military pedant would have been almost equally fatal. From the beginning we started out to secure the essentials of discipline, while laying just as little stress as possible on the non-essentials. The men were singularly quick to respond to any appeal to their intelligence and patriotism. The faults they committed were those of ignorance merely. When Holderman, in announcing dinner to the Colonel and the three Majors, genially remarked, "If you fellars don't come soon, everything 'll get cold," he had no thought of other than a kindly and respectful regard for their welfare, and was glad to modify his form of address on being told that it was not what could be described as conventionally military. When one of our sentinels, who had with much labor learned the manual of arms, saluted with great pride as I passed, and added, with a friendly nod, "Good-evening, Colonel," this variation in the accepted formula on such occasions was meant, and was accepted, as mere friendly interest. In both cases the needed instruction was given and received in the same kindly spirit.

One of the new Indian Territory recruits, after twenty-four hours' stay in camp, during which he had held himself distinctly aloof from the general interests, called on the Colonel in his tent, and remarked, "Well, Colonel, I want to shake hands and say we're with you. We didn't know how we would like you fellars at first; but you're all right, and you know your business, and you mean business, and you can count on us every time!"

That same night, which was hot, mosquitoes were very annoying; and shortly after midnight both the Colonel and I came to the doors of our respective tents, which adjoined one another. The sentinel in front was also fighting mosquitoes. As we came out we saw him pitch his gun about ten feet off, and sit down to attack some of the pests that had swarmed up his trousers' legs. Happening to glance in our direction, he nodded pleasantly and, with unabashed and friendly feeling, remarked, "Ain't they bad?"

It was astonishing how soon the men got over these little peculiarities. They speedily grew to recognize the fact that the observance of certain forms was essential to the maintenance of proper discipline. They became scrupulously careful in touching their hats, and always came to attention when spoken to. They saw that we did not insist upon the observance of these forms to humiliate them; that we were as anxious to learn our own duties as we were to have them learn theirs, and as scrupulous in paying respect to our superiors as we were in exacting the acknowledgment due our rank from those below us; moreover, what was very important, they saw that we were careful to look after their interests in every way, and were doing all that was possible to hurry up the equipment and drill of the regiment, so as to get into the war.

Rigid guard duty was established at once, and everyone was impressed with the necessity for vigilance and watchfulness. The policing of the camp was likewise attended to with the utmost rigor. As always with new troops, they were at first indifferent to the necessity for cleanliness in camp arrangements; but on this point Colonel Wood brooked no laxity, and in a very little while the hygienic conditions of the camp were as good as those of any regular regiment. Meanwhile the men were being drilled, on foot at first, with the utmost assiduity. Every night we had officers' school, the non-commissioned officers of each troop being given similar schooling by the Captain or one of the Lieutenants of the troop; and every day we practised hard, by squad, by troop, by squadron and battalion. The earnestness and intelligence with which the men went to work rendered the task of instruction much less difficult than would be supposed. It soon grew easy to handle the regiment in all the simpler forms of close and open order. When they had grown so that they could be handled with ease in marching, and in the ordinary manœuvres of the drill-ground, we began to train them in open-order work, skirmishing and firing. Here their woodcraft and plainscraft, their knowledge of the rifle, helped us very much. Skirmishing they took to naturally, which was fortunate, as practically all our fighting was done in open order.

Meanwhile we were purchasing horses. Judging from what I saw I do not think that we got heavy enough animals, and of those purchased certainly a half were nearly unbroken. It was no easy matter to handle them on the picket-lines, and to provide for feeding and watering; and the efforts to shoe and ride them were at first productive of much vigorous excitement. Of course, those that were wild from the range had to be thrown and tied down before they could be shod. Half the horses of the regiment bucked, or possessed some other of the amiable weaknesses incident to horse life on the great ranches; but we had abundance of men who were utterly unmoved by any antic a horse might commit. Every animal was speedily mastered, though a large number remained to the end mounts upon which an ordinary rider would have felt very uncomfortable.

My own horses were purchased for me by a Texas friend, John Moore, with whom I had once hunted peccaries on the Nueces. I only paid fifty dollars apiece, and the animals were not showy; but they were tough and hardy, and answered my purpose well.

Mounted drill with such horses and men bade fair to offer opportunities for excitement; yet it usually went off smoothly enough. Before drilling the men on horseback they had all been drilled on foot, and having gone at their work with hearty zest, they knew well the simple movements to form any kind of line or column. Wood was busy from morning till night in hurrying the final details of the equipment, and he turned the drill of the men over to me. To drill perfectly needs long practice, but to drill roughly is a thing very easy to learn indeed. We were not always right about our intervals, our lines were somewhat irregular, and our more difficult movements were executed at times in rather a haphazard way; but the essential commands and the essential movements we learned without any difficulty, and the men performed them with great dash. When we put them on horseback, there was, of course, trouble with the horses; but the horsemanship of the riders was consummate. In fact, the men were immensely interested in making their horses perform each evolution with the utmost speed and accuracy, and in forcing each unquiet, vicious brute to get into line and stay in line, whether he would or not. The guidon-bearers held their plunging steeds true to the line, no matter what they tried to do; and each wild rider brought his wild horse into his proper place with a dash and ease which showed the natural cavalryman.

In short, from the very beginning the horseback drills were good fun, and everyone enjoyed them. We marched out through the adjoining country to drill wherever we found open ground, practising all the different column formations as we went. On the open ground we threw out the line to one side or the other, and in one position and the other, sometimes at the trot, sometimes at the gallop. As the men grew accustomed to the simple evolutions, we tried them more and more in skirmish drills, practising them so that they might get accustomed to advance in open order and to skirmish in any country, while the horses were held in the rear.

Our arms were the regular cavalry carbine, the "Krag," a splendid weapon, and the revolver. A few carried their favorite Winchesters, using, of course, the new model, which took the Government cartridge. We felt very strongly that it would be worse than a waste of time to try to train our men to use the sabre—a weapon utterly alien to them; but with the rifle and revolver they were already thoroughly familiar. Many of my cavalry friends in the past had insisted to me that the revolver was a better weapon than the sword—among them Basil Duke, the noted Confederate cavalry leader, and Captain Frank Edwards, whom I had met when elk-hunting on the headwaters of the Yellowstone and the Snake. Personally, I knew too little to decide as to the comparative merits of the two arms; but I did know that it was a great deal better to use the arm with which our men were already proficient. They were therefore armed with what might be called their natural weapon, the revolver.

As it turned out, we were not used mounted at all, so that our preparations on this point came to nothing. In a way, I have always regretted this. We thought we should at least be employed as cavalry in the great campaign against Havana in the fall; and from the beginning I began to train my men in shock tactics for use against hostile cavalry. My belief was that the horse was really the weapon with which to strike the first blow. I felt that if my men could be trained to hit their adversaries with their horses, it was a matter of small amount whether, at the moment when the onset occurred, sabres, lances, or revolvers were used; while in the subsequent mêlée I believed the revolver would outclass cold steel as a weapon. But this is all guesswork, for we never had occasion to try the experiment.

It was astonishing what a difference was made by two or three weeks' training. The mere thorough performance of guard and police duties helped the men very rapidly to become soldiers. The officers studied hard, and both officers and men worked hard in the drill-field. It was, of course, rough and ready drill; but it was very efficient, and it was suited to the men who made up the regiment. Their uniform also suited them. In their slouch hats, blue flannel shirts, brown trousers, leggings and boots, with handkerchiefs knotted loosely around their necks, they looked exactly as a body of cow-boy cavalry should look. The officers speedily grew to realize that they must not be over-familiar with their men, and yet that they must care for them in every way. The men, in return, began to acquire those habits of attention to soldierly detail which mean so much in making a regiment. Above all, every man felt, and had constantly instilled into him, a keen pride of the regiment, and a resolute purpose to do his whole duty uncomplainingly, and, above all, to win glory by the way he handled himself in battle.

II

To Cuba

Up to the last moment we were spending every ounce of energy we had in getting the regiment into shape. Fortunately, there were a good many vacancies among the officers, as the original number of 780 men was increased to 1,000; so that two companies were organized entirely anew. This gave the chance to promote some first-rate men.

One of the most useful members of the regiment was Dr. Robb Church, formerly a Princeton foot-ball player. He was appointed as Assistant Surgeon, but acted throughout almost all the Cuban campaign as the Regimental Surgeon. It was Dr. Church who first gave me an idea of Bucky O'Neill's versatility, for I happened to overhear them discussing Aryan word-roots together, and then sliding off into a review of the novels of Balzac, and a discussion as to how far Balzac could be said to be the founder of the modern realistic school of fiction. Church had led almost as varied a life as Bucky himself, his career including incidents as far apart as exploring and elk-hunting in the Olympic Mountains, cooking in a lumber-camp, and serving as doctor on an emigrant ship.

Woodbury Kane was given a commission, and also Horace Devereux, of Princeton. Kane was older than the other college men who entered in the ranks; and as he had the same good qualities to start with, this resulted in his ultimately becoming perhaps the most useful soldier in the regiment. He escaped wounds and serious sickness, and was able to serve through every day of the regiment's existence.

Two of the men made Second Lieutenants by promotion from the ranks while in San Antonio were John Greenway, a noted Yale foot-ball player and catcher on her base-ball nine, and David Goodrich, for two years captain of the Harvard crew. They were young men, Goodrich having only just graduated; while Greenway, whose father had served with honor in the Confederate Army, had been out of Yale three or four years. They were natural soldiers, and it would be well-nigh impossible to overestimate the amount of good they did the regiment. They were strapping fellows, entirely fearless, modest, and quiet. Their only thought was how to perfect themselves in their own duties, and how to take care of the men under them, so as to bring them to the highest point of soldierly perfection. I grew steadily to rely upon them, as men who could be counted upon with absolute certainty, not only in every emergency, but in all routine work. They were never so tired as not to respond with eagerness to the slightest suggestion of doing something new, whether it was dangerous or merely difficult and laborious. They not merely did their duty, but were always on the watch to find out some new duty which they could construe to be theirs. Whether it was policing camp, or keeping guard, or preventing straggling on the march, or procuring food for the men, or seeing that they took care of themselves in camp, or performing some feat of unusual hazard in the fight—no call was ever made upon them to which they did not respond with eager thankfulness for being given the chance to answer it. Later on I worked them as hard as I knew how, and the regiment will always be their debtor.

Greenway was from Arkansas. We could have filled up the whole regiment many times over from the South Atlantic and Gulf States alone, but were only able to accept a very few applicants. One of them was John McIlhenny, of Louisiana; a planter and manufacturer, a big-game hunter and book-lover, who could have had a commission in the Louisiana troops, but who preferred to go as a trooper in the Rough Riders because he believed we would surely see fighting. He could have commanded any influence, social or political, he wished; but he never asked a favor of any kind. He went into one of the New Mexican troops, and by his high qualities and zealous attention to duty speedily rose to a sergeantcy, and finally won his lieutenancy for gallantry in action.

The tone of the officers' mess was very high. Everyone seemed to realize that he had undertaken most serious work. They all earnestly wished for a chance to distinguish themselves, and fully appreciated that they ran the risk not merely of death, but of what was infinitely worse—namely, failure at the crisis to perform duty well; and they strove earnestly so to train themselves, and the men under them, as to minimize the possibility of such disgrace. Every officer and every man was taught continually to look forward to the day of battle eagerly, but with an entire sense of the drain that would then be made upon his endurance and resolution. They were also taught that, before the battle came, the rigorous performance of the countless irksome duties of the camp and the march was demanded from all alike, and that no excuse would be tolerated for failure to perform duty. Very few of the men had gone into the regiment lightly, and the fact that they did their duty so well may be largely attributed to the seriousness with which these eager, adventurous young fellows approached their work. This seriousness, and a certain simple manliness which accompanied it, had one very pleasant side. During our entire time of service, I never heard in the officers' mess a foul story or a foul word; and though there was occasional hard swearing in moments of emergency, yet even this was the exception.

The regiment attracted adventurous spirits from everywhere. Our chief trumpeter was a native American, our second trumpeter was from the Mediterranean—I think an Italian—who had been a soldier of fortune not only in Egypt, but in the French Army in Southern China. Two excellent men were Osborne, a tall Australian, who had been an officer in the New South Wales Mounted Rifles; and Cook, an Englishman, who had served in South Africa.

Both, when the regiment disbanded, were plaintive in expressing their fond regret that it could not be used against the Transvaal Boers!

One of our best soldiers was a man whose real and assumed names I, for obvious reasons conceal. He usually went by a nickname which I will call Tennessee. He was a tall, gaunt fellow, with a quiet and distinctly sinister eye, who did his duty excellently, especially when a fight was on, and who, being an expert gambler, always contrived to reap a rich harvest after pay-day. When the regiment was mustered out, he asked me to put a brief memorandum of his services on his discharge certificate, which I gladly did. He much appreciated this, and added, in explanation, "You see, Colonel, my real name isn't Smith, its Yancy. I had to change it, because three or four years ago I had a little trouble with a gentleman, and—er—well, in fact, I had to kill him; and the District Attorney, he had it in for me, and so I just skipped the country; and now, if it ever should be brought up against me, I should like to show your certificate as to my character!" The course of frontier justice sometimes moves in unexpected zigzags; so I did not express the doubt I felt as to whether my certificate that he had been a good soldier would help him much if he was tried for a murder committed three or four years previously.

The men worked hard and faithfully. As a rule, in spite of the number of rough characters among them, they behaved very well. One night a few of them went on a spree, and proceeded "to paint San Antonio red." One was captured by the city authorities, and we had to leave him behind us in jail. The others we dealt with ourselves, in a way that prevented a repetition of the occurrence.

The men speedily gave one another nicknames, largely conferred in a spirit of derision, their basis lying in contrast. A brave but fastidious member of a well-known Eastern club, who was serving in the ranks, was christened "Tough Ike"; and his bunkie, the man who shared his shelter-tent, who was a decidedly rough cow-puncher, gradually acquired the name of "The Dude." One unlucky and simple-minded cow-puncher, who had never been east of the great plains in his life, unwarily boasted that he had an aunt in New York, and ever afterward went by the name of "Metropolitan Bill." A huge redheaded Irishman was named "Sheeny Solomon." A young Jew who developed into one of the best fighters in the regiment accepted, with entire equanimity, the name of "Pork-chop." We had quite a number of professional gamblers, who, I am bound to say, usually made good soldiers. One, who was almost abnormally quiet and gentle, was called "Hell Roarer"; while another, who in point of language and deportment was his exact antithesis, was christened "Prayerful James."

While the officers and men were learning their duties, and learning to know one another, Colonel Wood was straining every nerve to get our equipments—an effort which was complicated by the tendency of the Ordnance Bureau to send whatever we really needed by freight instead of express. Finally, just as the last rifles, revolvers, and saddles came, we were ordered by wire at once to proceed by train to Tampa.

Instantly, all was joyful excitement. We had enjoyed San Antonio, and were glad that our regiment had been organized in the city where the Alamo commemorates the death fight of Crockett, Bowie, and their famous band of frontier heroes. All of us had worked hard, so that we had had no time to be homesick or downcast; but we were glad to leave the hot camp, where every day the strong wind sifted the dust through everything, and to start for the gathering-place of the army which was to invade Cuba. Our horses and men were getting into good shape. We were well enough equipped to warrant our starting on the campaign, and every man was filled with dread of being out of the fighting. We had a pack-train of 150 mules, so we had close on to 1,200 animals to carry.

Of course, our train was split up into sections, seven, all told; Colonel Wood commanding the first three, and I the last four. The journey by rail from San Antonio to Tampa took just four days, and I doubt if anybody who was on the trip will soon forget it. To occupy my few spare moments, I was reading M. Demolins's "Supériorité des Anglo-Saxons." M. Demolins, in giving the reasons why the English-speaking peoples are superior to those of Continental Europe, lays much stress upon the way in which "militarism" deadens the power of individual initiative, the soldier being trained to complete suppression of individual will, while his faculties become atrophied in consequence of his being merely a cog in a vast and perfectly ordered machine. I can assure the excellent French publicist that American "militarism," at least of the volunteer sort, has points of difference from the militarism of Continental Europe. The battalion chief of a newly raised American regiment, when striving to get into a war which the American people have undertaken with buoyant and light-hearted indifference to detail, has positively unlimited opportunity for the display of "individual initiative," and is in no danger whatever either of suffering from unhealthy suppression of personal will, or of finding his faculties of self-help numbed by becoming a cog in a gigantic and smooth-running machine. If such a battalion chief wants to get anything or go anywhere he must do it by exercising every pound of resource, inventiveness, and audacity he possesses. The help, advice, and superintendence he gets from outside will be of the most general, not to say superficial, character. If he is a cavalry officer, he has got to hurry and push the purchase of his horses, plunging into and out of the meshes of red-tape as best he can. He will have to fight for his rifles and his tents and his clothes. He will have to keep his men healthy largely by the light that nature has given him. When he wishes to embark his regiment, he will have to fight for his railway-cars exactly as he fights for his transport when it comes to going across the sea; and on his journey his men will or will not have food, and his horses will or will not have water and hay, and the trains will or will not make connections, in exact correspondence to the energy and success of his own efforts to keep things moving straight.

It was on Sunday, May 29th, that we marched out of our hot, windy, dusty camp to take the cars for Tampa. Colonel Wood went first, with the three sections under his special care. I followed with the other four. The railway had promised us a forty-eight hours' trip, but our experience in loading was enough to show that the promise would not be made good. There were no proper facilities for getting the horses on or off the cars, or for feeding or watering them; and there was endless confusion and delay among the railway officials. I marched my four sections over in the afternoon, the first three having taken the entire day to get off. We occupied the night. As far as the regiment itself was concerned, we worked an excellent system, Wood instructing me exactly how to proceed so as to avoid confusion. Being a veteran campaigner, he had all along insisted that for such work as we had before us we must travel with the minimum possible luggage. The men had merely what they could carry on their own backs, and the officers very little more. My own roll of clothes and bedding could be put on my spare horse. The mule-train was to be used simply for food, forage, and spare ammunition. As it turned out, we were not allowed to take either it or the horses.

It was dusk when I marched my long files of dusty troopers into the station-yard. I then made all dismount, excepting the troop which I first intended to load. This was brought up to the first freight-car. Here every man unsaddled, and left his saddle, bridle, and all that he did not himself need in the car, each individual's property being corded together. A guard was left in the car, and the rest of the men took the naked horses into the pens to be fed and watered. The other troops were loaded in the same way in succession. With each section there were thus a couple of baggage-cars in which the horse-gear, the superfluous baggage, and the travel rations were carried; and I also put aboard, not only at starting, but at every other opportunity, what oats and hay I could get, so as to provide against accidents for the horses. By the time the baggage-cars were loaded the horses of the first section had eaten and drunk their fill, and we loaded them on cattle-cars. The officers of each troop saw to the loading, taking a dozen picked men to help them; for some of the wild creatures, half broken and fresh from the ranges, were with difficulty driven up the chutes. Meanwhile I superintended not merely my own men, but the railroad men; and when the delays of the latter, and their inability to understand what was necessary, grew past bearing, I took charge of the trains myself, so as to insure the horse-cars of each section being coupled with the baggage-cars of that section.

We worked until long past midnight before we got the horses

and baggage aboard, and then found that for some reason the passenger-cars were delayed and would not be out for some hours. In the confusion and darkness men of the different troops had become scattered, and some had drifted off to the vile drinking-booths around the stock-yards; so I sent details to search the latter, while the trumpeters blew the assembly until the First Sergeants could account for all the men. Then the troops were arranged in order, and the men of each lay down where they were, by the tracks and in the brush, to sleep until morning.

At dawn the passenger-trains arrived. The senior Captain of each section saw to it that his own horses, troopers, and baggage were together; and one by one they started off, I taking the last in person. Captain Capron had at the very beginning shown himself to be simply invaluable, from his extraordinary energy, executive capacity, and mastery over men; and I kept his section next mine, so that we generally came together at the different yards.

The next four days were very hot and very dusty. I tried to arrange so the sections would be far enough apart to allow each ample time to unload, feed, water, and load the horses at any stopping-place before the next section could arrive. There was enough delay and failure to make connections on the part of the railroad people to keep me entirely busy, not to speak of seeing at the stopping-places that the inexperienced officers got enough hay for their horses, and that the water given to them was both ample in quantity and drinkable. It happened that we usually made our longest stops at night, and this meant that we were up all night long.

Two or three times a day I got the men buckets of hot coffee, and when we made a long enough stop they were allowed liberty under the supervision of the non-commissioned officers. Some of them abused the privilege, and started to get drunk. These were promptly handled with the necessary severity, in the interest of the others; for it was only by putting an immediate check to every form of lawlessness or disobedience among the few men who were inclined to be bad that we were enabled to give full liberty to those who would not abuse it.

Everywhere the people came out to greet us and cheer us. They brought us flowers; they brought us watermelons and other fruits, and sometimes jugs and pails of milk—all of which we greatly appreciated. We were travelling through a region where practically all the older men had served in the Confederate Army, and where the younger men had all their lives long drunk in the endless tales told by their elders, at home, and at the cross-roads taverns, and in the court-house squares, about the cavalry of Forrest and Morgan and the infantry of Jackson and Hood. The blood of the old men stirred to the distant breath of battle; the blood of the young men leaped hot with eager desire to accompany us. The older women, who remembered the dreadful misery of war—the misery that presses its iron weight most heavily on the wives and the little ones—looked sadly at us; but the young girls drove down in bevies, arrayed in their finery, to wave flags in farewell to the troopers and to beg cartridges and buttons as mementos. Everywhere we saw the Stars and Stripes, and everywhere we were told, half-laughing, by grizzled ex-Confederates that they had never dreamed in the bygone days of bitterness to greet the old flag as they now were greeting it, and to send their sons, as now they were sending them, to fight and die under it.

It was four days later that we disembarked, in a perfect welter of confusion. Tampa lay in the pine-covered sand-flats at the end of a one-track railroad, and everything connected with both military and railroad matters was in an almost inextricable tangle. There was no one to meet us or to tell us where we were to camp, and no one to issue us food for the first twenty-four hours; while the railroad people unloaded us wherever they pleased, or rather wherever the jam of all kinds of trains rendered it possible. We had to buy the men food out of our own pockets, and to seize wagons in order to get our spare baggage taken to the camping ground which we at last found had been allotted to us.

Once on the ground, we speedily got order out of confusion. Under Wood's eye the tents were put up in long streets, the picket-line of each troop stretching down its side of each street. The officers' quarters were at the upper ends of the streets, the company kitchens and sinks at the opposite ends. The camp was strictly policed, and drill promptly begun. For thirty-six hours we let the horses rest, drilling on foot, and then began the mounted drill again. The regiments with which we were afterward to serve were camped near us, and the sandy streets of the little town were thronged with soldiers, almost all of them regulars; for there were but one or two volunteer organizations besides ourselves. The regulars wore the canonical dark blue of Uncle Sam. Our own men were clad in dusty brown blouses, trousers and leggings being of the same hue, while the broad-brimmed soft hat was of dark gray; and very workmanlike they looked as, in column of fours, each troop trotted down its company street to form by squadron or battalion, the troopers sitting steadily in the saddles as they made their half-trained horses conform to the movement of the guidons.

Over in Tampa town the huge winter hotel was gay with general-officers and their staffs, with women in pretty dresses, with newspaper correspondents by the score, with military attachés of foreign powers, and with onlookers of all sorts; but we spent very little time there.

We worked with the utmost industry, special attention being given by each troop-commander to skirmish-drill in the woods. Once or twice we had mounted drill of the regiment as a whole. The military attachés came out to look on—English, German, Russian, French, and Japanese. With the Englishman, Captain Arthur Lee, a capital fellow, we soon struck up an especially close friendship; and we saw much of him throughout the campaign. So we did of several of the newspaper correspondents—Richard Harding Davis, John Fox, Jr., Caspar Whitney, and Frederic Remington. On Sunday Chaplain Brown, of Arizona, held service, as he did almost every Sunday during the campaign.

There were but four or five days at Tampa, however. We were notified that the expedition would start for destination unknown at once, and that we were to go with it; but that our horses were to be left behind, and only eight troops of seventy men each taken. Our sorrow at leaving the horses was entirely outweighed by our joy at going; but it was very hard indeed to select the four troops that were to stay, and the men who had to be left behind from each of the troops that went. Colonel Wood took Major Brodie and myself to command the two squadrons, being allowed only two squadron commanders. The men who were left behind felt the most bitter heart-burn. To the great bulk of them I think it will be a life-long sorrow. I saw more than one, both among the officers and privates, burst into tears when he found he could not go. No outsider can appreciate the bitterness of the disappointment. Of course, really, those that stayed were entitled to precisely as much honor as those that went. Each man was doing his duty, and much the hardest and most disagreeable duty was to stay. Credit should go with the performance of duty, and not with what is very often the accident of glory. All this and much more we explained, but our explanations could not alter the fact that some had to be chosen and some had to be left. One of the Captains chosen was Captain Maximilian Luna, who commanded Troop F, from New Mexico. The Captain's people had been on the banks of the Rio Grande before my forefathers came to the mouth of the Hudson or Wood's landed at Plymouth; and he made the plea that it was his right to go as a representative of his race, for he was the only man of pure Spanish blood who bore a commission in the army, and he demanded the privilege of proving that his people were precisely as loyal Americans as any others. I was glad when it was decided to take him.

It was the evening of June 7th when we suddenly received orders that the expedition was to start from Port Tampa, nine miles distant by rail, at daybreak the following morning; and that if we were not aboard our transport by that time we could not go. We had no intention of getting left, and prepared at once for the scramble which was evidently about to take place. As the number and capacity of the transports were known, or ought to have been known, and as the number and size of the regiments to go were also known, the task of allotting each regiment or fraction of a regiment to its proper transport, and arranging that the regiments and the transports should meet in due order on the dock, ought not to have been difficult. However, no arrangements were made in advance; and we were allowed to shove and hustle for ourselves as best we could, on much the same principles that had governed our preparations hitherto.

We were ordered to be at a certain track with all our baggage at midnight, there to take a train for Port Tampa. At the appointed time we turned up, but the train did not. The men slept heavily, while Wood and I and various other officers wandered about in search of information which no one could give. We now and then came across a Brigadier-General, or even a Major-General; but nobody knew anything. Some regiments got aboard the trains and some did not, but as none of the trains started this made little difference. At three o'clock we received orders to march over to an entirely different track, and away we went. No train appeared on this track either; but at six o'clock some coal-cars came by, and these we seized. By various arguments we persuaded the engineer in charge of the train to back us down the nine miles to Port Tampa, where we arrived covered with coal-dust, but with all our belongings.

The railway tracks ran out on the quay, and the transports, which had been anchored in midstream, were gradually being brought up alongside the quay and loaded. The trains were unloading wherever they happened to be, no attention whatever being paid to the possible position of the transport on which the soldiers were to go. Colonel Wood and I jumped off and started on a hunt, which soon convinced us that we had our work cut out if we were to get a transport at all. From the highest General down, nobody could tell us where to go to find out what transport we were to have. At last we were informed that we were to hunt up the depot quartermaster, Colonel Humphrey. We found his office, where his assistant informed us that he didn't know where the Colonel was, but believed him to be asleep upon one of the transports. This seemed odd at such a time; but so many of the methods in vogue were odd, that we were quite prepared to accept it as a fact. However, it proved not to be such; but for an hour Colonel Humphrey might just as well have been asleep, as nobody knew where he was and nobody could find him, and the quay was crammed with some ten thousand men, most of whom were working at cross purposes.

At last, however, after over an hour's industrious and rapid search through this swarming ant-heap of humanity, Wood and I, who had separated, found Colonel Humphrey at nearly the same time and were alloted a transport—the Yucatan. She was out in midstream, so Wood seized a stray launch and boarded her. At the same time I happened to find out that she had previously been allotted to two other regiments—the Second Regular Infantry and the Seventy-first New York Volunteers, which latter regiment alone contained more men than could be put aboard her. Accordingly, I ran at full speed to our train; and leaving a strong guard with the baggage, I double-quicked the rest of the regiment up to the boat, just in time to board her as she came into the quay, and then to hold her against the Second Regulars and the Seventy-first, who had arrived a little too late, being a shade less ready than we were in the matter of individual initiative. There was a good deal of expostulation, but we had possession; and as the ship could not contain half of the men who had been told to go aboard her, the Seventy-first went away, as did all but four companies of the Second. These latter we took aboard. Meanwhile a General had caused our train to be unloaded at the end of the quay farthest from where the ship was; and the hungry, tired men spent most of the day in the labor of bringing down their baggage and the food and ammunition.

The officers' horses were on another boat, my own being accompanied by my colored body-servant, Marshall, the most faithful and loyal of men, himself an old soldier of the Ninth Cavalry. Marshall had been in Indian campaigns, and he christened my larger horse "Rain-in-the-Face," while the other, a pony, went by the name of "Texas."

By the time that night fell, and our transport pulled off and anchored in midstream, we felt we had spent thirty-six tolerably active hours. The transport was overloaded, the men being packed like sardines, not only below but upon the decks; so that at night it was only possible to walk about by continually stepping over the bodies of the sleepers. The travel rations which had been issued to the men for the voyage were not sufficient, because the meat was very bad indeed; and when a ration consists of only four or five items, which taken together just meet the requirements of a strong and healthy man, the loss of one item is a serious thing. If we had been given canned corn-beef we would have been all right, but instead of this the soldiers were issued horrible stuff called "canned fresh beef." There was no salt in it. At the best it was stringy and tasteless; at the worst it was nauseating. Not one-fourth of it was ever eaten at all, even when the men became very hungry. There were no facilities for the men to cook anything. There was no ice for them; the water was not good; and they had no fresh meat or fresh vegetables.

However, all these things seemed of small importance compared with the fact that we were really embarked, and were with the first expedition to leave our shores. But by next morning came the news that the order to sail had been countermanded, and that we were to stay where we were for the time being. What this meant none of us could understand. It turned out later to be due to the blunder of a naval officer who mistook some of our vessels for Spaniards, and by his report caused consternation in Washington, until by vigorous scouting on the part of our other ships the illusion was dispelled.

Meanwhile the troop-ships, packed tight with their living freight, sweltered in the burning heat of Tampa Harbor. There was nothing whatever for the men to do, space being too cramped for amusement or for more drill than was implied in the manual of arms. In this we drilled them assiduously, and we also continued to hold school for both the officers and the non-commissioned officers. Each troop commander was regarded as responsible for his own non-commissioned officers, and Wood or myself simply dropped in to superintend, just as we did with the manual at arms. In the officers' school Captain Capron was the special instructor, and a most admirable one he was.

The heat, the steaming discomfort, and the confinement, together with the forced inaction, were very irksome; but everyone made the best of it, and there was little or no grumbling even among the men. All, from the highest to the lowest, were bent upon perfecting themselves according to their slender opportunities. Every book of tactics in the regiment was in use from morning until night, and the officers and non-commissioned officers were always studying the problems presented at the schools. About the only amusement was bathing over the side, in which we indulged both in the morning and evening. Many of the men from the Far West had never seen the ocean. One of them who knew how to swim was much interested in finding that the ocean water was not drinkable. Another, who had never in his life before seen any water more extensive that the head-stream of the Rio Grande, met with an accident later in the voyage; that is, his hat blew away while we were in mid-ocean, and I heard him explaining the accident to a friend in the following words: "Oh-o-h, Jim! Ma hat blew into the creek!" So we lay for nearly a week, the vessels swinging around on their anchor chains, while the hot water of the bay flowed to and fro around them and the sun burned overhead.

At last, on the evening of June 13th, we received the welcome order to start. Ship after ship weighed anchor and went slowly ahead under half-steam for the distant mouth of the harbor, the bands playing, the flags flying, the rigging black with the clustered soldiers, cheering and shouting to those left behind on the quay and to their fellows on the other ships. The channel was very tortuous; and we anchored before we had gone far down it, after coming within an ace of a bad collision with another transport. The next morning we were all again under way, and in the afternoon the great fleet steamed southeast until Tampa Light sank in the distance.

For the next six days we sailed steadily southward and eastward through the wonderful sapphire seas of the West Indies. The thirty odd transports moved in long parallel lines, while ahead and behind and on their flanks the gray hulls of the war-ships surged through the blue water. We had every variety of craft to guard us, from the mighty battle-ship and swift cruiser to the converted yachts and the frail, venomous-looking torpedo-boats. The war-ships watched with ceaseless vigilance by day and night. When a sail of any kind appeared, instantly one of our guardians steamed toward it. Ordinarily, the torpedo-boats were towed. Once a strange ship steamed up too close, and instantly the nearest torpedo-boat was slipped like a greyhound from the leash, and sped across the water toward it; but the stranger proved harmless, and the swift, delicate, death-fraught craft returned again.

It was very pleasant, sailing southward through the tropic seas toward the unknown. We knew not whither we were bound, nor what we were to do; but we believed that the nearing future held for us many chances of death and hardship, of honor and renown. If we failed, we would share the fate of all who fail; but we were sure that we would win, that we should score the first great triumph in a mighty world-movement. At night we looked at the new stars, and hailed the Southern Cross when at last we raised it above the horizon. In the daytime we drilled, and in the evening we held officers' school; but there was much time when we had little to do, save to scan the wonderful blue sea and watch the flying-fish. Toward evening, when the officers clustered together on the forward bridge, the band of the Second Infantry played tune after tune, until on our quarter the glorious sun sunk in the red west, and, one by one, the lights blazed out on troop-ship and war-ship for miles ahead and astern, as they steamed onward through the brilliant tropic night.

The men on the ship were young and strong, eager to face what lay hidden before them, eager for adventure where risk was the price of gain. Sometimes they talked of what they might do in the future, and wondered whether we were to attack Santiago or Porto Rico. At other times, as they lounged in groups, they told stories of their past—stories of the mining camps and the cattle ranges, of hunting bear and deer, of war-trails against the Indians, of lawless deeds of violence and the lawful violence by which they were avenged, of brawls in saloons, of shrewd deals in cattle and sheep, of successful quest for the precious metals; stories of brutal wrong and brutal appetite, melancholy love-tales, and memories of nameless heroes—masters of men and tamers of horses.

The officers, too, had many strange experiences to relate; none, not even Llewellen or O'Neill, had been through what was better worth telling, or could tell it better, than Capron. He had spent years among the Apaches, the wildest and fiercest of tribes, and again and again had owed his life to his own cool judgment and extraordinary personal prowess. He knew the sign language, familiar to all the Indians of the mountains and the plains; and it was curious to find that the signs for different animals, for water, for sleep and death, which he knew from holding intercourse with the tribes of the Southeast, were exactly like those which I had picked up on my occasional hunting or trading trips among the Sioux and Mandans of the North. He was a great rifle shot and wolf hunter, and had many tales to tell of the deeds of gallant hounds and the feats of famous horses. He had handled his Indian scouts and dealt with the "bronco" Indians, the renegades from the tribes, in circumstances of extreme peril; for he had seen the sullen, moody Apaches when they suddenly went crazy with wolfish blood-lust, and in their madness wished to kill whomever was nearest. He knew, so far as white man could know, their ways of thought, and how to humor and divert them when on the brink of some dangerous outbreak. Capron's training and temper fitted him to do great work in war; and he looked forward with eager confidence to what the future held, for he was sure that for him it held either triumph or death. Death was the prize he drew.

Most of the men had simple souls. They could relate facts, but they said very little about what they dimly felt. Bucky O'Neill, however, the iron-nerved, iron-willed fighter from Arizona, the Sheriff whose name was a by-word of terror to every wrong-doer, white or red, the gambler who with unmoved face would stake and lose every dollar he had in the world—he, alone among his comrades, was a visionary, an articulate emotionalist. He was very quiet about it, never talking unless he was sure of his listener; but at night, when we leaned on the railing to look at the Southern Cross, he was less apt to tell tales of his hard and stormy past than he was to speak of the mysteries which lie behind courage, and fear, and love, behind animal hatred, and animal lust for the pleasures that have tangible shape. He had keenly enjoyed life, and he could breast its turbulent torrent as few men could; he was a practical man, who knew how to wrest personal success from adverse forces, among money-makers, politicians, and desperadoes alike; yet, down at bottom, what seemed to interest him most was the philosophy of life itself, of our understanding of it, and of the limitations set to that understanding. But he was as far as possible from being a mere dreamer of dreams. A stanchly loyal and generous friend, he was also exceedingly ambitious on his own account. If, by risking his life, no matter how great the risk, he could gain high military distinction, he was bent on gaining it. He had taken so many chances when death lay on the hazard, that he felt the odds were now against him; but, said he, "Who would not risk his life for a star?" Had he lived, and had the war lasted, he would surely have won the eagle, if not the star.

We had a good deal of trouble with the transports, chiefly because they were not under the control of the navy. One of them was towing a schooner, and another a scow; both, of course, kept lagging behind. Finally, when we had gone nearly the length of Cuba, the transport with the schooner sagged very far behind, and then our wretched transport was directed by General Shafter to fall out of line and keep her company. Of course, we executed the order, greatly to the wrath of Captain Clover, who, in the gunboat Bancroft, had charge of the rear of the column—for we could be of no earthly use to the other transport, and by our presence simply added just so much to Captain Clover's anxiety, as he had two transports to protect instead of one. Next morning the rest of the convoy were out of sight, but we reached them just as they finally turned.

Until this we had steamed with the trade-wind blowing steadily in our faces; but once we were well to eastward of Cuba, we ran southwest with the wind behind on our quarter, and we all knew that our destination was Santiago. On the morning of the 20th we were close to the Cuban coast. High mountains rose almost from the water's edge, looking huge and barren across the sea. We sped onward past Guantanamo Bay, where we saw the little picket-ships of the fleet; and in the afternoon we sighted Santiago Harbor, with the great war-ships standing off and on in front of it, gray and sullen in their war-paint.

All next day we rolled and wallowed in the seaway, waiting until a decision was reached as to where we should land. On the morning of June 22d the welcome order for landing came. We did the landing as we had done everything else—that is, in a scramble, each commander shifting for himself. The port at which we landed was called Daiquiri, a squalid little village where there had been a railway and iron-works. There were no facilities for landing, and the fleet did not have a quarter the number of boats it should have had for the purpose. All we could do was to stand in with the transports as close as possible, and then row ashore in our own few boats and the boats of the war-ships. Luck favored our regiment. My former naval aide, while I was Assistant Secretary of the Navy, Lieutenant Sharp, was in command of the Vixen, a converted yacht; and everything being managed on the go-as-you-please principle, he steamed by us and offered to help put us ashore. Of course, we jumped at the chance. Wood and I boarded the Vixen, and there we got Lieutenant Sharp's black Cuban pilot, who told us he could take our transport right in to within a few hundred yards of the land. Accordingly, we put him aboard; and in he brought her, gaining at least a mile and a half by the manœuvre. The other transports followed; but we had our berth, and were all right.

There was plenty of excitement to the landing. In the first place, the smaller war-vessels shelled Daiquiri, so as to dislodge any Spaniards who might be lurking in the neighborhood, and also shelled other places along the coast, to keep the enemy puzzled as to our intentions. Then the surf was high, and the landing difficult; so that the task of getting the men, the ammunition, and provisions ashore was not easy. Each man carried three days' field rations and a hundred rounds of ammunition. Our regiment had accumulated two rapid-fire Colt automatic guns, the gift of Stevens, Kane, Tiffany, and one or two others of the New York men, and also a dynamite gun, under the immediate charge of Sergeant Borrowe. To get these, and especially the last, ashore, involved no little work and hazard. Meanwhile, from another transport, our horses were being landed, together with the mules, by the simple process of throwing them overboard and letting them swim ashore, if they could. Both of Wood's got safely through. One of mine was drowned. The other, little Texas, got ashore all right. While I was superintending the landing at the ruined dock, with Bucky O'Neill, a boatful of colored infantry soldiers capsized, and two of the men went to the bottom; Bucky O'Neill plunging in, in full uniform, to save them, but in vain.

However, by the late afternoon we had all our men, with what ammunition and provisions they could themselves carry, landed, and were ready for anything that might turn up.

III

General Young's Fight at
Las Guasimas

Just before leaving Tampa we had been brigaded with the First
(white) and Tenth (colored) Regular Cavalry under Brigadier-
General S. B. M. Young. We were the Second Brigade, the First
Brigade consisting of the Third and Sixth (white), and the Ninth
(colored) Regular Cavalry under Brigadier-General Sumner. The
two brigades of the cavalry division were under Major-General
Joseph Wheeler, the gallant old Confederate cavalry commander.

General Young was—and is—as fine a type of the American
fighting soldier as a man can hope to see. He had been in command,
as Colonel, of the Yellowstone National Park, and I had seen a
good deal of him in connection therewith, as I was President of the
Boone and Crockett Club, an organization devoted to hunting big
game, to its preservation, and to forest preservation. During the
preceding winter, while he was in Washington, he had lunched with
me at the Metropolitan Club, Wood being one of the other guests.
Of course, we talked of the war, which all of us present believed to
be impending, and Wood and I told him we were going to make
every effort to get in, somehow; and he answered that we must be
sure to get into his brigade, if he had one, and he would guarantee
to show us fighting. None of us forgot the conversation. As soon as

our regiment was raised General Young applied for it to be put in his brigade. We were put in; and he made his word good; for he fought and won the first fight on Cuban soil.

Yet, even though under him, we should not have been in this fight at all if we had not taken advantage of the chance to disembark among the first troops, and if it had not been for Wood's energy in pushing our regiment to the front.

On landing we spent some active hours in marching our men a quarter of a mile or so inland, as boat-load by boat-load they disembarked. Meanwhile one of the men, Knoblauch, a New Yorker, who was a great athlete and a champion swimmer, by diving in the surf off the dock, recovered most of the rifles which had been lost when the boat-load of colored cavalry capsized. The country would have offered very great difficulties to an attacking force had there been resistance. It was little but a mass of rugged and precipitous hills, covered for the most part by dense jungle. Five hundred resolute men could have prevented the disembarkation at very little cost to themselves. There had been about that number of Spaniards at Daiquiri that morning, but they had fled even before the ships began shelling. In their place we found hundreds of Cuban insurgents, a crew of as utter tatterdemalions as human eyes ever looked on, armed with every kind of rifle in all stages of dilapidation. It was evident, at a glance, that they would be no use in serious fighting, but it was hoped that they might be of service in scouting. From a variety of causes, however, they turned out to be nearly useless, even for this purpose, so far as the Santiago campaign was concerned.

We were camped on a dusty, brush-covered flat, with jungle on one side, and on the other a shallow, fetid pool fringed with palm-trees. Huge land-crabs scuttled noisily through the underbrush, exciting much interest among the men. Camping was a simple matter, as each man carried all he had, and the officers had nothing. I took a light mackintosh and a tooth-brush. Fortunately, that night it did not rain; and from the palm-leaves we built shelters from the sun.

General Lawton, a tall, fine-looking man, had taken the advance. A thorough soldier, he at once established outposts and pushed reconnoitring parties ahead on the trails. He had as little baggage as the rest of us. Our own Brigade-Commander, General Young, had exactly the same impedimenta that I had, namely, a mackintosh and a tooth-brush.

Next morning we were hard at work trying to get the stuff unloaded from the ship, and succeeded in getting most of it ashore, but were utterly unable to get transportation for anything but a very small quantity. The great shortcoming throughout the campaign was the utterly inadequate transportation. If we had been allowed to take our mule-train, we could have kept the whole cavalry division supplied.

In the afternoon word came to us to march. General Wheeler, a regular game-cock, was as anxious as Lawton to get first blood, and he was bent upon putting the cavalry division to the front as quickly as possible. Lawton's advance-guard was in touch with the Spaniards, and there had been a skirmish between the latter and some Cubans, who were repulsed. General Wheeler made a reconnoissance in person, found out where the enemy was, and directed General Young to take our brigade and move forward so as to strike him next morning. He had the power to do this, as when General Shafter was afloat he had command ashore.

I had succeeded in finding Texas, my surviving horse, much the worse for his fortnight on the transport and his experience in getting off, but still able to carry me.

It was mid-afternoon and the tropic sun was beating fiercely down when Colonel Wood started our regiment—the First and Tenth Cavalry and some of the infantry regiments having already marched. Colonel Wood himself rode in advance, while I led my squadron, and Major Brodie followed with his. It was a hard march, the hilly jungle trail being so narrow that often we had to go in single file. We marched fast, for Wood was bound to get us ahead of the other regiments, so as to be sure of our place in the body that struck the enemy next morning. If it had not been for his energy in pushing forward, we should certainly have missed the fight. As it was, we did not halt until we were at the extreme front.

The men were not in very good shape for marching, and moreover they were really horsemen, the majority being cow-boys who had never done much walking. The heat was intense and their burdens very heavy. Yet there was very little straggling. Whenever we halted they instantly took off their packs and threw themselves on their backs. Then at the word to start they would spring into place again. The captains and lieutenants tramped along, encouraging the men by example and word. A good part of the time I was by Captain Llewellen, and was greatly pleased to see the way in which he kept his men up to their work. He never pitied or coddled his troopers, but he always looked after them. He helped them whenever he could, and took rather more than his full share of hardship and danger, so that his men naturally followed him with entire devotion. Jack Greenway was under him as lieutenant, and to him the entire march was nothing but an enjoyable outing, the chance of fight on the morrow simply adding the needed spice of excitement.

It was long after nightfall when we tramped through the darkness into the squalid coast hamlet of Siboney. As usual when we made a night camp, we simply drew the men up in column of troops, and then let each man lie down where he was. Black thunder-clouds were gathering. Before they broke the fires were made and the men cooked their coffee and pork, some frying the hard-tack with the pork. The officers, of course, fared just as the men did. Hardly had we finished eating when the rain came, a regular tropic downpour. We sat about, sheltering ourselves as best we could, for the hour or two it lasted; then the fires were relighted and we closed around them, the men taking off their wet things to dry them, so far as possible, by the blaze.

Wood had gone off to see General Young, as General Wheeler had instructed General Young to hit the Spaniards, who were about four miles away, as soon after daybreak as possible. Meanwhile I strolled over to Captain Capron's troop. He and I, with his two lieutenants, Day and Thomas, stood around the fire, together with two or three non-commissioned officers and privates; among the latter were Sergeant Hamilton Fish and Trooper Elliot Cowdin, both of New York. Cowdin, together with two other troopers, Harry Thorpe and Munro Ferguson, had been on my Oyster Bay Polo

Team some years before. Hamilton Fish had already shown himself one of the best non-commissioned officers we had. A huge fellow, of enormous strength and endurance and dauntless courage, he took naturally to a soldier's life. He never complained and never shirked any duty of any kind, while his power over his men was great. So good a sergeant had he made that Captain Capron, keen to get the best men under him, took him when he left Tampa—for Fish's troop remained behind. As we stood around the flickering blaze that night I caught myself admiring the splendid bodily vigor of Capron and Fish—the captain and the sergeant. Their frames seemed of steel, to withstand all fatigue; they were flushed with health; in their eyes shone high resolve and fiery desire. Two finer types of the fighting man, two better representatives of the American soldier, there were not in the whole army. Capron was going over his plans for the fight when we should meet the Spaniards on the morrow, Fish occasionally asking a question. They were both filled with eager longing to show their mettle, and both were rightly confident that if they lived they would win honorable renown and would rise high in their chosen profession. Within twelve hours they both were dead.

I had lain down when toward midnight Wood returned. He had gone over the whole plan with General Young. We were to start by sunrise toward Santiago, General Young taking four troops of the Tenth and four troops of the First up the road which led through the valley; while Colonel Wood was to lead our eight troops along a hill-trail to the left, which joined the valley road about four miles on, at a point where the road went over a spur of the mountain chain and from thence went down hill toward Santiago. The Spaniards had their lines at the junction of the road and the trail.

Before describing our part in the fight, it is necessary to say a word about General Young's share, for, of course, the whole fight was under his direction, and the fight on the right wing under his immediate supervision. General Young had obtained from General Castillo, the commander of the Cuban forces, a full description of the country in front. General Castillo promised Young the aid of eight hundred Cubans, if he made a reconnoissance in force to find out exactly what the Spanish strength was. This promised Cuban aid did not, however, materialize, the Cubans, who had been beaten back by the Spaniards the day before, not appearing on the firing-line until the fight was over.

General Young had in his immediate command a squadron of the First Regular Cavalry, two hundred and forty-four strong, under the command of Major Bell, and a squadron of the Tenth Regular Cavalry, two hundred and twenty strong, under the command of Major Norvell. He also had two Hotchkiss mountain guns, under Captain Watson of the Tenth. He started at a quarter before six in the morning, accompanied by Captain A. L. Mills, as aide. It was at half-past seven that Captain Mills, with a patrol of two men in advance, discovered the Spaniards as they lay across where the two roads came together, some of them in pits, others simply lying in the heavy jungle, while on their extreme right they occupied a big ranch. Where General Young struck them they held a high ridge a little to the left of his front, this ridge being separated by a deep ravine from the hill-trail still farther to the left, down which the Rough Riders were advancing. That is, their forces occupied a range of high hills in the form of an obtuse angle, the salient being toward the space between the American forces, while there were advance parties along both roads. There were stone breastworks flanked by block-houses on that part of the ridge where the two trails came together. The place was called Las Guasimas, from trees of that name in the neighborhood.

General Young, who was riding a mule, carefully examined the Spanish position in person. He ordered the canteens of the troops to be filled, placed the Hotchkiss battery in concealment about nine hundred yards from the Spanish lines, and then deployed the white regulars, with the colored regulars in support, having sent a Cuban guide to try to find Colonel Wood and warn him. He did not attack immediately, because he knew that Colonel Wood, having a more difficult route, would require a longer time to reach the position. During the delay General Wheeler arrived; he had been up since long before dawn, to see that everything went well. Young informed him of the dispositions and plan of attack he made. General Wheeler approved of them, and with excellent judgment left General Young a free hand to fight his battle.

So, about eight o'clock Young began the fight with his Hotchkiss guns, he himself being up on the firing-line. No sooner had the Hotchkiss one-pounders opened than the Spaniards opened fire in return, most of the time firing by volleys executed in perfect time, almost as on parade. They had a couple of light guns, which our people thought were quick firers. The denseness of the jungle and the fact that they used absolutely smokeless powder, made it exceedingly difficult to place exactly where they were, and almost immediately Young, who always liked to get as close as possible to his enemy, began to push his troops forward. They were deployed on both sides of the road in such thick jungle that it was only here and there that they could possibly see ahead, and some confusion, of course, ensued, the support gradually getting mixed with the advance. Captain Beck took A Troop of the Tenth in on the left, next Captain Galbraith's troop of the First; two other troops of the Tenth were on the extreme right. Through the jungle ran wire fences here and there, and as the troops got to the ridge they encountered precipitous heights. They were led most gallantly, as American regular officers always lead their men; and the men followed their leaders with the splendid courage always shown by the American regular soldier. There was not a single straggler among them, and in not one instance was an attempt made by any trooper to fall out in order to assist the wounded or carry back the dead, while so cool were they and so perfect their fire discipline, that in the entire engagement the expenditure of ammunition was not over ten rounds per man. Major Bell, who commanded the squadron, had his leg broken by a shot as he was leading his men. Captain Wainwright succeeded to the command of the squadron. Captain Knox was shot in the abdomen. He continued for some time giving orders to his troops, and refused to allow a man in the firing-line to assist him to the rear. His First Lieutenant, Byram, was himself shot, but continued to lead his men until the wound and the heat overcame him and he fell in a faint. The advance was pushed forward under General Young's eye with the utmost energy, until the enemy's voices could be heard in the entrenchments. The Spaniards kept up a very heavy firing, but the regulars would not be denied, and as they climbed the ridges the Spaniards broke and fled.

Meanwhile, at six o'clock, the Rough Riders began their advance. We first had to climb a very steep hill. Many of the men, foot-sore and weary from their march of the preceding day, found the pace up this hill too hard, and either dropped their bundles or fell out of line, with the result that we went into action with less than five hundred men—as, in addition to the stragglers, a detachment had been left to guard the baggage on shore. At the time I was rather inclined to grumble to myself about Wood setting so fast a pace, but when the fight began I realized that it had been absolutely necessary, as otherwise we should have arrived late and the regulars would have had very hard work indeed.

Tiffany, by great exertions, had corralled a couple of mules and was using them to transport the Colt automatic guns in the rear of the regiment. The dynamite gun was not with us, as mules for it could not be obtained in time.

Captain Capron's troop was in the lead, it being chosen for the most responsible and dangerous position because of Capron's capacity. Four men, headed by Sergeant Hamilton Fish, went first; a support of twenty men followed some distance behind; and then came Capron and the rest of his troop, followed by Wood, with whom General Young had sent Lieutenants Smedburg and Rivers as aides. I rode close behind, at the head of the other three troops of my squadron, and then came Brodie at the head of his squadron. The trail was so narrow that for the most part the men marched in single file, and it was bordered by dense, tangled jungle, through which a man could with difficulty force his way; so that to put out flankers was impossible, for they could not possibly have kept up with the march of the column. Every man had his canteen full. There was a Cuban guide at the head of the column, but he ran away as soon as the fighting began. There were also with us, at the head of the column, two men who did not run away, who, though non-combatants—newspaper correspondents—showed as much gallantry as any soldier in the field. They were Edward Marshall and Richard Harding Davis.

After reaching the top of the hill the walk was very pleasant. Now and then we came to glades or rounded hill-shoulders, whence we could look off for some distance. The tropical forest was very beautiful, and it was a delight to see the strange trees, the splendid royal palms and a tree which looked like a flat-topped acacia, and which was covered with a mass of brilliant scarlet flowers. We heard many bird-notes, too, the cooing of doves and the call of a great brush cuckoo. Afterward we found that the Spanish guerillas imitated these bird-calls, but the sounds we heard that morning, as we advanced through the tropic forest, were from birds, not guerillas, until we came right up to the Spanish lines. It was very beautiful and very peaceful, and it seemed more as if we were off on some hunting excursion than as if we were about to go into a sharp and bloody little fight.

Of course, we accommodated our movements to those of the men in front. After marching for somewhat over an hour, we suddenly came to a halt, and immediately afterward Colonel Wood sent word down the line that the advance guard had come upon a Spanish outpost. Then the order was passed to fill the magazines, which was done.

The men were totally unconcerned, and I do not think they realized that any fighting was at hand; at any rate, I could hear the group nearest me discussing in low murmurs, not the Spaniards, but the conduct of a certain cow-puncher in quitting work on a ranch and starting a saloon in some New Mexican town. In another minute, however, Wood sent me orders to deploy three troops to the right of the trail, and to advance when we became engaged; while, at the same time, the other troops, under Major Brodie, were deployed to the left of the trail where the ground was more open than elsewhere—one troop being held in reserve in the centre, besides the reserves on each wing. Later all the reserves were put into the firing-line.

To the right the jungle was quite thick, and we had barely begun to deploy when a crash in front announced that the fight was on. It was evidently very hot, and L Troop had its hands full; so I hurried my men up abreast of them. So thick was the jungle that it was very difficult to keep together, especially when there was no time for delay, and while I got up Llewellen's troops and Kane's platoon of K Troop, the rest of K Troop under Captain Jenkins which, with Bucky O'Neill's troop, made up the right wing, were behind, and it was some time before they got into the fight at all.

Meanwhile I had gone forward with Llewellen, Greenway, Kane and their troopers until we came out on a kind of shoulder, jutting over a ravine, which separated us from a great ridge on our right. It was on this ridge that the Spaniards had some of their intrench-ments, and it was just beyond this ridge that the Valley Road led, up which the regulars were at that very time pushing their attack; but, of course, at the moment we knew nothing of this. The effect of the smokeless powder was remarkable. The air seemed full of the rustling sound of the Mauser bullets, for the Spaniards knew the trails by which we were advancing, and opened heavily on our po-sition. Moreover, as we advanced we were, of course, exposed, and they could see us and fire. But they themselves were entirely invis-ible. The jungle covered everything, and not the faintest trace of smoke was to be seen in any direction to indicate from whence the bullets came. It was some time before the men fired; Llewellen, Kane, and I anxiously studying the ground to see where our oppo-nents were, and utterly unable to find out.

We could hear the faint reports of the Hotchkiss guns and the reply of two Spanish guns, and the Mauser bullets were singing through the trees over our heads, making a noise like the humming of telephone wires; but exactly where they came from we could not tell. The Spaniards were firing high and for the most part by volleys, and their shooting was not very good, which perhaps was not to be wondered at, as they were a long way off. Gradually, how-ever, they began to get the range and occasionally one of our men would crumple up. In no case did the man make any outcry when hit, seeming to take it as a matter of course; at the outside, making only such a remark as, "Well, I got it that time." With hardly an ex-ception, there was no sign of flinching. I say with hardly an exception, for though I personally did not see an instance, and though all the men at the front behaved excellently, yet there were a very few men who lagged behind and drifted back to the trail over which we had come. The character of the fight put a premium upon such conduct, and afforded a very severe test for raw troops; because the jungle was so dense that as we advanced in open order, every man was, from time to time, left almost alone and away from the eyes of his officers. There was unlimited opportunity for dropping out without attracting notice, while it was peculiarly hard to be exposed to the fire of an unseen foe, and to see men dropping under it, and yet to be, for some time, unable to return it, and also to be entirely ignorant of what was going on in any other part of the field.

It was Richard Harding Davis who gave us our first opportunity to shoot back with effect. He was behaving precisely like my officers, being on the extreme front of the line, and taking every opportunity to study with his glasses the ground where we thought the Spaniards were. I had tried some volley firing at points where I rather doubtfully believed the Spaniards to be, but had stopped firing and was myself studying the jungle-covered mountain ahead with my glasses, when Davis suddenly said: "There they are, Colonel; look over there; I can see their hats near that glade," pointing across the valley to our right. In a minute I, too, made out the hats, and then pointed them out to three or four of our best shots, giving them my estimate of the range. For a minute or two no result followed, and I kept raising the range, at the same time getting more men on the firing-line. Then, evidently, the shots told, for the Spaniards suddenly sprang out of the cover through which we had seen their hats, and ran to another spot; and we could now make out a large number of them.

I accordingly got all of my men up in line and began quick firing. In a very few minutes our bullets began to do damage, for the Spaniards retreated to the left into the jungle, and we lost sight of them. At the same moment a big body of men who, it afterward turned out, were Spaniards, came in sight along the glade, following the retreat of those whom we had just driven from the trenches.

We supposed that there was a large force of Cubans with General Young, not being aware that these Cubans had failed to make their appearance, and as it was impossible to tell the Cubans from the Spaniards, and as we could not decide whether these were Cubans following the Spaniards we had put to flight, or merely another troop of Spaniards retreating after the first (which was really the case) we dared not fire, and in a minute they had passed the glade and were out of sight.

At every halt we took advantage of the cover, sinking down behind any mound, bush, or tree-trunk in the neighborhood. The trees, of course, furnished no protection from the Mauser bullets. Once I was standing behind a large palm with my head out to one side, very fortunately; for a bullet passed through the palm, filling my left eye and ear with the dust and splinters.

No man was allowed to drop out to help the wounded. It was hard to leave them there in the jungle, where they might not be found again until the vultures and the land-crabs came, but war is a grim game and there was no choice. One of the men shot was Harry Heffner of G Troop, who was mortally wounded through the hips. He fell without uttering a sound, and two of his companions dragged him behind a tree. Here he propped himself up and asked to be given his canteen and his rifle, which I handed to him. He then again began shooting, and continued loading and firing until the line moved forward and we left him alone, dying in the gloomy shade. When we found him again, after the fight, he was dead.

At one time, as I was out of touch with that part of my wing commanded by Jenkins and O'Neill, I sent Greenway, with Sergeant Russell, a New Yorker, and trooper Rowland, a New Mexican cow-puncher, down in the valley to find out where they were. To do this the three had to expose themselves to a very severe fire, but they were not men to whom this mattered. Russell was killed; the other two returned and reported to me the position of Jenkins and O'Neill. They then resumed their places on the firing-line. After awhile I noticed blood coming out of Rowland's side and discovered that he had been shot, although he did not seem to be taking any notice of it. He said the wound was only slight, but as I saw he had broken a rib, I told him to go to the rear to the hospital. After some grumbling he went, but fifteen minutes later he was back on the firing-line again and said he could not find the hospital—which I doubted. However, I then let him stay until the end of the fight.

After we had driven the Spaniards off from their position to our right, the firing seemed to die away so far as we were concerned, for the bullets no longer struck around us in such a storm as before, though along the rest of the line the battle was as brisk as ever. Soon we saw troops appearing across the ravine, not very far from where we had seen the Spaniards whom we had thought might be Cubans. Again we dared not fire, and carefully studied the new-comers with our glasses; and this time we were right, for we recognized our own cavalry-men. We were by no means sure that they recognized us, however, and were anxious that they should, but it was very difficult to find a clear spot in the jungle from which to signal; so Sergeant Lee of Troop K climbed a tree and from its summit waved the troop guidon. They waved their guidon back, and as our right wing was now in touch with the regulars, I left Jenkins and O'Neill to keep the connection, and led Llewellen's troop back to the path to join the rest of the regiment, which was evidently still in the thick of the fight. I was still very much in the dark as to where the main body of the Spanish forces were, or exactly what lines the battle was following, and was very uncertain what I ought to do; but I knew it could not be wrong to go forward, and I thought I would find Wood and then see what he wished me to do. I was in a mood to cordially welcome guidance, for it was most bewildering to fight an enemy whom one so rarely saw.

I had not seen Wood since the beginning of the skirmish, when he hurried forward. When the firing opened some of the men began to curse. "Don't swear—shoot!" growled Wood, as he strode along the path leading his horse, and everyone laughed and became cool again. The Spanish outposts were very near our advance guard, and some minutes of the hottest kind of firing followed before they were driven back and slipped off through the jungle to their main lines in the rear.

Here, at the very outset of our active service, we suffered the loss of two as gallant men as ever wore uniform. Sergeant Hamilton Fish at the extreme front, while holding the point up to its work and firing back where the Spanish advance guards lay, was shot and instantly killed; three of the men with him were likewise hit. Captain Capron, leading the advance guard in person, and displaying equal courage and coolness in the way that he handled them, was also struck, and died a few minutes afterward. The command of the troop then devolved upon the First Lieutenant, young Thomas. Like Capron, Thomas was the fifth in line from father to son who had served in the American army, though in his case it was in the volunteer and not the regular service; the four preceding generations had furnished soldiers respectively to the Revolutionary War, the War of 1812, the Mexican War, and the Civil War. In a few minutes Thomas was shot through the leg, and the command devolved upon the Second Lieutenant, Day (a nephew of "Albemarle" Cushing, he who sunk the great Confederate ram). Day, who proved himself to be one of our most efficient officers, continued to handle the men to the best possible advantage, and brought them steadily forward. L Troop was from the Indian Territory. The whites, Indians, and half-breeds in it, all fought with equal courage. Captain McClintock was hurried forward to its relief with his Troop B of Arizona men. In a few minutes he was shot through the leg and his place was taken by his First Lieutenant, Wilcox, who handled his men in the same soldierly manner that Day did.

Among the men who showed marked courage and coolness was the tall color-sergeant, Wright; the colors were shot through three times.

When I had led G Troop back to the trail I ran ahead of them, passing the dead and wounded men of L Troop, passing young Fish as he lay with glazed eyes under the rank tropic growth to one side of the trail. When I came to the front I found the men spread out in a very thin skirmish line, advancing through comparatively open ground, each man taking advantage of what cover he could, while Wood strolled about leading his horse, Brodie being close at hand. How Wood escaped being hit, I do not see, and still less how his horse escaped. I had left mine at the beginning of the action, and was only regretting that I had not left my sword with it, as it kept getting between my legs when I was tearing my way through the jungle. I never wore it again in action. Lieutenant Rivers was with Wood, also leading his horse. Smedburg had been sent off on the by no means pleasant task of establishing communications with Young.

Very soon after I reached the front, Brodie was hit, the bullet shattering one arm and whirling him around as he stood. He had kept on the extreme front all through, his presence and example keeping his men entirely steady, and he at first refused to go to the rear; but the wound was very painful, and he became so faint that he had to be sent. Thereupon, Wood directed me to take charge of the left wing in Brodie's place, and to bring it forward; so over I went.

I now had under me Captains Luna, Muller, and Houston, and I began to take them forward, well spread out, through the high grass of a rather open forest. I noticed Goodrich, of Houston's troop, tramping along behind his men, absorbed in making them keep at good intervals from one another and fire slowly with careful aim. As I came close up to the edge of the troop, he caught a glimpse of me, mistook me for one of his own skirmishers who was crowding in too closely, and called out, "Keep your interval, sir; keep your interval, and go forward."

A perfect hail of bullets was sweeping over us as we advanced. Once I got a glimpse of some Spaniards, apparently retreating, far in the front, and to our right, and we fired a couple of rounds after them. Then I became convinced, after much anxious study, that we were being fired at from some large red-tiled buildings, part of a ranch on our front. Smokeless powder, and the thick cover in our front, continued to puzzle us, and I more than once consulted anxiously the officers as to the exact whereabouts of our opponents. I took a rifle from a wounded man and began to try shots with it myself. It was very hot and the men were getting exhausted, though at this particular time we were not suffering heavily from bullets, the Spanish fire going high. As we advanced, the cover became a little thicker and I lost touch of the main body under Wood; so I halted and we fired industriously at the ranch buildings ahead of us, some five hundred yards off. Then we heard cheering on the right, and I supposed that this meant a charge on the part of Wood's men, so I sprang up and ordered the men to rush the buildings ahead of us. They came forward with a will. There was a moment's heavy firing from the Spaniards, which all went over our heads, and then it ceased entirely. When we arrived at the buildings, panting and out of breath, they contained nothing but heaps of empty cartridge-shells and two dead Spaniards, shot through the head.

The country all around us was thickly forested, so that it was very difficult to see any distance in any direction. The firing had now died out, but I was still entirely uncertain as to exactly what had happened. I did not know whether the enemy had been driven back or whether it was merely a lull in the fight, and we might be attacked again; nor did I know what had happened in any other part of the line, while as I occupied the extreme left, I was not sure whether or not my flank was in danger. At this moment one of our men who had dropped out, arrived with the information (fortunately false) that Wood was dead. Of course, this meant that the command devolved upon me, and I hastily set about taking charge of the regiment. I had been particularly struck by the coolness and courage shown by Sergeants Dame and McIlhenny, and sent them out with small pickets to keep watch in front and to the left of the left wing. I sent other men to fill the canteens with water, and threw the rest out in a long line in a disused sunken road, which gave them cover, putting two or three wounded men, who had hitherto kept up with the fighting-line, and a dozen men who were suffering from heat exhaustion—for the fighting and running under that blazing sun through the thick dry jungle was heart-breaking—into the ranch buildings. Then I started over toward the main body, but to my delight encountered Wood himself, who told me the fight was over and the Spaniards had retreated. He also informed me that other troops were just coming up. The first to appear was a squadron of the Ninth Cavalry, under Major Dimick, which had hurried up to get into the fight, and was greatly disappointed to find it over.

They took post in front of our lines, so that our tired men were able to get a rest, Captain McBlain, of the Ninth, good-naturedly giving us some points as to the best way to station our outposts. Then General Chaffee, rather glum at not having been in the fight himself, rode up at the head of some of his infantry, and I marched my squadron back to where the rest of the regiment was going into camp, just where the two trails came together, and beyond—that is, on the Santiago side of—the original Spanish lines.

The Rough Riders had lost eight men killed and thirty-four wounded, aside from two or three who were merely scratched and whose wounds were not reported. The First Cavalry, white, lost seven men killed and eight wounded; the Tenth Cavalry, colored, one man killed and ten wounded; so, out of 964 men engaged on our side, 16 were killed and 52 wounded. The Spaniards were under General Rubin, with, as second in command, Colonel Alcarez. They had two guns, and eleven companies of about a hundred men each: three belonging to the Porto Rico regiment, three to the San Fernandino, two to the Talavero, two being so-called mobilized companies from the mineral districts, and one a company of engineers; over twelve hundred men in all, together with two guns.*

General Rubin reported that he had repulsed the American attack, and Lieutenant Tejeiro states in his book that General Rubin forced the Americans to retreat, and enumerates the attacking force as consisting of three regular regiments of infantry, the Second Massachusetts and the Seventy-first New York (not one of which fired a gun or were anywhere near the battle), in addition to

---

* See Lieutenant Müller y Tejeiro, "Combates y Capitulación de Santiago de Cuba," page 136. The Lieutenant speaks as if only one échelon, of seven companies and two guns, was engaged on the 24th. The official report says distinctly, "General Rubin's column," which consisted of the companies detailed above. By turning to page 146, where Lieutenant Tejeiro enumerates the strength of the various companies, it will be seen that they averaged over 110 men apiece; this probably does not include officers, and is probably an understatement anyhow. On page 261 he makes the Spanish loss at Las Guasimas, which he calls Sevilla, 9 killed and 27 wounded. Very possibly he includes only the Spanish regulars; two of the Spaniards we slew, over on the left, were in brown, instead of the light blue of the regulars, and were doubtless guerillas.

the sixteen dismounted troops of cavalry. In other words, as the five infantry regiments each included twelve companies, he makes the attacking force consist of just five times the actual amount. As for the "repulse," our line never went back ten yards in any place, and the advance was practically steady; while an hour and a half after the fight began we were in complete possession of the entire Spanish position, and their troops were fleeing in masses down the road, our men being too exhausted to follow them.

General Rubin also reports that he lost but seven men killed. This is certainly incorrect, for Captain O'Neill and I went over the ground very carefully and counted eleven dead Spaniards, all of whom were actually buried by our burying squads. There were probably two or three men whom we missed, but I think that our official reports are incorrect in stating that forty-two dead Spaniards were found; this being based upon reports in which I think some of the Spanish dead were counted two or three times. Indeed, I should doubt whether their loss was as heavy as ours, for they were under cover, while we advanced, often in the open, and their main lines fled long before we could get to close quarters. It was a very difficult country, and a force of good soldiers resolutely handled could have held the pass with ease against two or three times their number. As it was, with a force half of regulars and half of volunteers, we drove out a superior number of Spanish regular troops, strongly posted, without suffering a very heavy loss. Although the Spanish fire was very heavy, it does not seem to me it was very well directed; and though they fired with great spirit while we merely stood at a distance and fired at them, they did not show much resolution, and when we advanced, always went back long before there was any chance of our coming into contact with them. Our men behaved very well indeed—white regulars, colored regulars, and Rough Riders alike. The newspaper press failed to do full justice to the white regulars, in my opinion, from the simple reason that everybody knew that they would fight, whereas there had been a good deal of question as to how the Rough Riders, who were volunteer troops, and the Tenth Cavalry, who were colored, would behave; so there was a tendency to exalt our deeds at the expense of those of the First Regulars, whose courage and good conduct were taken for granted. It was a trying fight beyond what the losses show, for it is hard upon raw soldiers to be pitted against an unseen foe, and to advance steadily when their comrades are falling around them, and when they can only occasionally see a chance to retaliate. Wood's experience in fighting Apaches stood him in good stead. An entirely raw man at the head of the regiment, conducting, as Wood was, what was practically an independent fight, would have been in a very trying position. The fight cleared the way toward Santiago, and we experienced no further resistance.

That afternoon we made camp and dined, subsisting chiefly on a load of beans which we found on one of the Spanish mules which had been shot. We also looked after the wounded. Dr. Church had himself gone out to the firing-line during the fight, and carried to the rear some of the worst wounded on his back or in his arms. Those who could walk had walked in to where the little field-hospital of the regiment was established on the trail. We found all our dead and all the badly wounded. Around one of the latter the big, hideous land-crabs had gathered in a grewsome ring, waiting for life to be extinct. One of our own men and most of the Spanish dead had been found by the vultures before we got to them; and their bodies were mangled, the eyes and wounds being torn.

The Rough Rider who had been thus treated was in Bucky O'Neill's troop; and as we looked at the body, O'Neill turned to me and asked, "Colonel, isn't it Whitman who says of the vultures that 'they pluck the eyes of princes and tear the flesh of kings'?" I answered that I could not place the quotation. Just a week afterward we were shielding his own body from the birds of prey.

One of the men who fired first, and who displayed conspicuous gallantry was a Cherokee half-breed, who was hit seven times, and of course had to go back to the States. Before he rejoined us at Montauk Point he had gone through a little private war of his own; for on his return he found that a cow-boy had gone off with his sweetheart, and in the fight that ensued he shot his rival. Another man of L Troop who also showed marked gallantry was Elliot Cowdin. The men of the plains and mountains were trained by life-long habit to look on life and death with iron philosophy. As I passed by a couple of tall, lank, Oklahoma cow-punchers, I heard one say, "Well, some of the boys got it in the neck!" to which the other answered with the grim plains proverb of the South: "Many a good horse dies."

Thomas Isbell, a half-breed Cherokee in the squad under Hamilton Fish, was among the first to shoot and be shot at. He was wounded no less than seven times. The first wound was received by him two minutes after he had fired his first shot, the bullet going through his neck. The second hit him in the left thumb. The third struck near his right hip, passing entirely through the body. The fourth bullet (which was apparently from a Remington and not from a Mauser) went into his neck and lodged against the bone, being afterward cut out. The fifth bullet again hit his left hand. The sixth scraped his head and the seventh his neck. He did not receive all of the wounds at the same time, over half an hour elapsing between the first and the last. Up to receiving the last wound he had declined to leave the firing-line, but by that time he had lost so much blood that he had to be sent to the rear. The man's wiry toughness was as notable as his courage.

We improvised litters, and carried the more sorely wounded back to Siboney that afternoon and the next morning; the others walked. One of the men who had been most severely wounded was Edward Marshall, the correspondent, and he showed as much heroism as any soldier in the whole army. He was shot through the spine, a terrible and very painful wound, which we supposed meant that he would surely die; but he made no complaint of any kind, and while he retained consciousness persisted in dictating the story of the fight. A very touching incident happened in the improvised open-air hospital after the fight, where the wounded were lying. They did not groan, and made no complaint, trying to help one another. One of them suddenly began to hum, "My Country 'tis of Thee," and one by one the others joined in the chorus, which swelled out through the tropic woods, where the victors lay in camp beside their dead. I did not see any sign among the fighting men, whether wounded or unwounded, of the very complicated emotions assigned to their kind by some of the realistic modern novelists who have written about battles. At the front everyone behaved quite simply and took things as they came, in a matter-of-course way; but there was doubtless, as is always the case, a good deal of panic and confusion in the rear where the wounded, the stragglers, a few of the packers, and two or three newspaper correspondents were, and in consequence the first reports sent back to the coast were of a most alarming character, describing, with minute inaccuracy, how we had run into an ambush, etc. The packers with the mules which carried the rapid-fire guns were among those who ran, and they let the mules go in the jungle; in consequence the guns were never even brought to the firing-line, and only Fred Herrig's skill as a trailer enabled us to recover them. By patient work he followed up the mules' tracks in the forest until he found the animals.

Among the wounded who walked to the temporary hospital at Siboney was the trooper, Rowland, of whom I spoke before. There the doctors examined him, and decreed that his wound was so serious that he must go back to the States. This was enough for Rowland, who waited until nightfall and then escaped, slipping out of the window and making his way back to camp with his rifle and pack, though his wound must have made all movement very painful to him. After this, we felt that he was entitled to stay, and he never left us for a day, distinguishing himself again in the fight at San Juan.

Next morning we buried seven dead Rough Riders in a grave on the summit of the trail, Chaplain Brown reading the solemn burial service of the Episcopalians, while the men stood around with bared heads and joined in singing, "Rock of Ages." Vast numbers of vultures were wheeling round and round in great circles through the blue sky overhead. There could be no more honorable burial than that of these men in a common grave—Indian and cow-boy, miner, packer, and college athlete—the man of unknown ancestry from the lonely Western plains, and the man who carried on his watch the crests of the Stuyvesants and the Fishes, one in the way they had met death, just as during life they had been one in their daring and their loyalty.

On the afternoon of the 25th we moved on a couple of miles, and camped in a marshy open spot close to a beautiful stream. Here we lay for several days. Captain Lee, the British attaché, spent some time with us; we had begun to regard him as almost a member of the regiment. Count von Götzen, the German attaché, another good fellow, also visited us. General Young was struck down with the fever, and Wood took charge of the brigade. This left me in command of the regiment, of which I was very glad, for such experience as we had had is a quick teacher. By this time the men and I knew one another, and I felt able to make them do themselves justice in march or battle. They understood that I paid no heed to where they came from; no heed to their creed, politics, or social standing; that I would care for them to the utmost of my power, but that I demanded the highest performance of duty; while in return I had seen them tested, and knew I could depend absolutely on their courage, hardihood, obedience, and individual initiative.

There was nothing like enough transportation with the army, whether in the way of wagons or mule-trains; exactly as there had been no sufficient number of landing-boats with the transports. The officers' baggage had come up, but none of us had much, and the shelter-tents proved only a partial protection against the terrific downpours of rain. These occurred almost every afternoon, and turned the camp into a tarn, and the trails into torrents and quagmires. We were not given quite the proper amount of food, and what we did get, like most of the clothing issued us, was fitter for the Klondyke than for Cuba. We got enough salt port and hardtack for the men, but not the full ration of coffee and sugar, and nothing else. I organized a couple of expeditions back to the seacoast, taking the strongest and best walkers and also some of the officers' horses and a stray mule or two, and brought back beans and canned tomatoes. These I got partly by great exertions on my part, and partly by the aid of Colonel Weston of the Commissary Department, a particularly energetic man whose services were of great value. A silly regulation forbade my purchasing canned vegetables, etc., except for the officers; and I had no little difficulty in getting round this regulation, and purchasing (with my own money, of course) what I needed for the men.

One of the men I took with me on one of these trips was Sherman Bell, the former Deputy Marshal of Cripple Creek, and Wells-Fargo Express rider. In coming home with his load, through a blinding storm, he slipped and opened the old rupture. The agony was very great and one of his comrades took his load. He himself, sometimes walking, and sometimes crawling, got back to camp, where Dr. Church fixed him up with a spike bandage, but informed him that he would have to be sent back to the States when an ambulance came along. The ambulance did not come until the next day, which was the day before we marched to San Juan. It arrived after nightfall, and as soon as Bell heard it coming, he crawled out of the hospital tent into the jungle, where he lay all night; and the ambulance went off without him. The men shielded him just as school-boys would shield a companion, carrying his gun, belt, and bedding; while Bell kept out of sight until the column started, and then staggered along behind it. I found him the morning of the San Juan fight. He told me that he wanted to die fighting, if die he must, and I hadn't the heart to send him back. He did splendid service that day, and afterward in the trenches, and though the rupture opened twice again, and on each occasion he was within a hair's breadth of death, he escaped, and came back with us to the United States.

The army was camped along the valley, ahead of and behind us, our outposts being established on either side. From the generals to the privates all were eager to march against Santiago. At daybreak, when the tall palms began to show dimly through the rising mist, the scream of the cavalry trumpets tore the tropic dawn; and in the evening, as the bands of regiment after regiment played the "Star-Spangled Banner," all, officers and men alike, stood with heads uncovered, wherever they were, until the last strains of the anthem died away in the hot sunset air.

IV

THE CAVALRY AT SANTIAGO

On June 30th we received orders to hold ourselves in readiness to march against Santiago, and all the men were greatly overjoyed, for the inaction was trying. The one narrow road, a mere muddy track along which the army was encamped, was choked with the marching columns. As always happened when we had to change camp, everything that the men could not carry, including, of course, the officers' baggage, was left behind.

About noon the Rough Riders struck camp and drew up in column beside the road in the rear of the First Cavalry. Then we sat down and waited for hours before the order came to march, while regiment after regiment passed by, varied by bands of tatterdemalion Cuban insurgents, and by mule-trains with ammunition. Every man carried three days' provisions. We had succeeded in borrowing mules sufficient to carry along the dynamite gun and the automatic Colts.

At last, toward mid-afternoon, the First and Tenth Cavalry, ahead of us, marched, and we followed. The First was under the command of Lieutenant-Colonel Veile, the Tenth under Lieutenant-Colonel Baldwin. Every few minutes there would be a stoppage in front, and at the halt I would make the men sit or lie down beside the track, loosening their packs. The heat was intense as we passed through the still, close jungle, which formed a wall on either hand. Occasionally we came to gaps or open spaces, where some regiment was camped, and now and then one of these regiments, which apparently had been left out of its proper place, would file into the road, breaking up our line of march. As a result, we finally found ourselves following merely the tail of the regiment ahead of us, an infantry regiment being thrust into the interval. Once or twice we had to wade streams. Darkness came on, but we still continued to march. It was about eight o'clock when we turned to the left and climbed El Poso hill, on whose summit there was a ruined ranch and sugar factory, now, of course, deserted. Here I found General Wood, who was arranging for the camping of the brigade. Our own arrangements for the night were simple. I extended each troop across the road into the jungle, and then the men threw down their belongings where they stood and slept on their arms. Fortunately, there was no rain. Wood and I curled up under our rain-coats on the saddle-blankets, while his two aides, Captain A. L. Mills and Lieutenant W. N. Ship, slept near us. We were up before dawn and getting breakfast. Mills and Ship had nothing to eat, and they breakfasted with Wood and myself, as we had been able to get some handfuls of beans, and some coffee and sugar, as well as the ordinary bacon and hardtack.

We did not talk much, for though we were in ignorance as to precisely what the day would bring forth, we knew that we should see fighting. We had slept soundly enough, although, of course, both Wood and I during the night had made a round of the sentries, he of the brigade, and I of the regiment; and I suppose that, excepting among hardened veterans, there is always a certain feeling of uneasy excitement the night before the battle.

Mills and Ship were both tall, fine-looking men, of tried courage, and thoroughly trained in every detail of their profession; I remember being struck by the quiet, soldierly way they were going about their work early that morning. Before noon one was killed and the other dangerously wounded.

General Wheeler was sick, but with his usual indomitable pluck and entire indifference to his own personal comfort, he kept to the front. He was unable to retain command of the cavalry division, which accordingly devolved upon General Samuel Sumner, who commanded it until mid-afternoon, when the bulk of the fighting was over. General Sumner's own brigade fell to Colonel Henry Carroll. General Sumner led the advance with the cavalry, and the battle was fought by him and by General Kent, who commanded the infantry division, and whose foremost brigade was led by General Hawkins.

As the sun rose the men fell in, and at the same time a battery of field-guns was brought up on the hill-crest just beyond, between us and toward Santiago. It was a fine sight to see the great horses straining under the lash as they whirled the guns up the hill and into position.

Our brigade was drawn up on the hither side of a kind of half basin, a big band of Cubans being off to the left. As yet we had received no orders, except that we were told that the main fighting was to be done by Lawton's infantry division, which was to take El Caney, several miles to our right, while we were simply to make a diversion. This diversion was to be made mainly with the artillery, and the battery which had taken position immediately in front of us was to begin when Lawton began.

It was about six o'clock that the first report of the cannon from El Caney came booming to us across the miles of still jungle. It was a very lovely morning, the sky of cloudless blue, while the level, shimmering rays from the just-risen sun brought into fine relief the splendid palms which here and there towered above the lower growth. The lofty and beautiful mountains hemmed in the Santiago plain, making it an amphitheatre for the battle.

Immediately our guns opened, and at the report great clouds of white smoke hung on the ridge crest. For a minute or two there was no response. Wood and I were sitting together, and Wood remarked to me that he wished our brigade could be moved somewhere else, for we were directly in line of any return fire aimed by the Spaniards at the battery. Hardly had he spoken when there was a peculiar whistling, singing sound in the air, and immediately afterward the noise of something exploding over our heads. It was shrapnel from the Spanish batteries. We sprung to our feet and leaped on our horses. Immediately afterward a second shot came which burst directly above us; and then a third. From the second shell one of the shrapnel bullets dropped on my wrist, hardly breaking the skin, but raising a bump about as big as a hickory-nut. The same shell wounded four of my regiment, one of them being Mason Mitchell, and two or three of the regulars were also hit, one losing his leg by a great fragment of shell. Another shell exploded right in the middle of the Cubans, killing and wounding a good many, while the remainder scattered like guinea-hens. Wood's led horse was also shot through the lungs. I at once hustled my regiment over the crest of the hill into the thick underbrush, where I had no little difficulty in getting them together again into column.

Meanwhile the firing continued for fifteen or twenty minutes, until it gradually died away. As the Spaniards used smokeless powder, their artillery had an enormous advantage over ours, and, moreover, we did not have the best type of modern guns, our fire being slow.

As soon as the firing ceased, Wood formed his brigade, with my regiment in front, and gave me orders to follow behind the First Brigade, which was just moving off the ground. In column of fours we marched down the trail toward the ford of the San Juan River. We passed two or three regiments of infantry, and were several times halted before we came to the ford. The First Brigade, which was under Colonel Carroll—Lieutenant-Colonel Hamilton commanding the Ninth Regiment, Major Wessels the Third, and Captain Kerr the Sixth—had already crossed and was marching to the right, parallel to, but a little distance from, the river. The Spaniards in the trenches and block-houses on top of the hills in front were already firing at the brigade in desultory fashion. The extreme advance of the Ninth Cavalry was under Lieutenants McNamee and Hartwick. They were joined by General Hawkins, with his staff, who was looking over the ground and deciding on the route he should take his infantry brigade.

Our orders had been of the vaguest kind, being simply to march to the right and connect with Lawton—with whom, of course, there was no chance of our connecting. No reconnoissance had been made, and the exact position and strength of the Spaniards was not known. A captive balloon was up in the air at this moment, but it was worse than useless. A previous proper reconnoissance and proper look-out from the hills would have given us exact information. As it was, Generals Kent, Sumner, and Hawkins had to be their own reconnoissance, and they fought their troops so well that we won anyhow.

I was now ordered to cross the ford, march half a mile or so to the right, and then halt and await further orders; and I promptly hurried my men across, for the fire was getting hot, and the captive balloon, to the horror of everybody, was coming down to the ford. Of course, it was a special target for the enemy's fire. I got my men across before it reached the ford. There it partly collapsed and remained, causing severe loss of life, as it indicated the exact position where the Tenth and the First Cavalry, and the infantry, were crossing.

As I led my column slowly along, under the intense heat, through the high grass of the open jungle, the First Brigade was to our left, and the firing between it and the Spaniards on the hills grew steadily hotter and hotter. After awhile I came to a sunken lane, and as by this time the First Brigade had stopped and was engaged in a stand-up fight, I halted my men and sent back word for orders. As we faced toward the Spanish hills my regiment was on the right with next to it and a little in advance the First Cavalry, and behind them the Tenth. In our front the Ninth held the right, the Sixth the centre, and the Third the left; but in the jungle the lines were already overlapping in places. Kent's infantry were coming up, farther to the left.

Captain Mills was with me. The sunken lane, which had a wire fence on either side, led straight up toward, and between, the two hills in our front, the hill on the left, which contained heavy blockhouses, being farther away from us than the hill on our right, which we afterward grew to call Kettle Hill, and which was surmounted merely by some large ranch buildings or haciendas, with sunken brick-lined walls and cellars. I got the men as well-sheltered as I could. Many of them lay close under the bank of the lane, others slipped into the San Juan River and crouched under its hither bank, while the rest lay down behind the patches of bushy jungle in the tall grass. The heat was intense, and many of the men were already showing signs of exhaustion. The sides of the hills in front were bare; but the country up to them was, for the most part, covered with such dense jungle that in charging through it no accuracy of formation could possibly be preserved.

The fight was now on in good earnest, and the Spaniards on the hills were engaged in heavy volley firing. The Mauser bullets drove in sheets through the trees and the tall jungle grass, making a peculiar whirring or rustling sound; some of the bullets seemed to pop in the air, so that we thought they were explosive; and, indeed, many of those which were coated with brass did explode, in the sense that the brass coat was ripped off, making a thin plate of hard metal with a jagged edge, which inflicted a ghastly wound. These bullets were shot from a .45-calibre rifle carrying smokeless powder, which was much used by the guerillas and irregular Spanish troops. The Mauser bullets themselves made a small clean hole, with the result that the wound healed in a most astonishing manner. One or two of our men who were shot in the head had the skull blown open, but elsewhere the wounds from the minute steel-coated bullet, with its very high velocity, were certainly nothing like as serious as those made by the old large-calibre, low-power rifle. If a man was shot through the heart, spine, or brain he was, of course, killed instantly; but very few of the wounded died—even under the appalling conditions which prevailed, owing to the lack of attendance and supplies in the field-hospitals with the army.

While we were lying in reserve we were suffering nearly as much as afterward when we charged. I think that the bulk of the Spanish fire was practically unaimed, or at least not aimed at any particular man, and only occasionally at a particular body of men; but they swept the whole field of battle up to the edge of the river, and man after man in our ranks fell dead or wounded, although I had the troopers scattered out far apart, taking advantage of every scrap of cover.

Devereux was dangerously shot while he lay with his men on the edge of the river. A young West Point cadet, Ernest Haskell, who had taken his holiday with us as an acting second lieutenant, was shot through the stomach. He had shown great coolness and gallantry, which he displayed to an even more marked degree after being wounded, shaking my hand and saying, "All right, Colonel, I'm going to get well. Don't bother about me, and don't let any man come away with me." When I shook hands with him, I thought he would surely die; yet he recovered.

The most serious loss that I and the regiment could have suffered befell just before we charged. Bucky O'Neill was strolling up and down in front of his men, smoking his cigarette, for he was inveterately addicted to the habit. He had a theory that an officer ought never to take cover—a theory which was, of course, wrong, though in a volunteer organization the officers should certainly expose themselves very fully, simply for the effect on the men; our regimental toast on the transport running, "The officers; may the war last until each is killed, wounded, or promoted." As O'Neill moved to and fro, his men begged him to lie down, and one of the sergeants said, "Captain, a bullet is sure to hit you." O'Neill took his cigarette out of his mouth, and blowing out a cloud of smoke laughed and said, "Sergeant, the Spanish bullet isn't made that will kill me." A little later he discussed for a moment with one of the regular officers the direction from which the Spanish fire was coming. As he turned on his heel a bullet struck him in the mouth and came out at the back of his head; so that even before he fell his wild and gallant soul had gone out into the darkness.

My orderly was a brave young Harvard boy, Sanders, from the quaint old Massachusetts town of Salem. The work of an orderly on foot, under the blazing sun, through the hot and matted jungle, was very severe, and finally the heat overcame him. He dropped; nor did he ever recover fully, and later he died from fever. In his place I summoned a trooper whose name I did not know. Shortly afterward, while sitting beside the bank, I directed him to go back and ask whatever general he came across if I could not advance, as my men were being much cut up. He stood up to salute and then pitched forward across my knees, a bullet having gone through his throat, cutting the carotid.

When O'Neill was shot, his troop, who were devoted to him, were for the moment at a loss whom to follow. One of their number, Henry Bardshar, a huge Arizona miner, immediately attached himself to me as my orderly, and from that moment he was closer to me, not only in the fight, but throughout the rest of the campaign, than any other man, not even excepting the color-sergeant, Wright.

Captain Mills was with me; gallant Ship had already been killed. Mills was an invaluable aide, absolutely cool, absolutely unmoved or flurried in any way.

I sent messenger after messenger to try to find General Sumner or General Wood and get permission to advance, and was just about making up my mind that in the absence of orders I had better "march toward the guns," when Lieutenant-Colonel Dorst came riding up through the storm of bullets with the welcome command "to move forward and support the regulars in the assault on the hills in front." General Sumner had obtained authority to advance from Lieutenant Miley, who was representing General Shafter at the front, and was in the thick of the fire. The General at once ordered the first brigade to advance on the hills, and the second to support it. He himself was riding his horse along the lines, superintending the fight. Later I overheard a couple of my men talking together about him. What they said illustrates the value of a display of courage among the officers in hardening their soldiers; for their theme was how, as they were lying down under a fire which they could not return, and were in consequence feeling rather nervous, General Sumner suddenly appeared on horseback, sauntering by quite unmoved; and, said one of the men, "That made us feel all right. If the General could stand it, we could."

The instant I received the order I sprang on my horse and then my "crowded hour" began. The guerillas had been shooting at us from the edges of the jungle and from their perches in the leafy trees, and as they used smokeless powder, it was almost impossible to see them, though a few of my men had from time to time responded. We had also suffered from the hill on our right front, which was held chiefly by guerillas, although there were also some Spanish regulars with them, for we found their dead. I formed my men in column of troops, each troop extended in open skirmishing order, the right resting on the wire fences which bordered the sunken lane. Captain Jenkins led the first squadron, his eyes literally dancing with joyous excitement.

I started in the rear of the regiment, the position in which the colonel should theoretically stay. Captain Mills and Captain McCormick were both with me as aides; but I speedily had to send them off on special duty in getting the different bodies of men forward. I had intended to go into action on foot as at Las Guasimas, but the heat was so oppressive that I found I should be quite unable to run up and down the line and superintend matters unless I was mounted; and, moreover, when on horseback, I could see the men better and they could see me better.

A curious incident happened as I was getting the men started forward. Always when men have been lying down under cover for some time, and are required to advance, there is a little hesitation, each looking to see whether the others are going forward. As I rode down the line, calling to the troopers to go forward, and rasping brief directions to the captains and lieutenants, I came upon a man lying behind a little bush, and I ordered him to jump up. I do not think he understood that we were making a forward move, and he looked up at me for a moment with hesitation, and I again bade him rise, jeering him and saying: "Are you afraid to stand up when I am on horseback?" As I spoke, he suddenly fell forward on his face, a bullet having struck him and gone through him lengthwise. I suppose the bullet had been aimed at me; at any rate, I, who was on horseback in the open, was unhurt, and the man lying flat on the ground in the cover beside me was killed. There were several pairs of brothers with us; of the two Nortons one was killed; of the two McCurdys one was wounded.

I soon found that I could get that line, behind which I personally was, faster forward than the one immediately in front of it, with the result that the two rearmost lines of the regiment began to crowd together; so I rode through them both, the better to move on the one in front. This happened with every line in succession, until I found myself at the head of the regiment.

Both lieutenants of B Troop from Arizona had been exerting themselves greatly, and both were overcome by the heat; but Sergeants Campbell and Davidson took it forward in splendid shape. Some of the men from this troop and from the other Arizona troop (Bucky O'Neill's) joined me as a kind of fighting tail.

The Ninth Regiment was immediately in front of me, and the First on my left, and these went up Kettle Hill with my regiment. The Third, Sixth, and Tenth went partly up Kettle Hill (following the Rough Riders and the Ninth and First), and partly between that and the block-house hill, which the infantry were assailing. General Sumner in person gave the Tenth the order to charge the hills; and it went forward at a rapid gait. The three regiments went forward more or less intermingled, advancing steadily and keeping up a heavy fire. Up Kettle Hill Sergeant George Berry, of the Tenth, bore not only his own regimental colors but those of the Third, the color-sergeant of the Third having been shot down; he kept shouting, "Dress on the colors, boys, dress on the colors!" as he followed Captain Ayres, who was running in advance of his men, shouting and waving his hat. The Tenth Cavalry lost a greater proportion of its officers than any other regiment in the battle—eleven out of twenty-two.

By the time I had come to the head of the regiment we ran into the left wing of the Ninth Regulars, and some of the First Regulars, who were lying down; that is, the troopers were lying down, while the officers were walking to and fro. The officers of the white and colored regiments alike took the greatest pride in seeing that the men more than did their duty; and the mortality among them was great.

I spoke to the captain in command of the rear platoons, saying that I had been ordered to support the regulars in the attack upon the hills, and that in my judgment we could not take these hills by firing at them, and that we must rush them. He answered that his orders were to keep his men lying where they were, and that he could not charge without orders. I asked where the Colonel was, and as he was not in sight, said, "Then I am the ranking officer here and I give the order to charge"—for I did not want to keep the men longer in the open suffering under a fire which they could not effectively return. Naturally the Captain hesitated to obey this order when no word had been received from his own Colonel. So I said, "Then let my men through, sir," and rode on through the lines, followed by the grinning Rough Riders, whose attention had been completely taken off the Spanish bullets, partly by my dialogue with the regulars, and partly by the language I had been using to themselves as I got the lines forward, for I had been joking with some and swearing at others, as the exigencies of the case seemed to demand. When we started to go through, however, it proved too much for the regulars, and they jumped up and came along, their officers and troops mingling with mine, all being delighted at the chance. When I got to where the head of the left wing of the Ninth was lying, through the courtesy of Lieutenant Hartwick, two of whose colored troopers threw down the fence, I was enabled to get back into the lane, at the same time waving my hat, and giving the order to charge the hill on our right front. Out of my sight, over on the right, Captains McBlain and Taylor, of the Ninth, made up their minds independently to charge at just about this time; and at almost the same moment Colonels Carroll and Hamilton, who were off, I believe, to my left, where we could see neither them nor their men, gave the order to advance. But of all this I knew nothing at the time. The whole line, tired of waiting, and eager to close with the enemy, was straining to go forward; and it seems that different parts slipped the leash at almost the same moment. The First Cavalry came up the hill just behind, and partly mixed with my regiment and the Ninth. As already said, portions of the Third, Sixth, and Tenth followed, while the rest of the members of these three regiments kept more in touch with the infantry on our left.

By this time we were all in the spirit of the thing and greatly excited by the charge, the men cheering and running forward between shots, while the delighted faces of the foremost officers, like

Captain C. J. Stevens, of the Ninth, as they ran at the head of their troops, will always stay in my mind. As soon as I was in the line I galloped forward a few yards until I saw that the men were well started, and then galloped back to help Goodrich, who was in command of his troop, get his men across the road so as to attack the hill from that side. Captain Mills had already thrown three of the other troops of the regiment across this road for the same purpose. Wheeling around, I then again galloped toward the hill, passing the shouting, cheering, firing men, and went up the lane, splashing through a small stream; when I got abreast of the ranch buildings on the top of Kettle Hill, I turned and went up the slope. Being on horseback I was, of course, able to get ahead of the men on foot, excepting my orderly, Henry Bardshar, who had run ahead very fast in order to get better shots at the Spaniards, who were now running out of the ranch buildings. Sergeant Campbell and a number of the Arizona men, and Dudley Dean, among others, were very close behind. Stevens, with his platoon of the Ninth, was abreast of us; so were McNamee and Hartwick. Some forty yards from the top I ran into a wire fence and jumped off Little Texas, turning him loose. He had been scraped by a couple of bullets, one of which nicked my elbow, and I never expected to see him again. As I ran up to the hill, Bardshar stopped to shoot, and two Spaniards fell as he emptied his magazine. These were the only Spaniards I actually saw fall to aimed shots by any one of my men, with the exception of two guerillas in trees.

Almost immediately afterward the hill was covered by the troops, both Rough Riders and the colored troopers of the Ninth, and some men of the First. There was the usual confusion, and afterward there was much discussion as to exactly who had been on the hill first. The first guidons planted there were those of the three New Mexican troops, G, E, and F, of my regiment, under their Captains, Llewellen, Luna, and Muller, but on the extreme right of the hill, at the opposite end from where we struck it, Captains Taylor and McBlain and their men of the Ninth were first up. Each of the five captains was firm in the belief that his troop was first up. As for the individual men, each of whom honestly thought he was first on the summit, their name was legion. One Spaniard was captured in the buildings, another was shot as he tried to hide himself, and a few others were killed as they ran.

Among the many deeds of conspicuous gallantry here performed, two, both to the credit of the First Cavalry, may be mentioned as examples of the others, not as exceptions. Sergeant Charles Karsten, while close beside Captain Tutherly, the squadron commander, was hit by a shrapnel bullet. He continued on the line, firing until his arm grew numb; and he then refused to go to the rear, and devoted himself to taking care of the wounded, utterly unmoved by the heavy fire. Trooper Hugo Brittain, when wounded, brought the regimental standard forward, waving it to and fro, to cheer the men.

No sooner were we on the crest than the Spaniards from the line of hills in our front, where they were strongly intrenched, opened a very heavy fire upon us with their rifles. They also opened upon us with one or two pieces of artillery, using time fuses which burned very accurately, the shells exploding right over our heads.

On the top of the hill was a huge iron kettle, or something of the kind, probably used for sugar refining. Several of our men took shelter behind this. We had a splendid view of the charge on the San Juan block-house to our left, where the infantry of Kent, led by Hawkins, were climbing the hill. Obviously the proper thing to do was to help them, and I got the men together and started them volley-firing against the Spaniards in the San Juan block-house and in the trenches around it. We could only see their heads; of course this was all we ever could see when we were firing at them in their trenches. Stevens was directing not only his own colored troopers, but a number of Rough Riders; for in a mêlée good soldiers are always prompt to recognize a good officer, and are eager to follow him.

We kept up a brisk fire for some five or ten minutes; meanwhile we were much cut up ourselves. Gallant Colonel Hamilton, than whom there was never a braver man, was killed, and equally gallant

Colonel Carroll wounded. When near the summit Captain Mills had been shot through the head, the bullet destroying the sight of one eye permanently and of the other temporarily. He would not go back or let any man assist him, sitting down where he was and waiting until one of the men brought him word that the hill was stormed. Colonel Veile planted the standard of the First Cavalry on the hill, and General Sumner rode up. He was fighting his division in great form, and was always himself in the thick of the fire. As the men were much excited by the firing, they seemed to pay very little heed to their own losses.

Suddenly, above the cracking of the carbines, rose a peculiar drumming sound, and some of the men cried, "The Spanish machine-guns!" Listening, I made out that it came from the flat ground to the left, and jumped to my feet, smiting my hand on my thigh, and shouting aloud with exultation, "It's the Gatlings, men, our Gatlings!" Lieutenant Parker was bringing his four Gatlings into action, and shoving them nearer and nearer the front. Now and then the drumming ceased for a moment; then it would resound again, always closer to San Juan hill, which Parker, like ourselves, was hammering to assist the infantry attack. Our men cheered lustily. We saw much of Parker after that, and there was never a more welcome sound than his Gatlings as they opened. It was the only sound which I ever heard my men cheer in battle.

The infantry got nearer and nearer the crest of the hill. At last we could see the Spaniards running from the rifle-pits as the Americans came on in their final rush. Then I stopped my men for fear they should injure their comrades, and called to them to charge the next line of trenches, on the hills in our front, from which we had been undergoing a good deal of punishment. Thinking that the men would all come, I jumped over the wire fence in front of us and started at the double; but, as a matter of fact, the troopers were so excited, what with shooting and being shot, and shouting and cheering, that they did not hear, or did not heed me; and after running about a hundred yards I found I had only five men along with me. Bullets were ripping the grass all around us, and one of the men, Clay Green, was mortally wounded; another, Winslow Clark, a Harvard man, was shot first in the leg and then through the body. He made not the slightest murmur, only asking me to put his water canteen where he could get at it, which I did; he ultimately recovered. There was no use going on with the remaining three men, and I bade them stay where they were while I went back and brought up the rest of the brigade. This was a decidedly cool request, for there was really no possible point in letting them stay there while I went back; but at the moment it seemed perfectly natural to me, and apparently so to them, for they cheerfully nodded, and sat down in the grass, firing back at the line of trenches from which the Spaniards were shooting at them. Meanwhile, I ran back, jumped over the wire fence, and went over the crest of the hill, filled with anger against the troopers, and especially those of my own regiment, for not having accompanied me. They, of course, were quite innocent of wrong-doing; and even while I taunted them bitterly for not having followed me, it was all I could do not to smile at the look of injury and surprise that came over their faces, while they cried out, "We didn't hear you, we didn't see you go, Colonel; lead on now, we'll sure follow you." I wanted the other regiments to come too, so I ran down to where General Sumner was and asked him if I might make the charge; and he told me to go and that he would see that the men followed. By this time everybody had his attention attracted, and when I leaped over the fence again, with Major Jenkins beside me, the men of the various regiments which were already on the hill came with a rush, and we started across the wide valley which lay between us and the Spanish intrenchments. Captain Dimmick, now in command of the Ninth, was bringing it forward; Captain McBlain had a number of Rough Riders mixed in with his troop, and led them all together; Captain Taylor had been severely wounded. The long-legged men like Greenway, Goodrich, sharp-shooter Proffit, and others, outstripped the rest of us, as we had a considerable distance to go. Long before we got near them the Spaniards ran, save a few here and there, who either surrendered or were shot down. When we reached the trenches we found them filled with dead bodies in the light blue and white uniform of the Spanish regular army. There were very few wounded. Most of the fallen had little holes in their heads from which their brains were oozing; for they were covered from the neck down by the trenches.

It was at this place that Major Wessels, of the Third Cavalry, was shot in the back of the head. It was a severe wound, but after having it bound up he again came to the front in command of his regiment. Among the men who were foremost was Lieutenant Milton F. Davis, of the First Cavalry. He had been joined by three men of the Seventy-first New York, who ran up, and, saluting, said, "Lieutenant, we want to go with you, our officers won't lead us." One of the brave fellows was soon afterward shot in the face. Lieutenant Davis's first sergeant, Clarence Gould, killed a Spanish soldier with his revolver, just as the Spaniard was aiming at one of my Rough Riders. At about the same time I also shot one. I was with Henry Bardshar, running up at the double, and two Spaniards leaped from the trenches and fired at us, not ten yards away. As they turned to run I closed in and fired twice, missing the first and killing the second. My revolver was from the sunken battle-ship Maine, and had been given me by my brother-in-law, Captain W. S. Cowles, of the Navy. At the time I did not know of Gould's exploit, and supposed my feat to be unique; and although Gould had killed his Spaniard in the trenches, not very far from me, I never learned of it until weeks after. It is astonishing what a limited area of vision and experience one has in the hurly-burly of a battle.

There was very great confusion at this time, the different regiments being completely intermingled—white regulars, colored regulars, and Rough Riders. General Sumner had kept a considerable force in reserve on Kettle Hill, under Major Jackson, of the Third Cavalry. We were still under a heavy fire and I got together a mixed lot of men and pushed on from the trenches and ranch-houses which we had just taken, driving the Spaniards through a line of palm-trees, and over the crest of a chain of hills. When we reached these crests we found ourselves overlooking Santiago. Some of the men, including Jenkins, Greenway, and Goodrich, pushed on almost by themselves far ahead. Lieutenant Hugh

Berkely, of the First, with a sergeant and two troopers, reached the extreme front. He was, at the time, ahead of everyone; the sergeant was killed and one trooper wounded; but the lieutenant and the remaining trooper stuck to their post for the rest of the afternoon until our line was gradually extended to include them.

While I was re-forming the troops on the chain of hills, one of General Sumner's aides, Captain Robert Howze—as dashing and gallant an officer as there was in the whole gallant cavalry division, by the way—came up with orders to me to halt where I was, not advancing farther, but to hold the hill at all hazards. Howze had his horse, and I had some difficulty in making him take proper shelter; he stayed with us for quite a time, unable to make up his mind to leave the extreme front, and meanwhile jumping at the chance to render any service, of risk or otherwise, which the moment developed.

I now had under me all the fragments of the six cavalry regiments which were at the extreme front, being the highest officer left there, and I was in immediate command of them for the remainder of the afternoon and that night. The Ninth was over to the right, and the Thirteenth Infantry afterward came up beside it. The rest of Kent's infantry was to our left. Of the Tenth, Lieutenants Anderson, Muller, and Fleming reported to me; Anderson was slightly wounded, but he paid no heed to this. All three, like every other officer, had troopers of various regiments under them; such mixing was inevitable in making repeated charges through thick jungle; it was essentially a troop commanders', indeed, almost a squad leaders', fight. The Spaniards who had been holding the trenches and the line of hills, had fallen back upon their supports and we were under a very heavy fire both from rifles and great guns. At the point where we were, the grass-covered hill-crest was gently rounded, giving poor cover, and I made my men lie down on the hither slope.

On the extreme left Captain Beck, of the Tenth, with his own troop, and small bodies of the men of other regiments, was exercising a practically independent command, driving back the Spaniards whenever they showed any symptoms of advancing. He had received his orders to hold the line at all hazards from Lieutenant Andrews, one of General Sumner's aides, just as I had received mine from Captain Howze. Finally, he was relieved by some infantry, and then rejoined the rest of the Tenth, which was engaged heavily until dark, Major Wint being among the severely wounded. Lieutenant W. N. Smith was killed. Captain Bigelow had been wounded three times.

Our artillery made one or two efforts to come into action on the firing-line of the infantry, but the black powder rendered each attempt fruitless. The Spanish guns used smokeless powder, so that it was difficult to place them. In this respect they were on a par with their own infantry and with our regular infantry and dismounted cavalry; but our only two volunteer infantry regiments, the Second Massachusetts and the Seventy-first New York, and our artillery, all had black powder. This rendered the two volunteer regiments, which were armed with the antiquated Springfield, almost useless in the battle, and did practically the same thing for the artillery wherever it was formed within rifle range. When one of the guns was discharged a thick cloud of smoke shot out and hung over the place, making an ideal target, and in a half minute every Spanish gun and rifle within range was directed at the particular spot thus indicated; the consequence was that after a more or less lengthy stand the gun was silenced or driven off. We got no appreciable help from our guns on July 1st. Our men were quick to realize the defects of our artillery, but they were entirely philosophic about it, not showing the least concern at its failure. On the contrary, whenever they heard our artillery open they would grin as they looked at one another and remark, "There go the guns again; wonder how soon they'll be shut up," and shut up they were sure to be. The light battery of Hotchkiss one-pounders, under Lieutenant J. B. Hughes, of the Tenth Cavalry, was handled with conspicuous gallantry.

On the hill-slope immediately around me I had a mixed force composed of members of most of the cavalry regiments, and a few infantrymen. There were about fifty of my Rough Riders with

Lieutenants Goodrich and Carr. Among the rest were perhaps a score of colored infantrymen, but, as it happened, at this particular point without any of their officers. No troops could have behaved better that the colored soldiers had behaved so far; but they are, of course, peculiarly dependent upon their white officers. Occasionally they produce non-commissioned officers who can take the initiative and accept responsibility precisely like the best class of whites; but this cannot be expected normally, nor is it fair to expect it. With the colored troops there should always be some of their own officers; whereas, with the white regulars, as with my own Rough Riders, experience showed that the non-commissioned officers could usually carry on the fight by themselves if they were once started, no matter whether their officers were killed or not.

At this particular time it was trying for the men, as they were lying flat on their faces, very rarely responding to the bullets, shells, and shrapnel which swept over the hill-top, and which occasionally killed or wounded one of their number. Major Albert G. Forse, of the First Cavalry, a noted Indian fighter, was killed about this time. One of my best men, Sergeant Greenly, of Arizona, who was lying beside me, suddenly said, "Beg pardon, Colonel; but I've been hit in the leg." I asked, "Badly?" He said, "Yes, Colonel; quite badly." After one of his comrades had helped him fix up his leg with a first-aid-to-the-injured bandage, he limped off to the rear.

None of the white regulars or Rough Riders showed the slightest sign of weakening; but under the strain the colored infantrymen (who had none of their officers) began to get a little uneasy and to drift to the rear, either helping wounded men, or saying that they wished to find their own regiments. This I could not allow, as it was depleting my line, so I jumped up, and walking a few yards to the rear, drew my revolver, halted the retreating soldiers, and called out to them that I appreciated the gallantry with which they had fought and would be sorry to hurt them, but that I should shoot the first man who, on any pretence whatever, went to the rear. My own men had all sat up and were watching my movements with the utmost interest; so was Captain Howze. I ended my statement to the colored soldiers by saying: "Now, I shall be very sorry to hurt you, and you don't know whether or not I will keep my word, but my men can tell you that I always do"; whereupon my cow-punchers, hunters, and miners solemnly nodded their heads and commented in chorus, exactly as if in a comic opera, "He always does; he always does!"

This was the end of the trouble, for the "smoked Yankees"—as the Spaniards called the colored soldiers—flashed their white teeth at one another, as they broke into broad grins, and I had no more trouble with them, they seeming to accept me as one of their own officers. The colored cavalrymen had already so accepted me; in return, the Rough Riders, although for the most part Southwesterners, who have a strong color prejudice, grew to accept them with hearty good-will as comrades, and were entirely willing, in their own phrase, "to drink out of the same canteen." Where all the regular officers did so well, it is hard to draw any distinction; but in the cavalry division a peculiar meed of praise should be given to the officers of the Ninth and Tenth for their work, and under their leadership the colored troops did as well as any soldiers could possibly do.

In the course of the afternoon the Spaniards in our front made the only offensive movement which I saw them make during the entire campaign; for what were ordinarily called "attacks" upon our lines consisted merely of heavy firing from their trenches and from their skirmishers. In this case they did actually begin to make a forward movement, their cavalry coming up as well as the marines and reserve infantry,* while their skirmishers, who were always bold, redoubled their activity. It could not be called a charge, and not only was it not pushed home, but it was stopped almost as soon as it began, our men immediately running forward to the crest of the hill with shouts of delight at seeing their enemies at last came into the open. A few seconds' firing stopped their advance and drove them into the cover of the trenches.

---

* Lieutenant Tejeiro, pp. 94–95, speaks of this attempt to retake San Juan and its failure.

They kept up a very heavy fire for some time longer, and our men again lay down, only replying occasionally. Suddenly we heard on our right the peculiar drumming sound which had been so welcome in the morning, when the infantry were assailing the San Juan block-house. The Gatlings were up again! I started over to inquire, and found that Lieutenant Parker, not content with using his guns in support of the attacking forces, had thrust them forward to the extreme front of the fighting line, where he was handling them with great effect. From this time on, throughout the fighting, Parker's Gatlings were on the right of my regiment, and his men and mine fraternized in every way. He kept his pieces at the extreme front, using them on every occasion until the last Spanish shot was fired. Indeed, the dash and efficiency with which the Gatlings were handled by Parker was one of the most striking features of the campaign; he showed that a first-rate officer could use machine-guns, on wheels, in battle and skirmish, in attacking and defending trenches, alongside of the best troops, and to their great advantage.

As night came on, the firing gradually died away. Before this happened, however, Captains Morton and Boughton, of the Third Cavalry, came over to tell me that a rumor had reached them to the effect that there had been some talk of retiring and that they wished to protest in the strongest manner. I had been watching them both, as they handled their troops with the cool confidence of the veteran regular officer, and had been congratulating myself that they were off toward the right flank, for as long as they were there, I knew I was perfectly safe in that direction. I had heard no rumor about retiring, and I cordially agreed with them that it would be far worse than a blunder to abandon our position.

To attack the Spaniards by rushing across open ground, or through wire entanglements and low, almost impassable jungle, without the help of artillery, and to force unbroken infantry, fighting behind earthworks and armed with the best repeating weapons, supported by cannon, was one thing; to repel such an attack ourselves, or to fight our foes on anything like even terms in the open, was quite another thing. No possible number of Spaniards coming at us from in front could have driven us from our position, and there was not a man on the crest who did not eagerly and devoutly hope that our opponents would make the attempt, for it would surely have been followed, not merely by a repulse, but by our immediately taking the city. There was not an officer or a man on the firing-line, so far as I saw them, who did not feel this way.

As night fell, some of my men went back to the buildings in our rear and foraged through them, for we had now been fourteen hours charging and fighting without food. They came across what was evidently the Spanish officers' mess, where their dinner was still cooking, and they brought it to the front in high glee. It was evident that the Spanish officers were living well, however the Spanish rank and file were faring. There were three big iron pots, one filled with beef-stew, one with boiled rice, and one with boiled peas; there was a big demijohn of rum (all along the trenches which the Spaniards held were empty wine and liquor bottles); there were a number of loaves of rice-bread; and there were even some small cans of preserves and a few salt fish. Of course, among so many men, the food, which was equally divided, did not give very much to each, but it freshened us all.

Soon after dark, General Wheeler, who in the afternoon had resumed command of the cavalry division, came to the front. A very few words with General Wheeler reassured us about retiring. He had been through too much heavy fighting in the Civil War to regard the present fight as very serious, and he told us not to be under any apprehension, for he had sent word that there was no need whatever of retiring, and was sure we would stay where we were until the chance came to advance. He was second in command; and to him more than to any other one man was due the prompt abandonment of the proposal to fall back—a proposal which, if adopted, would have meant shame and disaster.

Shortly afterward General Wheeler sent us orders to intrench. The men of the different regiments were now getting in place again and sifting themselves out. All of our troops who had been kept at Kettle Hill came forward and rejoined us after nightfall. During the afternoon Greenway, apparently not having enough to do in the fighting, had taken advantage of a lull to explore the buildings himself, and had found a number of Spanish intrenching tools, picks, and shovels, and these we used in digging trenches along our line. The men were very tired indeed, but they went cheerfully to work, all the officers doing their part.

Crockett, the ex-Revenue officer from Georgia, was a slight man, not physically very strong. He came to me and told me he didn't think he would be much use in digging, but that he had found a lot of Spanish coffee and would spend his time making coffee for the men, if I approved. I did approve very heartily, and Crockett officiated as cook for the next three or four hours until the trench was dug, his coffee being much appreciated by all of us.

So many acts of gallantry were performed during the day that it is quite impossible to notice them all, and it seems unjust to single out any; yet I shall mention a few, which it must always be remembered are to stand, not as exceptions, but as instances of what very many men did. It happened that I saw these myself. There were innumerable others, which either were not seen at all, or were seen only by officers who happened not to mention them; and, of course, I know chiefly those that happened in my own regiment.

Captain Llewellen was a large, heavy man, who had a grown-up son in the ranks. On the march he had frequently carried the load of some man who weakened, and he was not feeling well on the morning of the fight. Nevertheless, he kept at the head of his troop all day. In the charging and rushing, he not only became very much exhausted, but finally fell, wrenching himself terribly, and though he remained with us all night, he was so sick by morning that we had to take him behind the hill into an improvised hospital. Lieutenant Day, after handling his troop with equal gallantry and efficiency, was shot, on the summit of Kettle Hill. He was hit in the arm and was forced to go to the rear, but he would not return to the States, and rejoined us at the front long before his wound was healed. Lieutenant Leahy was also wounded, not far from him.

Thirteen of the men were wounded and yet kept on fighting until the end of the day, and in some cases never went to the rear at all, even to have their wounds dressed. They were Corporals Waller and Fortescue and Trooper McKinley of Troop E; Corporal Roades of Troop D; Troopers Albertson, Winter, McGregor, and Ray Clark of Troop F; Troopers Bugbee, Jackson, and Waller of Troop A; Trumpeter McDonald of Troop L; Sergeant Hughes of Troop B; and Trooper Gievers of Troop G. One of the Wallers was a cow-puncher from New Mexico, the other the champion Yale high-jumper. The first was shot through the left arm so as to paralyze the fingers, but he continued in battle, pointing his rifle over the wounded arm as though it had been a rest. The other Waller, and Bugbee, were hit in the head, the bullets merely inflicting scalp wounds. Neither of them paid any heed to the wounds except that after nightfall each had his head done up in a bandage. Fortescue I was at times using as an extra orderly. I noticed he limped, but supposed that his foot was skinned. It proved, however, that he had been struck in the foot, though not very seriously, by a bullet, and I never knew what was the matter until the next day I saw him making wry faces as he drew off his bloody boot, which was stuck fast to the foot. Trooper Rowland again distinguished himself by his fearlessness.

For gallantry on the field of action Sergeants Dame, Ferguson, Tiffany, Greenwald, and, later on, McIlhenny, were promoted to second lieutenancies, as Sergeant Hayes had already been. Lieutenant Carr, who commanded his troop, and behaved with great gallantry throughout the day, was shot and severely wounded at nightfall. He was the son of a Confederate officer; his was the fifth generation which, from father to son, had fought in every war of the United States. Among the men whom I noticed as leading in the charges and always being nearest the enemy, were the Pawnee, Pollock, Simpson of Texas, and Dudley Dean. Jenkins was made major, Woodbury Kane, Day, and Frantz captains, and Greenway and Goodrich first lieutenants, for gallantry in action, and for the efficiency with which the first had handled his squadron, and the other five their troops—for each of them, owing to some accident to his superior, found himself in command of his troop.

Dr. Church had worked quite as hard as any man at the front in caring for the wounded; as had Chaplain Brown. Lieutenant Keyes, who acted as adjutant, did so well that he was given the position permanently. Lieutenant Coleman similarly won the position of quartermaster.

We finished digging the trench soon after midnight, and then the worn-out men laid down in rows on their rifles and dropped heavily to sleep. About one in ten of them had blankets taken from the Spaniards. Henry Bardshar, my orderly, had procured one for me. He, Goodrich, and I slept together. If the men without blankets had not been so tired that they fell asleep anyhow, they would have been very cold, for, of course, we were all drenched with sweat, and above the waist had on nothing but our flannel shirts, while the night was cool, with a heavy dew. Before anyone had time to wake from the cold, however, we were all awakened by the Spaniards, whose skirmishers suddenly opened fire on us. Of course, we could not tell whether or not this was the forerunner of a heavy attack, for our Cossack posts were responding briskly. It was about three o'clock in the morning, at which time men's courage is said to be at the lowest ebb; but the cavalry division was certainly free from any weakness in that direction. At the alarm everybody jumped to his feet and the stiff, shivering, haggard men, their eyes only half-opened, all clutched their rifles and ran forward to the trench on the crest of the hill.

The sputtering shots died away and we went to sleep again. But in another hour dawn broke and the Spaniards opened fire in good earnest. There was a little tree only a few feet away, under which I made my head-quarters, and while I was lying there, with Goodrich and Keyes, a shrapnel burst among us, not hurting us in the least, but with the sweep of its bullets killing or wounding five men in our rear, one of whom was a singularly gallant young Harvard fellow, Stanley Hollister. An equally gallant young fellow from Yale, Theodore Miller, had already been mortally wounded. Hollister also died.

The Second Brigade lost more heavily than the First; but neither its brigade commander nor any of its regimental commanders were touched, while the commander of the First Brigade and two of its three regimental commanders had been killed or wounded.

In this fight our regiment had numbered 490 men, as, in addition to the killed and wounded of the first fight, some had had to go to the hospital for sickness and some had been left behind with the baggage, or were detailed on other duty. Eighty-nine were killed and wounded: the heaviest loss suffered by any regiment in the cavalry division. The Spaniards made a stiff fight, standing firm until we charged home. They fought much more stubbornly than at Las Guasimas. We ought to have expected this, for they have always done well in holding intrenchments. On this day they showed themselves to be brave foes, worthy of honor for their gallantry.

In the attack on the San Juan hills our forces numbered about 6,600.* There were about 4,500 Spaniards against us.† Our total loss in killed and wounded was 1,071. Of the cavalry division there were, all told, some 2,300 officers and men, of whom 375 were killed and wounded. In the division over a fourth of the officers

---

* According to the official reports, 5,104 officers and men of Kent's infantry, and 2,649 of the cavalry had been landed. My regiment is put down as 542 strong, instead of the real figure, 490, the difference being due to men who were in hospital and on guard at the sea-shore, etc. In other words, the total represents the total landed; the details, etc., are included. General Wheeler, in his report of July 7th, puts these details as about fifteen per cent. of the whole of the force which was on the transports; about eighty-five per cent. got forward and was in the fight.

† The total Spanish force in Santiago under General Linares was 6,000: 4,000 regulars, 1,000 volunteers, and 1,000 marines and sailors from the ships. (Diary of the British Consul, Frederick W. Ramsden, entry of July 1st.) Four thousand more troops entered next day. Of the 6,000 troops, 600 or thereabouts were at El Caney, and 900 in the forts at the mouth of the harbor. Lieutenant Tejeiro states that there were 520 men at El Caney, 970 in the forts at the mouth of the harbor, and 3,000 in the lines, not counting the cavalry and civil guard which were in reserve. He certainly very much understates the Spanish force; thus he nowhere accounts for the engineers mentioned on p. 135; and his figures would make the total number of Spanish artillerymen but 32. He excludes the cavalry, the civil guard, and the marines which had been stationed at the Plaza del Toros; yet he later mentions that these marines were brought up, and their commander, Bustamente, severely wounded; he states

that the cavalry advanced to cover the retreat of the infantry, and I myself saw the cavalry come forward, for the most part dismounted, when the Spaniards attempted a forward movement late in the afternoon, and we shot many of their horses; while later I saw and conversed with officers and men of the civil guard who had been wounded at the same time—this in connection with returning them their wives and children, after the latter had fled from the city. Although the engineers are excluded, Lieutenant Tejeiro mentions that their colonel, as well as the colonel of the artillery, was wounded. Four thousand five hundred is surely an understatement of the forces which resisted the attack of the forces under Wheeler. Lieutenant Tejeiro is very careless in his figures. Thus in one place he states that the position of San Juan was held by two companies comprising 250 soldiers. Later he says it was held by three companies, whose strength he puts at 300—thus making them average 100 instead of 125 men apiece. He then mentions another echelon of two companies, so situated as to cross their fire with the others. Doubtless the block-house and trenches at Fort San Juan proper were only held by three or four hundred men; they were taken by the Sixth and Sixteenth Infantry under Hawkins's immediate command; and they formed but one point in the line of hills, trenches, ranch-houses, and block-houses which the Spaniards held, and from which we drove them. When the city capitulated later, over 8,000 unwounded troops and over 16,000 rifles and carbines were surrendered; by that time the marines and sailors had of course gone, and the volunteers had disbanded.

In all these figures I have taken merely the statements from the Spanish side. I am inclined to think the actual numbers were much greater than those here given. Lieutenant Miley, in his book In Cuba with Shafter, which is practically an official statement, states that nearly 11,000 Spanish troops were surrendered; and this is the number given by the Spaniards themselves in the remarkable letter the captured soldiers addressed to General Shafter, which Miley quotes in full. Lieutenant Tejeiro, in his chap. xiv., explains that the volunteers had disbanded before the end came, and the marines and sailors had of course gone, while nearly a thousand men had been killed or captured or had died of wounds and disease, so that there must have been at least 14,000 all told. Subtracting the reinforcements who arrived on the 2d, this would mean about 10,000 Spaniards present on the 1st; in which case Kent and Wheeler were opposed by at least equal numbers.

In dealing with the Spanish losses, Lieutenant Tejeiro contradicts himself. He puts their total loss on this day at 593, including 94 killed, 121 missing, and 2 prisoners—217 in all. Yet he states that of the 520 men at Caney but 80 got back, the remaining 440 being killed, captured, or missing. When we captured the city we found in the hospitals over 2,000 seriously wounded and sick Spaniards; on making inquiries, I found that over a third were wounded. From these facts I feel that it is safe to put down the total Spanish loss in battle as at least 1,200, of whom over a thousand were killed and wounded.

Lieutenant Tejeiro, while rightly claiming credit for the courage shown by the Spaniards, also praises the courage and resolution of the Americans, saying that they fought, "con un arrojo y una decision verdaderamente admirables." He dwells repeatedly upon the determination with which our troops kept charging though themselves unprotected by cover. As for the Spanish troops, all who fought them that day will most freely admit the courage they showed. At El Caney, where they were nearly hemmed in, they made a most desperate defence; at San Juan the way to retreat was open, and so, though they were seven times as numerous, they fought with less desperation, but still very gallantly.

were killed or wounded, their loss being relatively half as great again as that of the enlisted men—which was as it should be.

I think we suffered more heavily than the Spaniards did in killed and wounded (though we also captured some scores of prisoners). It would have been very extraordinary if the reverse was the case, for we did the charging; and to carry earthworks on foot with dismounted cavalry, when these earthworks are held by unbroken infantry armed with the best modern rifles, is a serious task.

V

IN THE TRENCHES

When the shrapnel burst among us on the hill-side we made up our minds that we had better settle down to solid siege work. All of the men who were not in the trenches I took off to the right, back of the Gatling guns, where there was a valley, and dispersed them by troops in sheltered parts. It took us an hour or two's experimenting to find out exactly what spots were free from danger, because some of the Spanish sharp-shooters were in trees in our front, where we could not possibly place them from the trenches; and these were able to reach little hollows and depressions where the men were entirely safe from the Spanish artillery and from their trench-fire. Moreover, in one hollow, which we thought safe, the Spaniards succeeded in dropping a shell, a fragment of which went through the head of one of my men, who, astonishing to say, lived, although unconscious, for two hours afterward. Finally, I got all eight troops settled, and the men promptly proceeded to make themselves as much at home as possible. For the next twenty-four hours, however, the amount of comfort was small, as in the way of protection and covering we only had what blankets, rain-coats, and hammocks we took from the dead Spaniards. Ammunition, which was, of course, the most vital need, was brought up in abundance; but very little food reached us. That afternoon we had just enough to allow each man for his supper two hardtacks, and one hardtack extra for every four men.

During the first night we had dug trenches sufficient in length and depth to shelter our men and insure safety against attack, but we had not put in any traverses or approaches, nor had we arranged the trenches at all points in the best places for offensive work; for we were working at night on ground which we had but partially explored. Later on an engineer officer stated that he did not think our work had been scientific; and I assured him that I did not doubt that he was right, for I had never before seen a trench, excepting those we captured from the Spaniards, or heard of a traverse, save as I vaguely remembered reading about them in books. For such work as we were engaged in, however, the problem of intrenchment was comparatively simple, and the work we did proved entirely adequate. No man in my regiment was ever hit in the trenches or going in or out of them.

But on the first day there was plenty of excitement connected with relieving the firing line. Under the intense heat, crowded down in cramped attitudes in the rank, newly dug, poisonous soil of the trenches, the men needed to be relieved every six hours or so. Accordingly, in the late morning, and again in the afternoon, I arranged for their release. On each occasion I waited until there was a lull in the firing and then started a sudden rush by the relieving party, who tumbled into the trenches every which way. The movement resulted on each occasion in a terrific outburst of fire from the Spanish lines, which proved quite harmless; and as it gradually died away the men who had been relieved got out as best they could. Fortunately, by the next day I was able to abandon this primitive, though thrilling and wholly novel, military method of relief.

When the hardtack came up that afternoon I felt much sympathy for the hungry unfortunates in the trenches and hated to condemn them to six hours more without food; but I did not know how to get food into them. Little McGinty, the bronco buster, volunteered to make the attempt, and I gave him permission. He simply took a case of hardtack in his arms and darted toward the trenches.

The distance was but short, and though there was an outburst of fire, he was actually missed. One bullet, however, passed through the case of hardtack just before he disappeared with it into the trench. A trooper named Shanafelt repeated the feat, later, with a pail of coffee. Another trooper, George King, spent a leisure hour in the rear making soup out of some rice and other stuff he found in a Spanish house; he brought some of it to General Wood, Jack Greenway, and myself, and nothing could have tasted more delicious.

At this time our army in the trenches numbered about 11,000 men; and the Spaniards in Santiago about 9,000,* their reinforcements having just arrived. Nobody on the firing line, whatever was the case in the rear, felt the slightest uneasiness as to the Spaniards being able to break out; but there were plenty who doubted the advisability of trying to rush the heavy earthworks and wire defences in our front.

All day long the firing continued—musketry and cannon. Our artillery gave up the attempt to fight on the firing line, and was withdrawn well to the rear out of range of the Spanish rifles; so far as we could see, it accomplished very little. The dynamite gun was brought up to the right of the regimental line. It was more effective than the regular artillery because it was fired with smokeless powder, and as it was used like a mortar from behind the hill, it did not betray its presence, and those firing it suffered no loss. Every few shots it got out of order, and the Rough Rider machinists and those furnished by Lieutenant Parker—whom we by this time began to consider as an exceedingly valuable member of our own regiment—would spend an hour or two in setting it right. Sergeant Borrowe had charge of it and handled it well. With him was Sergeant Guitilias, a gallant old fellow, a veteran of the Civil War, whose duties were properly those of standard-bearer, he having

---

* This is probably an understatement. Lieutenant Müller, in chap. xxxviii. of his book, says that there were "eight or nine thousand"; this is exclusive of the men from the fleet, and apparently also of many of the volunteers (see chap. xiv.), all of whom were present on July 2d. I am inclined to think that on the evening of that day there were more Spanish troops inside Santiago than there were American troops outside.

charge of the yellow cavalry standard of the regiment; but in the Cuban campaign he was given the more active work of helping run the dynamite gun. The shots from the dynamite gun made a terrific explosion, but they did not seem to go accurately. Once one of them struck a Spanish trench and wrecked part of it. On another occasion one struck a big building, from which there promptly swarmed both Spanish cavalry and infantry, on whom the Colt automatic guns played with good effect, during the minute that elapsed before they could get other cover.

These Colt automatic guns were not, on the whole, very successful. The gun detail was under the charge of Sergeant (afterward Lieutenant) Tiffany, assisted by some of our best men, like Stephens, Crowninshield, Bradley, Smith, and Herrig. The guns were mounted on tripods. They were too heavy for men to carry any distance and we could not always get mules. They would have been more effective if mounted on wheels, as the Gatlings were. Moreover, they proved more delicate than the Gatlings, and very readily got out of order. A further and serious disadvantage was that they did not use the Krag ammunition, as the Gatlings did, but the Mauser ammunition. The Spanish cartridges which we captured came in quite handily for this reason. Parker took the same fatherly interest in these two Colts that he did in the dynamite gun, and finally I put all three and their men under his immediate care, so that he had a battery of seven guns.

In fact, I think Parker deserved rather more credit than any other one man in the entire campaign. I do not allude especially to his courage and energy, great though they were, for there were hundreds of his fellow-officers of the cavalry and infantry who possessed as much of the former quality, and scores who possessed as much of the latter; but he had the rare good judgment and foresight to see the possibilities of the machine-guns, and, thanks to the aid of General Shafter, he was able to organize his battery. He then, by his own exertions, got it to the front and proved that it could do invaluable work on the field of battle, as much in attack as in defence. Parker's Gatlings were our inseparable companions throughout the siege. After our trenches were put in final shape, he

Theodore Roosevelt at San Antonio.
(Theodore Roosevelt Collection/Harvard College Library)

Soldiers waiting for the train to Port Tampa.
(Theodore Roosevelt Collection/Harvard College Library)

The Rough Riders' camp at Tampa.
(Theodore Roosevelt Collection / Harvard College Library)

**Scene at the dock at Port Tampa on the Day
of Sailing of the Transports.**
(Theodore Roosevelt Collection / Harvard College Library)

Twenty-third Colored Infantry in the trenches, July 2, 1898.
(Theodore Roosevelt Collection / Harvard College Library)

African-American troops crossing Rio San Juan near San Juan Hill.
(Theodore Roosevelt Collection / Harvard College Library)

Troops forming for march at Daiquiri.
(Theodore Roosevelt Collection / Harvard College Library)

First Division field hospital on the road to Santiago.
(Theodore Roosevelt Collection / Harvard College Library)

Rough Riders bringing in the wounded from the firing line.
(Theodore Roosevelt Collection/Harvard College Library)

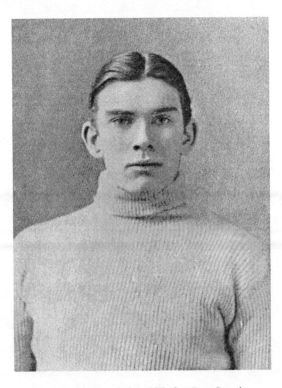

Sergeant Hamilton Fish, killed at Las Guasimas.
(Theodore Roosevelt Collection/Harvard College Library)

**View from San Juan trenches toward Kettle Hill,
showing country over which Rough Riders charged.**
(Theodore Roosevelt Collection / Harvard College Library)

Surgeon attending to the wounded in the field hospital.
(Theodore Roosevelt Collection / Harvard College Library)

Funeral for Rough Rider killed in combat.
(Theodore Roosevelt Collection/Harvard College Library)

Rough Riders cheering the surrender of Santiago, July 17, 1898.
(Theodore Roosevelt Collection/Harvard College Library)

Rough Riders' camp at Montauk.
(Theodore Roosevelt Collection/Harvard College Library)

Theodore Roosevelt at Montauk.
(Theodore Roosevelt Collection/Harvard College Library)

took off the wheels of a couple and placed them with our own two Colts in the trenches. His gunners slept beside the Rough Riders in the bomb-proofs, and the men shared with one another when either side got a supply of beans or of coffee and sugar; for Parker was as wide-awake and energetic in getting food for his men as we prided ourselves upon being in getting food for ours. Besides, he got oil, and let our men have plenty for their rifles. At no hour of the day or night was Parker anywhere but where we wished him to be in the event of an attack. If I was ordered to send a troop of Rough Riders to guard some road or some break in the lines, we usually got Parker to send a Gatling along, and whether the change was made by day or by night, the Gatling went, over any ground and in any weather. He never exposed the Gatlings needlessly or unless there was some object to be gained, but if serious fighting broke out, he always took a hand. Sometimes this fighting would be the result of an effort on our part to quell the fire from the Spanish trenches; sometimes the Spaniards took the initiative; but at whatever hour of the twenty-four serious fighting began, the drumming of the Gatlings was soon heard through the cracking of our own carbines.

I have spoken thus of Parker's Gatling detachment. How can I speak highly enough of the regular cavalry with whom it was our good fortune to serve? I do not believe that in any army of the world could be found a more gallant and soldierly body of fighters than the officers and men of the First, Third, Sixth, Ninth, and Tenth United States Cavalry, beside whom we marched to blood-bought victory under the tropic skies of Santiago. The American regular sets the standard of excellence. When we wish to give the utmost possible praise to a volunteer organization, we say that it is as good as the regulars. I was exceedingly proud of the fact that the regulars treated my regiment as on a complete equality with themselves, and were as ready to see it in a post of danger and responsibility as to see any of their own battalions. Lieutenant Colonel Dorst, a man from whom praise meant a good deal, christened us "the Eleventh United States Horse," and we endeavored, I think I may say successfully, to show that we deserved the title by our conduct, not only in fighting and in marching, but in guarding the trenches and in policing camp. In less than sixty days the regiment had been raised, organized, armed, equipped, drilled, mounted, dismounted, kept for a fortnight on transports, and put through two victorious aggressive fights in very difficult country, the loss in killed and wounded amounting to a quarter of those engaged. This is a record which it is not easy to match in the history of volunteer organizations. The loss was but small compared to that which befell hundreds of regiments in some of the great battles of the later years of the Civil War; but it may be doubted whether there was any regiment which made such a record during the first months of any of our wars.

After the battle of San Juan my men had really become veterans; they and I understood each other perfectly, and trusted each other implicitly; they knew I would share every hardship and danger with them, would do everything in my power to see that they were fed, and so far as might be, sheltered and spared; and in return I knew that they would endure every kind of hardship and fatigue without a murmur and face every danger with entire fearlessness. I felt utter confidence in them, and would have been more than willing to put them to any task which any crack regiment of the world, at home or abroad, could perform. They were natural fighters, men of great intelligence, great courage, great hardihood, and physical prowess; and I could draw on these qualities and upon their spirit of ready, soldierly obedience to make up for any deficiencies in the technique of the trade which they had temporarily adopted. It must be remembered that they were already good individual fighters, skilled in the use of the horse and the rifle, so that there was no need of putting them through the kind of training in which the ordinary raw recruit must spend his first year or two.

On July 2d, as the day wore on, the fight, though raging fitfully at intervals, gradually died away. The Spanish guerillas were causing us much trouble. They showed great courage, exactly as did their soldiers who were defending the trenches. In fact, the Spaniards throughout showed precisely the qualities they did early in the century, when, as every student will remember, their fleets were a helpless prey to the English war-ships, and their armies utterly unable to stand in the open against those of Napoleon's marshals, while on the other hand their guerillas performed marvellous feats, and their defence of intrenchments and walled towns, as at Saragossa and Gerona, were the wonder of the civilized world.

In our front their sharp-shooters crept up before dawn and either lay in the thick jungle or climbed into some tree with dense foliage. In these places it proved almost impossible to place them, as they kept cover very carefully, and their smokeless powder betrayed not the slightest sign of their whereabouts. They caused us a great deal of annoyance and some little loss, and though our own sharp-shooters were continually taking shots at the places where they supposed them to be, and though occasionally we would play a Gatling or a Colt all through the top of a suspicious tree, I but twice saw Spaniards brought down out of their perches from in front of our lines—on each occasion the fall of the Spaniard being hailed with loud cheers by our men.

These sharp-shooters in our front did perfectly legitimate work, and were entitled to all credit for their courage and skill. It was different with the guerillas in our rear. Quite a number of these had been posted in trees at the time of the San Juan fight. They were using, not Mausers, but Remingtons, which shot smokeless powder and a brass-coated bullet. It was one of these bullets which had hit Winslow Clark by my side on Kettle Hill; and though for long-range fighting the Remingtons were, of course, nothing like as good as the Mausers, they were equally serviceable for short-range bush work, as they used smokeless powder. When our troops advanced and the Spaniards in the trenches and in reserve behind the hill fled, the guerillas in the trees had no time to get away and in consequence were left in the rear of our lines. As we found out from the prisoners we took, the Spanish officers had been careful to instil into the minds of their soldiers the belief that the Americans never granted quarter, and I suppose it was in consequence of this that the guerillas did not surrender; for we found that the Spaniards were anxious enough to surrender as soon as they became convinced that we would treat them mercifully. At any rate, these guerillas kept up in their trees and showed not only courage but wanton cruelty and barbarity. At times they fired upon armed men in bodies, but they much preferred for their victims the unarmed attendants, the doctors, the chaplains, the hospital stewards. They fired at the men who were bearing off the wounded in litters; they fired at the doctors who came to the front, and at the chaplains who started to hold burial service; the conspicuous Red Cross brassard worn by all of these non-combatants, instead of serving as a protection, seemed to make them the special objects of the guerilla fire. So annoying did they become that I sent out that afternoon and next morning a detail of picked sharp-shooters to hunt them out, choosing, of course, first-class woodsmen and mountain men who were also good shots. My sharp-shooters felt very vindictively toward these guerillas and showed them no quarter. They started systematically to hunt them, and showed themselves much superior at the guerillas' own game, killing eleven, while not one of my men was scratched. Two of the men who did conspicuously good service in this work were Troopers Goodwin and Proffit, both of Arizona, but one by birth a Californian and the other a North Carolinian. Goodwin was a natural shot, not only with the rifle and revolver, but with the sling. Proffit might have stood as a type of the mountaineers described by John Fox and Miss Murfree. He was a tall, sinewy, handsome man of remarkable strength, an excellent shot and a thoroughly good soldier. His father had been a Confederate officer, rising from the ranks, and if the war had lasted long enough the son would have risen in the same manner. As it was, I should have been glad to have given him a commission, exactly as I should have been glad to have given a number of others in the regiment commissions, if I had only had them. Proffit was a saturnine, reserved man, who afterward fell very sick with the fever, and who, as a reward for his soldierly good conduct, was often granted unusual privileges; but he took the fever and the privileges with the same iron indifference, never grumbling, and never expressing satisfaction.

The sharp-shooters returned by nightfall. Soon afterward I established my pickets and outposts well to the front in the jungle, so as to prevent all possibility of surprise. After dark, fires suddenly shot up on the mountain passes far to our right. They all rose together and we could make nothing of them. After a good deal of consultation, we decided they must be some signals to the Spaniards in Santiago, from the troops marching to reinforce them from without—for we were ignorant that the reinforcements had already reached the city, the Cubans being quite unable to prevent the Spanish regulars from marching wherever they wished. While we were thus pondering over the watch-fires and attributing them to Spanish machinations of some sort, it appears that the Spaniards, equally puzzled, were setting them down as an attempt at communication between the insurgents and our army. Both sides were accordingly on the alert, and the Spaniards must have strengthened their outlying parties in the jungle ahead of us, for they suddenly attacked one of our pickets, wounding Crockett seriously. He was brought in by the other troopers. Evidently the Spanish lines felt a little nervous, for this sputter of shooting was immediately followed by a tremendous fire of great guns and rifles from their trenches and batteries. Our men in the trenches responded heavily, and word was sent back, not only to me, but to the commanders in the rear of the regiments along our line, that the Spaniards were attacking. It was imperative to see what was really going on, so I ran up to the trenches and looked out. At night it was far easier to place the Spanish lines than by day, because the flame-spurts shone in the darkness. I could soon tell that there were bodies of Spanish pickets or skirmishers in the jungle-covered valley, between their lines and ours, but that the bulk of the fire came from their trenches and showed not the slightest symptom of advancing; moreover, as is generally the case at night, the fire was almost all high, passing well overhead, with an occasional bullet near by.

I came to the conclusion that there was no use in our firing back under such circumstances; and I could tell that the same conclusion had been reached by Captain Ayres of the Tenth Cavalry on the right of my line, for even above the cracking of the carbines rose the Captain's voice as with varied and picturesque language he bade his black troopers cease firing. The Captain was as absolutely fearless as a man can be. He had command of his regimental trenches that night, and, having run up at the first alarm, had speedily satisfied himself that no particular purpose was served by blazing away in the dark, when the enormous majority of the Spaniards were simply shooting at random from their own trenches, and, if they ever had thought of advancing, had certainly given up the idea. His troopers were devoted to him, would follow him anywhere, and would do anything he said; but when men get firing at night it is rather difficult to stop them, especially when the fire of the enemy in front continues unabated. When he first reached the trenches it was impossible to say whether or not there was an actual night attack impending, and he had been instructing his men, as I instructed mine, to fire low, cutting the grass in front. As soon as he became convinced that there was no night attack, he ran up and down the line adjuring and commanding the troopers to cease shooting, with words and phrases which were doubtless not wholly unlike those which the Old Guard really did use at Waterloo. As I ran down my own line, I could see him coming up his, and he saved me all trouble in stopping the fire at the right, where the lines met, for my men there all dropped everything to listen to him and cheer and laugh. Soon we got the troopers in hand, and made them cease firing; then, after awhile, the Spanish fire died down. At the time we spoke of this as a night attack by the Spaniards, but it really was not an attack at all. Ever after my men had a great regard for Ayres, and would have followed him anywhere. I shall never forget the way in which he scolded his huge, devoted black troopers, generally ending with "I'm ashamed of you, ashamed of you! I wouldn't have believed it! Firing; when I told you to stop! I'm ashamed of you!"

That night we spent in perfecting the trenches and arranging entrances to them, doing about as much work as we had the preceding night. Greenway and Goodrich, from their energy, eagerness to do every duty, and great physical strength, were peculiarly useful in this work; as, indeed, they were in all work. They had been up practically the entire preceding night, but they were too good men for me to spare them, nor did they wish to be spared; and I kept them up all this night too. Goodrich had also been on guard as officer of the day the night we were at El Poso, so that it turned out that he spent nearly four days and three nights with practically hardly any sleep at all.

Next morning, at daybreak, the firing began again. This day, the 3d, we suffered nothing, save having one man wounded by a sharp-shooter, and, thanks to the approaches to the trenches, we were able to relieve the guards without any difficulty. The Spanish sharp-shooters in the trees and jungle nearby, however, annoyed us very much, and I made preparations to fix them next day. With this end in view I chose out some twenty first-class men, in many instances the same that I had sent after the guerillas, and arranged that each should take his canteen and a little food. They were to slip into the jungle between us and the Spanish lines before dawn next morning, and there to spend the day, getting as close to the Spanish lines as possible, moving about with great stealth, and picking off any hostile sharp-shooter, as well as any soldier who exposed himself in the trenches. I had plenty of men who possessed a training in wood-craft that fitted them for this work; and as soon as the rumor got abroad what I was planning, volunteers thronged to me. Daniels and Love were two of the men always to the front in any enterprise of this nature; so were Wadsworth, the two Bulls, Fortescue, and Cowdin. But I could not begin to name all the troopers who so eagerly craved the chance to win honor out of hazard and danger.

Among them was good, solemn Fred Herrig, the Alsatian. I knew Fred's patience and skill as a hunter from the trips we had taken together after deer and mountain sheep through the Bad Lands of the Little Missouri. He still spoke English with what might be called Alsatian variations—he always spoke of the gun detail as the "góndêtle," with the accent on the first syllable—and he expressed a wish to be allowed "a holiday from the gondetle to go after dem gorrillas." I told him he could have the holiday, but to his great disappointment the truce came first, and then Fred asked that, inasmuch as the "gorrillas" were now forbidden game, he might be allowed to go after guinea hens instead.

Even after the truce, however, some of my sharp-shooters had occupation, for two guerillas in our rear took occasional shots at the men who were bathing in a pond, until one of our men spied them, when they were both speedily brought down. One of my riflemen who did best at this kind of work, by the way, got into trouble because of it. He was much inflated by my commendation of him, and when he went back to his troop he declined to obey the first Sergeant's orders on the ground that he was "the Colonel's sharpshooter." The Lieutenant in command, being somewhat puzzled, brought him to me, and I had to explain that if the offence, disobedience of orders in face of the enemy, was repeated he might incur the death penalty; whereat he looked very crest-fallen. That afternoon he got permission, like Fred Herrig, to go after guinea-hens, which were found wild in some numbers round about; and he sent me the only one he got as a peace offering. The few guinea-hens thus procured were all used for the sick.

Dr. Church had established a little field hospital under the shoulder of the hill in our rear. He was himself very sick and had almost nothing in the way of medicine or supplies or apparatus of any kind, but the condition of the wounded in the big field hospitals in the rear was so horrible, from the lack of attendants as well as of medicines, that we kept all the men we possibly could at the front. Some of them had now begun to come down with fever. They were all very patient, but it was pitiful to see the sick and wounded soldiers lying on their blankets, if they had any, and if not then simply in the mud, with nothing to eat but hardtack and pork, which of course they could not touch when their fever got high, and with no chance to get more than the rudest attention. Among the very sick here was gallant Captain Llewellen. I feared he was going to die. We finally had to send him to one of the big hospitals in the rear. Doctors Brewer and Fuller of the Tenth had been unwearying in attending to the wounded, including many of those of my regiment.

At twelve o'clock we were notified to stop firing and a flag of truce was sent in to demand the surrender of the city. The negotiations gave us a breathing spell.

That afternoon I arranged to get our baggage up, sending back strong details of men to carry up their own goods, and, as usual, impressing into the service a kind of improvised pack-train consisting of the officers' horses, of two or three captured Spanish cavalry horses, two or three mules which had been shot and abandoned and which our men had taken and cured, and two or three Cuban ponies. Hitherto we had simply been sleeping by the trenches or immediately in their rear, with nothing in the way of shelter and only one blanket to every three or four men. Fortunately there had been little rain. We now got up the shelter tents of the men and some flies for the hospital and for the officers; and my personal baggage appeared. I celebrated its advent by a thorough wash and shave.

Later, I twice snatched a few hours to go to the rear and visit such of my men as I could find in the hospitals. Their patience was extraordinary. Kenneth Robinson, a gallant young trooper, though himself severely (I supposed at the time mortally) wounded, was noteworthy for the way in which he tended those among the wounded who were even more helpless, and the cheery courage with which he kept up their spirits. Gievers, who was shot through the hips, rejoined us at the front in a fortnight. Captain Day was hardly longer away. Jack Hammer, who, with poor Race Smith, a gallant Texas lad who was mortally hurt beside me on the summit of the hill, had been on kitchen detail, was wounded and sent to the rear; he was ordered to go to the United States, but he heard that we were to assault Santiago, so he struggled out to rejoin us, and thereafter stayed at the front. Cosby, badly wounded, made his way down to the sea-coast in three days, unassisted.

With all volunteer troops, and I am inclined to think with regulars, too, in time of trial, the best work can be got out of the men only if the officers endure the same hardships and face the same risks. In my regiment, as in the whole cavalry division, the proportion of loss in killed and wounded was considerably greater among the officers than among the troopers, and this was exactly as it should be. Moreover, when we got down to hard pan, we all, officers and men, fared exactly alike as regards both shelter and food. This prevented any grumbling. When the troopers saw that the officers had nothing but hardtack, there was not a man in the regiment who would not have been ashamed to grumble at faring no worse, and when all alike slept out in the open, in the rear of the trenches, and when the men always saw the field officers up at night, during the digging of the trenches, and going the rounds of the outposts, they would not tolerate, in any of their number, either complaint or shirking work. When things got easier I put up my tent and lived a little apart, for it is a mistake for an officer ever to grow too familiar with his men, no matter how good they are; and it is of course the greatest possible mistake to seek popularity either by showing weakness or by mollycoddling the men. They will never respect a commander who does not enforce discipline, who does not know his duty, and who is not willing both himself to encounter and to make them encounter every species of danger and hardship when necessary. The soldiers who do not feel this way are not worthy of the name and should be handled with iron severity until they become fighting men and not shams. In return the officer should carefully look after his men, should see that they are well fed and well sheltered, and that, no matter how much they may grumble, they keep the camp thoroughly policed.

After the cessation of the three days' fighting we began to get our rations regularly and had plenty of hardtack and salt pork, and usually about half the ordinary amount of sugar and coffee. It was not a very good ration for the tropics, however, and was of very little use indeed to the sick and half sick. On two or three occasions during the siege I got my improvised pack-train together and either took or sent it down to the sea-coast for beans, canned tomatoes, and the like. We got these either from the transports which were still landing stores on the beach or from the Red Cross. If I did not go myself I sent some man who had shown that he was a driving, energetic, tactful fellow, who would somehow get what we wanted. Chaplain Brown developed great capacity in this line, and so did one of the troopers named Knoblauch, he who had dived after the rifles that had sunk off the pier at Daiquiri. The supplies of food we got in this way had a very beneficial effect, not only upon the men's health, but upon their spirits. To the Red Cross and similar charitable organizations we owe a great deal. We also owed much to Colonel Weston of the Commissary Department, who always helped us and never let himself be hindered by red tape; thus he always let me violate the absurd regulation which forbade me, even in war time, to purchase food for my men from the stores, although letting me purchase for the officers. I, of course, paid no heed to the regulation when by violating it I could get beans, canned tomatoes, or tobacco. Sometimes I used my own money, sometimes what was given me by Woody Kane, or what was sent me by my brother-in-law, Douglas Robinson, or by the other Red Cross people in New York. My regiment did not fare very well; but I think it fared better than any other. Of course no one would have minded in the least such hardships as we endured had there been any need of enduring them; but there was none. System and sufficiency of transportation were all that were needed.

On one occasion a foreign military attaché visited my headquarters together with a foreign correspondent who had been through the Turco-Greek war. They were both most friendly critics, and as they knew I was aware of this, the correspondent finally ventured the remark, that he thought our soldiers fought even better than the Turks, but that on the whole our system of military administration seemed rather worse than that of the Greeks. As a nation we had prided ourselves on our business ability and adroitness in the arts of peace, while outsiders, at any rate, did not credit us with any especial warlike prowess; and it was curious that when war came we should have broken down precisely on the business and administrative side, while the fighting edge of the troops certainly left little to be desired.

I was very much touched by the devotion my men showed to me. After they had once become convinced that I would share their hardships, they made it a point that I should not suffer any hardships at all; and I really had an extremely easy time. Whether I had any food or not myself made no difference, as there were sure to be certain troopers, and, indeed, certain troop messes, on the lookout for me. If they had any beans they would send me over a cupful, or I would suddenly receive a present of doughnuts from some ex-roundup cook who had succeeded in obtaining a little flour and sugar, and if a man shot a guinea-hen it was all I could do to make him keep half of it for himself. Wright, the color sergeant, and Henry Bardshar, my orderly, always pitched and struck my tent and built me a bunk of bamboo poles, whenever we changed camp. So I personally endured very little discomfort; for, of course, no one minded the two or three days preceding or following each fight, when we all had to get along as best we could. Indeed, as long as we were under fire or in the immediate presence of the enemy, and I had plenty to do, there was nothing of which I could legitimately complain; and what I really did regard as hardships, my men did not object to—for later on, when we had some leisure, I would have given much for complete solitude and some good books.

Whether there was a truce, or whether, as sometimes happened, we were notified that there was no truce but merely a further cessation of hostilities by tacit agreement, or whether the fight was on, we kept equally vigilant watch, especially at night. In the trenches every fourth man kept awake, the others sleeping beside or behind him on their rifles; and the Cossack posts and pickets were pushed out in advance beyond the edge of the jungle. At least once a night at some irregular hour I tried to visit every part of our line, especially if it was dark and rainy, although sometimes, when the lines were in charge of some officer like Wilcox or Kane, Greenway or Goodrich, I became lazy, took off my boots, and slept all night through. Sometimes at night I went not only along the lines of our own brigade, but of the brigades adjoining. It was a matter of pride, not only with me, but with all our men, that the lines occupied by the Rough Riders should be at least as vigilantly guarded as the lines of any regular regiment.

Sometimes at night, when I met other officers inspecting their lines, we would sit and talk over matters, and wonder what shape the outcome of the siege would take. We knew we would capture Santiago, but exactly how we would do it we could not tell. The failure to establish any depot for provisions on the fighting-line, where there was hardly ever more than twenty-four hours' food ahead, made the risk very serious. If a hurricane had struck the transports, scattering them to the four winds, or if three days of heavy rain had completely broken up our communication, as they assuredly would have done, we would have been at starvation point on the front; and while, of course, we would have lived through it somehow and would have taken the city, it would only have been after very disagreeable experiences. As soon as I was able I accumulated for my own regiment about forty-eight hours' hardtack and salt pork, which I kept so far as possible intact to provide against any emergency.

If the city could be taken without direct assault on the intrenchments and wire entanglements, we earnestly hoped it would be, for such an assault meant, as we knew by past experience, the loss of a quarter of the attacking regiments (and we were bound that the Rough Riders should be one of these attacking regiments, if the attack had to be made). There was, of course, nobody who would not rather have assaulted than have run the risk of failure; but we hoped the city would fall without need arising for us to suffer the great loss of life which a further assault would have entailed.

Naturally, the colonels and captains had nothing to say in the peace negotiations which dragged along for the week following the sending in the flag of truce. Each day we expected either to see the city surrender, or to be told to begin fighting again, and toward the end it grew so irksome that we would have welcomed even an assault in preference to further inaction. I used to discuss matters with the officers of my own regiment now and then, and with a few of the officers of the neighboring regiments with whom I had struck up a friendship—Parker, Stevens, Beck, Ayres, Morton, and Boughton. I also saw a good deal of the excellent officers on the staffs of Generals Wheeler and Sumner, especially Colonel Dorst, Colonel Garlington, Captain Howze, Captain Steele, Lieutenant Andrews, and Captain Astor Chanler, who, like myself, was a volunteer. Chanler was an old friend and a fellow big-game hunter, who had done some good exploring work in Africa. I always wished I could have had him in my regiment. As for Dorst, he was peculiarly fitted to command a regiment. Although Howze and Andrews were not in my brigade, I saw a great deal of them, especially of Howze, who would have made a nearly ideal regimental commander. They were both natural cavalry-men and of most enterprising natures, ever desirous of pushing to the front and of taking the boldest course. The view Howze always took of every emergency (a view which found prompt expression in his actions when the opportunity offered) made me feel like an elderly conservative.

The week of non-fighting was not all a period of truce; part of the time was passed under a kind of nondescript arrangement, when we were told not to attack ourselves, but to be ready at any moment to repulse an attack and to make preparations for meeting it. During these times I busied myself in putting our trenches into first-rate shape and in building bomb-proofs and traverses. One night I got a detail of sixty men from the First, Ninth, and Tenth, whose officers always helped us in every way, and with these, and with sixty of my own men, I dug a long, zigzag trench in advance of the salient of my line out to a knoll well in front, from which we could command the Spanish trenches and block-houses immediately ahead of us. On this knoll we made a kind of bastion consisting of a deep, semi-circular trench with sand-bags arranged along the edge so as to constitute a wall with loop-holes. Of course, when I came to dig this trench, I kept both Greenway and Goodrich supervising the work all night, and equally of course I got Parker and Stevens to help me. By employing as many men as we did we were able to get the work so far advanced as to provide against interruption before the moon rose, which was about midnight. Our pickets were thrown far out in the jungle, to keep back the Spanish pickets and prevent any interference with the diggers. The men seemed to think the work rather good fun than otherwise, the possibility of a brush with the Spaniards lending a zest that prevented its growing monotonous.

Parker had taken two of his Gatlings, removed the wheels, and mounted them in the trenches; also mounting the two automatic Colts where he deemed they could do best service. With the completion of the trenches, bomb-proofs, and traverses, and the mounting of these guns, the fortifications of the hill assumed quite a respectable character, and the Gatling men christened it Fort Roosevelt, by which name it afterward went.*

During the truce various military attachés and foreign officers came out to visit us. Two or three of the newspaper men, including Richard Harding Davis, Caspar Whitney, and John Fox, had already been out to see us, and had been in the trenches during the firing. Among the others were Captains Lee and Paget of the British army and navy, fine fellows, who really seemed to take as much pride in the feats of our men as if we had been bound together by the ties of a common nationality instead of the ties of race and speech kinship. Another English visitor was Sir Bryan Leighton, a thrice-welcome guest, for he most thoughtfully brought to me half a dozen little jars of devilled ham and potted fruit, which enabled me to summon various officers down to my tent and hold a feast. Count von Götzen, and a Norwegian attaché, Gedde, very good fellows both, were also out. One day we were visited by a travelling Russian, Prince X., a large, blond man, smooth and impenetrable. I introduced him to one of the regular army officers, a capital fighter and excellent fellow, who, however, viewed foreign international politics from a strictly trans-Mississippi stand-point. He hailed the Russian with frank kindness and took him off to show him around the trenches, chatting volubly, and calling him "Prince," much as Kentuckians call one another "Colonel." As I returned I heard him remarking: "You see, Prince, the great result of this war is that it has united the two branches of the Anglo-Saxon people; and now that they are together they can whip the world, Prince! they can whip the world!"—being evidently filled with the pleasing belief that the Russian would cordially sympathize with this view.

The foreign attachés did not always get on well with our generals. The two English representatives never had any trouble, were heartily admired by everybody, and, indeed, were generally treated as if they were of our own number; and seemingly so regarded

* See Parker's "With the Gatlings at Santiago."

themselves. But this was not always true of the representatives from Continental Europe. One of the latter—a very good fellow, by the way—had not altogether approved of the way he was treated, and the climax came when he said good-by to the General who had special charge of him. The General in question was not accustomed to nice ethnic distinctions, and grouped all of the representatives from Continental Europe under the comprehensive title of "Dutchmen." When the attaché in question came to say farewell, the General responded with a bluff heartiness, in which perhaps the note of sincerity was more conspicuous than that of entire good breeding: "Well, good-by; sorry you're going; which are you anyhow—the German or the Russian?"

Shortly after midday on the 10th fighting began again, but it soon became evident that the Spaniards did not have much heart in it. The American field artillery was now under the command of General Randolph, and he fought it effectively. A mortar battery had also been established, though with an utterly inadequate supply of ammunition, and this rendered some service. Almost the only Rough Riders who had a chance to do much firing were the men with the Colt automatic guns, and the twenty picked sharpshooters, who were placed in the newly dug little fort out at the extreme front. Parker had a splendid time with the Gatlings and the Colts. With these machine guns he completely silenced the battery in front of us. This battery had caused us a good deal of trouble at first, as we could not place it. It was immediately in front of the hospital, from which many Red Cross flags were flying, one of them floating just above this battery, from where we looked at it. In consequence, for some time, we did not know it was a hostile battery at all, as, like all the other Spanish batteries, it was using smokeless powder. It was only by the aid of powerful glasses that we finally discovered its real nature. The Gatlings and Colts then actually put it out of action, silencing the big guns and the two field-pieces. Furthermore, the machine guns and our sharp-shooters together did good work in supplementing the effects of the dynamite gun; for when a shell from the latter struck near a Spanish trench, or a building in which there were Spanish troops, the shock was seemingly so great that the

Spaniards almost always showed themselves, and gave our men a chance to do some execution.

As the evening of the 10th came on, the men began to make their coffee in sheltered places. By this time they knew how to take care of themselves so well that not a man was touched by the Spaniards during the second bombardment. While I was lying with the officers just outside one of the bomb-proofs I saw a New Mexican trooper named Morrison making his coffee under the protection of a traverse high up on the hill. Morrison was originally a Baptist preacher who had joined the regiment purely from a sense of duty, leaving his wife and children, and had shown himself to be an excellent soldier. He had evidently exactly calculated the danger zone, and found that by getting close to the traverse he could sit up erect and make ready his supper without being cramped. I watched him solemnly pounding the coffee with the butt end of his revolver, and then boiling the water and frying his bacon, just as if he had been in the lee of the roundup wagon somewhere out on the plains.

By noon of the next day, the 11th, my regiment with one of the Gatlings was shifted over to the right to guard the Caney road. We did no fighting in our new position, for the last straggling shot had been fired by the time we got there. That evening there came up the worst storm we had had, and by midnight my tent blew over. I had for the first time in a fortnight undressed myself completely, and I felt fully punished for my love of luxury when I jumped out into the driving downpour of tropic rain, and groped blindly in the darkness for my clothes as they lay in the liquid mud. It was Kane's night on guard, and I knew the wretched Woody would be out along the line and taking care of the pickets, no matter what the storm might be; and so I basely made my way to the kitchen tent, where good Holderman, the Cherokee, wrapped me in dry blankets, and put me to sleep on a table which he had just procured from an abandoned Spanish house.

On the 17th the city formally surrendered and our regiment, like the rest of the army, was drawn up on the trenches. When the American flag was hoisted the trumpets blared and the men cheered, and we knew that the fighting part of our work was over.

Shortly after we took our new position the First Illinois Volunteers came up on our right. The next day, as a result of the storm and of further rain, the rivers were up and the roads quagmires, so that hardly any food reached the front. My regiment was all right, as we had provided for just such an emergency; but the Illinois newcomers had of course not done so, and they were literally without anything to eat. They were fine fellows and we could not see them suffer. I furnished them some beans and coffee for the elder officers and two or three cases of hardtack for the men, and then mounted my horse and rode down to head-quarters, half fording, half swimming the streams; and late in the evening I succeeded in getting half a mule-train of provisions for them.

On the morning of the 3d the Spaniards had sent out of Santiago many thousands of women, children, and other non-combatants, most of them belonging to the poorer classes, but among them not a few of the best families. These wretched creatures took very little with them. They came through our lines and for the most part went to El Caney in our rear, where we had to feed them and protect them from the Cubans. As we had barely enough food for our own men the rations of the refugees were scanty indeed and their sufferings great. Long before the surrender they had begun to come to our lines to ask for provisions, and my men gave them a good deal out of their own scanty stores, until I had positively to forbid it and to insist that the refugees should go to head-quarters; as, however hard and merciless it seemed, I was in duty bound to keep my own regiment at the highest pitch of fighting efficiency.

As soon as the surrender was assured the refugees came streaming back in an endless squalid procession down the Caney road to Santiago. My troopers, for all their roughness and their ferocity in fight, were rather tender-hearted than otherwise, and they helped the poor creatures, especially the women and children, in every way, giving them food and even carrying the children and the burdens borne by the women. I saw one man, Happy Jack, spend the entire day in walking to and fro for about a quarter of a mile on both sides of our lines along the road, carrying the bundles for a series of poor old women, or else carrying young children. Finally the doctor warned us that we must not touch the bundles of the refugees for fear of infection, as disease had broken out and was rife among them. Accordingly I had to put a stop to these acts of kindness on the part of my men; against which action Happy Jack respectfully but strongly protested upon the unexpected ground that "The Almighty would never let a man catch a disease while he was doing a good action." I did not venture to take so advanced a theological stand.

VI

THE RETURN HOME

Two or three days after the surrender the cavalry division was marched back to the foothills west of El Caney, and there went into camp, together with the artillery. It was a most beautiful spot beside a stream of clear water, but it was not healthy. In fact no ground in the neighborhood was healthy. For the tropics the climate was not bad, and I have no question but that a man who was able to take good care of himself could live there all the year round with comparative impunity; but the case was entirely different with an army which was obliged to suffer great exposure, and to live under conditions which almost insured being attacked by the severe malarial fever of the country. My own men were already suffering badly from fever, and they got worse rather than better in the new camp. The same was true of the other regiments in the cavalry division. A curious feature was that the colored troops seemed to suffer as heavily as the white. From week to week there were slight relative changes, but on the average all the six cavalry regiments, the Rough Riders, the white regulars, and the colored regulars seemed to suffer about alike, and we were all very much weakened; about as much as the regular infantry, although naturally not as much as the volunteer infantry.

Yet even under such circumstances adventurous spirits managed to make their way out to us. In the fortnight following the last bombardment of the city I enlisted no less than nine such recruits, six being from Harvard, Yale, or Princeton; and Bull, the former Harvard oar, who had been back to the States crippled after the first fight, actually got back to us as a stowaway on one of the transports, bound to share the luck of the regiment, even if it meant yellow fever.

There were but twelve ambulances with the army, and these were quite inadequate for their work; but the conditions in the large field hospitals were so bad, that as long as possible we kept all of our sick men in the regimental hospital at the front. Dr. Church did splendid work, although he himself was suffering much more than half the time from fever. Several of the men from the ranks did equally well, especially a young doctor from New York, Harry Thorpe, who had enlisted as a trooper, but who was now made acting assistant-surgeon. It was with the greatest difficulty that Church and Thorpe were able to get proper medicine for the sick, and it was almost the last day of our stay before we were able to get cots for them. Up to that time they lay on the ground. No food was issued suitable for them, or for the half-sick men who were not on the doctor's list; the two classes by this time included the bulk of the command. Occasionally we got hold of a wagon or of some Cuban carts, and at other times I used my improvised pack-train (the animals of which, however, were continually being taken away from us by our superiors) and went or sent back to the sea-coast at Siboney or into Santiago itself to get rice, flour, cornmeal, oatmeal, condensed milk, potatoes, and canned vegetables. The rice I bought in Santiago; the best of the other stuff I got from the Red Cross through Mr. George Kennan and Miss Clara Barton and Dr. Lesser; but some of it I got from our own transports. Colonel Weston, the Commissary-General, as always, rendered us every service in his power. This additional and varied food was of the utmost service, not merely to the sick but in preventing the well from becoming sick. Throughout the campaign the Division Inspector-

General, Lieutenant-Colonel Garlington, and Lieutenants West and Dickman, the acting division quartermaster and commissary, had done everything in their power to keep us supplied with food; but where there were so few mules and wagons even such able and zealous officers could not do the impossible.

We had the camp policed thoroughly, and I made the men build little bunks of poles to sleep on. By July 23d, when we had been ashore a month, we were able to get fresh meat, and from that time on we fared well; but the men were already sickening. The chief trouble was the malarial fever, which was recurrent. For a few days the man would be very sick indeed; then he would partially recover, and be able to go back to work; but after a little time he would be again struck down. Every officer other than myself except one was down with sickness at one time or another. Even Greenway and Goodrich succumbed to the fever and were knocked out for a few days. Very few of the men indeed retained their strength and energy, and though the percentage actually on the sick list never got over twenty, there were less than fifty per cent. who were fit for any kind of work. All the clothes were in rags; even the officers had neither socks nor underwear. The lithe college athletes had lost their spring; the tall, gaunt hunters and cow-punchers lounged listlessly in their dog-tents, which were steaming morasses during the torrential rains, and then ovens when the sun blazed down; but there were no complaints.

Through some blunder our march from the intrenchments to the camp on the foothills, after the surrender, was made during the heat of the day; and though it was only some five miles or thereabouts, very nearly half the men of the cavalry division dropped out. Captain Llewellen had come back, and led his troop on the march. He carried a pick and shovel for one of his sick men, and after we reached camp walked back with a mule to get another trooper who had fallen out from heat exhaustion. The result was that the captain himself went down and became exceedingly sick. We at last succeeded in sending him to the States. I never thought he would live, but he did, and when I met him again at Montauk

Point he had practically entirely recovered. My orderly, Henry Bardshar, was struck down, and though he ultimately recovered, he was a mere skeleton, having lost over eighty pounds.

Yellow fever also broke out in the rear, chiefly among the Cubans. It never became epidemic, but it caused a perfect panic among some of our own doctors, and especially in the minds of one or two generals and of the home authorities. We found that whenever we sent a man to the rear he was decreed to have yellow fever, whereas, if we kept him at the front, it always turned out that he had malarial fever, and after a few days he was back at work again. I doubt if there were ever more than a dozen genuine cases of yellow fever in the whole cavalry division; but the authorities at Washington, misled by the reports they received from one or two of their military and medical advisers at the front, became panic-struck, and under the influence of their fears hesitated to bring the army home, lest it might import yellow fever into the United States. Their panic was absolutely groundless, as shown by the fact that when brought home not a single case of yellow fever developed upon American soil. Our real foe was not the yellow fever at all, but malarial fever, which was not infectious, but which was certain, if the troops were left throughout the summer in Cuba, to destroy them, either killing them outright, or weakening them so that they would have fallen victims to any disease that attacked them.

However, for a time our prospects were gloomy, as the Washington authorities seemed determined that we should stay in Cuba. They unfortunately knew nothing of the country nor of the circumstances of the army, and the plans that were from time to time formulated in the Department (and even by an occasional general or surgeon at the front) for the management of the army would have been comic if they had not possessed such tragic possibilities. Thus, at one period it was proposed that we should shift camp every two or three days. Now, our transportation, as I have pointed out before, was utterly inadequate. In theory, under the regulations of the War Department, each regiment should have had at least twenty-five wagons. As a matter of fact our regiment often had none, sometimes one, rarely two, and never three; yet it was better off than any other in the cavalry division. In consequence it was impossible to carry much of anything save what the men had on their backs, and half of the men were too weak to walk three miles with their packs. Whenever we shifted camp the exertion among the half-sick caused our sick-roll to double next morning, and it took at least three days, even when the shift was for but a short distance, before we were able to bring up the officers' luggage, the hospital spare food, the ammunition, etc. Meanwhile the officers slept wherever they could, and those men who had not been able to carry their own bedding, slept as the officers did. In the weak condition of the men the labor of pitching camp was severe and told heavily upon them. In short, the scheme of continually shifting camp was impossible of fulfilment. It would merely have resulted in the early destruction of the army.

Again, it was proposed that we should go up the mountains and make our camps there. The palm and the bamboo grew to the summits of the mountains, and the soil along their sides was deep and soft, while the rains were very heavy, much more so than immediately on the coast—every mile or two inland bringing with it a great increase in the rainfall. We could, with much difficulty, have got our regiments up the mountains, but not half the men could have got up with their belongings; and once there it would have been an impossibility to feed them. It was all that could be done, with the limited number of wagons and mule-trains on hand, to feed the men in the existing camps, for the travel and the rain gradually rendered each road in succession wholly impassable. To have gone up the mountains would have meant early starvation.

The third plan of the Department was even more objectionable than either of the others. There was, some twenty-five miles in the interior, what was called a high interior plateau, and at one period we were informed that we were to be marched thither. As a matter of fact, this so-called high plateau was the sugar-cane country, where, during the summer, the rainfall was prodigious. It was a rich, deep soil, covered with a rank tropic growth, the guinea-grass being higher than the head of a man on horseback. It was a perfect hotbed of malaria, and there was no dry ground whatever in which to camp. To have sent the troops there would have been simple butchery.

Under these circumstances the alternative to leaving the country altogether was to stay where we were, with the hope that half the men would live through to the cool season. We did everything possible to keep up the spirits of the men, but it was exceedingly difficult because there was nothing for them to do. They were weak and languid, and in the wet heat they had lost energy, so that it was not possible for them to indulge in sports or pastimes. There were exceptions; but the average man who went off to shoot guinea-hens or tried some vigorous game always felt much the worse for his exertions. Once or twice I took some of my comrades with me, and climbed up one or another of the surrounding mountains, but the result generally was that half of the party were down with some kind of sickness next day. It was impossible to take heavy exercise in the heat of the day; the evening usually saw a rain-storm which made the country a quagmire; and in the early morning the drenching dew and wet, slimy soil made walking but little pleasure. Chaplain Brown held service every Sunday under a low tree outside my tent; and we always had a congregation of a few score troopers, lying or sitting round, their strong hard faces turned toward the preacher. I let a few of the men visit Santiago, but the long walk in and out was very tiring, and, moreover, wise restrictions had been put as to either officers or men coming in.

In any event there was very little to do in the quaint, dirty old Spanish city, though it was interesting to go in once or twice, and wander through the narrow streets with their curious little shops and low houses of stained stucco, with elaborately wrought iron trellises to the windows, and curiously carved balconies; or to sit in the central plaza where the cathedral was, and the clubs, and the Café Venus, and the low, bare, rambling building which was called the Governor's Palace. In this palace Wood had now been established as military governor, and Luna, and two or three of my other officers from the Mexican border, who knew Spanish, were sent in to do duty under him. A great many of my men knew Spanish, and some of the New Mexicans were of Spanish origin, although they behaved precisely like the other members of the regiment.

We should probably have spent the summer in our sick camps, losing half the men and hopelessly shattering the health of the remainder, if General Shafter had not summoned a council of officers, hoping by united action of a more or less public character to wake up the Washington authorities to the actual condition of things. As all the Spanish forces in the province of Santiago had surrendered, and as so-called immune regiments were coming to garrison the conquered territory, there was literally not one thing of any kind whatsoever for the army to do, and no purpose to serve by keeping it at Santiago. We did not suppose that peace was at hand, being ignorant of the negotiations. We were anxious to take part in the Porto Rico campaign, and would have been more than willing to suffer any amount of sickness, if by so doing we could get into action. But if we were not to take part in the Porto Rico campaign, then we knew it was absolutely indispensable to get our commands north immediately, if they were to be in trim for the great campaign against Havana, which would surely be the main event of the winter if peace were not declared in advance.

Our army included the great majority of the regulars, and was, therefore, the flower of the American force. It was on every account imperative to keep it in good trim; and to keep it in Santiago meant its entirely purposeless destruction. As soon as the surrender was an accomplished fact, the taking away of the army to the north should have begun.

Every officer, from the highest to the lowest, especially among the regulars, realized all of this, and about the last day of July, General Shafter called a conference, in the palace, of all the division and brigade commanders. By this time, owing to Wood's having been made Governor-General, I was in command of my brigade, so I went to the conference too, riding in with Generals Sumner and Wheeler, who were the other representatives of the cavalry division. Besides the line officers all the chief medical officers were present at the conference. The telegrams from the Secretary stating the position of himself and the Surgeon-General were read, and then almost every line and medical officer present expressed his views in turn. They were almost all regulars and had been brought up to life-long habits of obedience without protest. They were ready to obey still, but they felt, quite rightly, that it was their duty to protest rather than to see the flower of the United States forces destroyed as the culminating act of a campaign in which the blunders that had been committed had been retrieved only by the valor and splendid soldierly qualities of the officers and enlisted men of the infantry and dismounted cavalry. There was not a dissenting voice; for there could not be. There was but one side to the question. To talk of continually shifting camp or of moving up the mountains or of moving into the interior was idle, for not one of the plans could be carried out with our utterly insufficient transportation, and at that season and in that climate they would merely have resulted in aggravating the sickliness of the soldiers. It was deemed best to make some record of our opinion, in the shape of a letter or report, which would show that to keep the army in Santiago meant its absolute and objectless ruin, and that it should at once be recalled. At first there was naturally some hesitation on the part of the regular officers to take the initiative, for their entire future career might be sacrificed. So I wrote a letter to General Shafter, reading over the rough draft to the various Generals and adopting their corrections. Before I had finished making these corrections it was determined that we should send a circular letter on behalf of all of us to General Shafter, and when I returned from presenting him mine, I found this circular letter already prepared and we all of us signed it. Both letters were made public. The result was immediate. Within three days the army was ordered to be ready to sail for home.

As soon as it was known that we were to sail for home the spirits of the men changed for the better. In my regiment the officers began to plan methods of drilling the men on horseback, so as to fit them for use against the Spanish cavalry, if we should go against Havana in December. We had, all of us, eyed the captured Spanish cavalry with particular interest. The men were small, and the horses, though well trained and well built, were diminutive ponies, very much smaller than cow ponies. We were certain that if we ever got a chance to try shock tactics against them they would go down like nine-pins, provided only that our men could be trained to charge in any kind of line, and we made up our minds to devote our time to this. Dismounted work with the rifle we already felt thoroughly competent to perform.

My time was still much occupied with looking after the health of my brigade, but the fact that we were going home, where I knew that their health would improve, lightened my mind, and I was able thoroughly to enjoy the beauty of the country, and even of the storms, which hitherto I had regarded purely as enemies.

The surroundings of the city of Santiago are very grand. The circling mountains rise sheer and high. The plains are threaded by rapid winding brooks and are dotted here and there with quaint villages, curiously picturesque from their combining traces of an outworn old-world civilization with new and raw barbarism. The tall, graceful, feathery bamboos rise by the water's edge, and elsewhere, even on the mountain-crests, where the soil is wet and rank enough; and the splendid royal palms and cocoanut palms tower high above the matted green jungle.

Generally the thunder-storms came in the afternoon, but once I saw one at sunrise, driving down the high mountain valleys toward us. It was a very beautiful and almost terrible sight; for the sun rose behind the storm, and shone through the gusty rifts, lighting the mountain-crests here and there, while the plain below lay shrouded in the lingering night. The angry, level rays edged the dark clouds with crimson, and turned the downpour into sheets of golden rain; in the valleys the glimmering mists were tinted every wild hue; and the remotest heavens were lit with flaming glory.

One day General Lawton, General Wood and I, with Ferguson and poor Tiffany, went down the bay to visit Morro Castle. The shores were beautiful, especially where there were groves of palms and of the scarlet-flower tree, and the castle itself, on a jutting headland, overlooking the sea and guarding the deep, narrow entrance to the bay, showed just what it was, the splendid relic of a vanished power and a vanished age. We wandered all through it, among the castellated battlements, and in the dungeons, where we found hideous rusty implements of torture; and looked at the guns, some modern and some very old. It had been little hurt by the bombardment of the ships. Afterward I had a swim, not trusting much to the shark stories. We passed by the sunken hulks of the Merrimac and the Reina Mercedes, lying just outside the main channel. Our own people had tried to sink the first and the Spaniards had tried to sink the second, so as to block the entrance. Neither attempt was successful.

On August 6th we were ordered to embark, and next morning we sailed on the transport Miami. General Wheeler was with us and a squadron of the Third Cavalry under Major Jackson. The General put the policing and management of the ship into my hands, and I had great aid from Captain McCormick, who had been acting with me as adjutant-general of the brigade. I had profited by my experience coming down, and as Dr. Church knew his work well, although he was very sick, we kept the ship in such good sanitary condition, that we were one of the very few organizations allowed to land at Montauk immediately upon our arrival.

Soon after leaving port the captain of the ship notified me that his stokers and engineers were insubordinate and drunken, due, he thought, to liquor which my men had given them. I at once started a search of the ship, explaining to the men that they could not keep the liquor; that if they surrendered whatever they had to me I should return it to them when we went ashore; and that meanwhile I would allow the sick to drink when they really needed it; but that if they did not give the liquor to me of their own accord I would throw it overboard. About seventy flasks and bottles were handed to me, and I found and threw overboard about twenty. This at once put a stop to all drunkenness. The stokers and engineers were sullen and half mutinous, so I sent a detail of my men down to watch them and see that they did their work under the orders of the chief engineer; and we reduced them to obedience in short order. I could easily have drawn from the regiment sufficient skilled men to fill every position in the entire ship's crew, from captain to stoker.

We were very much crowded on board the ship, but rather better off than on the Yucatan, so far as the men were concerned, which was the important point. All the officers except General Wheeler slept in a kind of improvised shed, not unlike a chicken coop with bunks, on the aftermost part of the upper deck. The water was bad—some of it very bad. There was no ice. The canned beef proved practically uneatable, as we knew would be the case. There were not enough vegetables. We did not have enough disinfectants, and there was no provision whatever for a hospital or for isolating the sick; we simply put them on one portion of one deck. If, as so many of the high authorities had insisted, there had really been a yellow-fever epidemic, and if it had broken out on shipboard, the condition would have been frightful; but there was no yellow-fever epidemic. Three of our men had been kept behind as suspects, all three suffering simply from malarial fever. One of them, Lutz, a particularly good soldier, died; another, who was simply a malingerer and had nothing the matter with him whatever, of course recovered; the third was Tiffany who, I believe, would have lived had we been allowed to take him with us, but who was sent home later and died soon after landing.

I was very anxious to keep the men amused, and as the quarters were so crowded that it was out of the question for them to have any physical exercise, I did not interfere with their playing games of chance so long as no disorder followed. On shore this was not allowed; but in the particular emergency which we were meeting, the loss of a month's salary was as nothing compared to keeping the men thoroughly interested and diverted.

By care and diligence we succeeded in preventing any serious sickness. One man died, however. He had been suffering from dysentery ever since we landed, owing purely to his own fault, for on the very first night ashore he obtained a lot of fiery liquor from some of the Cubans, got very drunk, and had to march next day through the hot sun before he was entirely sober. He never recovered, and was useless from that time on. On board ship he died, and we gave him sea burial. Wrapped in a hammock, he was placed opposite a port, and the American flag thrown over him. The engine was stilled, and the great ship rocked on the waves unshaken by the screw, while the war-worn troopers clustered around with bare heads, to listen to Chaplain Brown read the funeral service, and to the band of the Third Cavalry as it played the funeral dirge. Then the port was knocked free, the flag withdrawn, and the shotted hammock plunged heavily over the side, rushing down through the dark water to lie, till the Judgment Day, in the ooze that holds the timbers of so many gallant ships, and the bones of so many fearless adventurers.

We were favored by good weather during our nine days' voyage, and much of the time when there was little to do we simply sat together and talked, each man contributing from the fund of his own experiences. Voyages around Cape Horn, yacht races for the America's cup, experiences on foot-ball teams which are famous in the annals of college sport; more serious feats of desperate prowess in Indian fighting and in breaking up gangs of white outlaws; adventures in hunting big game, in breaking wild horses, in tending great herds of cattle, and in wandering winter and summer among the mountains and across the lonely plains—the men who told the tales could draw upon countless memories such as these of the things they had done and the things they had seen others do. Sometimes General Wheeler joined us and told us about the great war, compared with which ours was such a small war—far-reaching in their importance though its effects were destined to be. When we had become convinced that we would escape an epidemic of sickness the homeward voyage became very pleasant.

On the eve of leaving Santiago I had received from Mr. Laffan of the Sun, a cable with the single word "Peace," and we speculated much on this, as the clumsy transport steamed slowly northward across the trade wind and then into the Gulf Stream. At last we sighted the low, sandy bluffs of the Long Island coast, and late on the afternoon of the 14th we steamed through the still waters of the Sound and cast anchor off Montauk. A gun-boat of the Mosquito fleet came out to greet us and to inform us that peace negotiations had begun.

Next morning we were marched on shore. Many of the men were very sick indeed. Of the three or four who had been closest to me among the enlisted men, Color-Sergeant Wright was the only one in good health. Henry Bardshar was a wreck, literally at death's door. I was myself in first-class health, all the better for having lost twenty pounds. Faithful Marshall, my colored body-servant, was so sick as to be nearly helpless.

Bob Wrenn nearly died. He had joined us very late and we could not get him a Krag carbine; so I had given him my Winchester, which carried the government cartridge; and when he was mustered out he carried it home in triumph, to the envy of his fellows, who themselves had to surrender their beloved rifles.

For the first few days there was great confusion and some want even after we got to Montauk. The men in hospitals suffered from lack of almost everything, even cots. But after these few days we were very well cared for and had abundance of all we needed, except that on several occasions there was a shortage of food for the horses, which I should have regarded as even more serious than a shortage for the men, had it not been that we were about to be disbanded. The men lived high, with milk, eggs, oranges, and any amount of tobacco, the lack of which during portions of the Cuban campaign had been felt as seriously as any lack of food. One of the distressing features of the malarial fever which had been ravaging the troops was that it was recurrent and persistent. Some of my men died after reaching home, and many were very sick. We owed much to the kindness not only of the New York hospitals and the Red Cross and kindred societies, but of individuals, notably Mr. Bayard Cutting and Mrs. Armitage, who took many of our men to their beautiful Long Island homes.

On the whole, however, the month we spent at Montauk before we disbanded was very pleasant. It was good to meet the rest of the regiment. They all felt dreadfully at not having been in Cuba. It was a sore trial to men who had given up much to go to the war, and who rebelled at nothing in the way of hardship or suffering, but who did bitterly feel the fact that their sacrifices seemed to have been useless. Of course those who stayed had done their duty precisely as did those who went, for the question of glory was not to be considered in comparison to the faithful performance of whatever was ordered; and no distinction of any kind was allowed in the regiment between those whose good fortune it had been to go and those whose harder fate it had been to remain. Nevertheless the latter could not be entirely comforted.

The regiment had three mascots; the two most characteristic—a young mountain lion brought by the Arizona troops, and a war eagle brought by the New Mexicans—we had been forced to leave behind in Tampa. The third, a rather disreputable but exceedingly knowing little dog named Cuba, had accompanied us through all the vicissitudes of the campaign. The mountain lion, Josephine, possessed an infernal temper; whereas both Cuba and the eagle, which have been named in my honor, were extremely good-humored. Josephine was kept tied up. She sometimes escaped. One cool night in early September she wandered off and, entering the tent of a Third Cavalry man, got into bed with him; whereupon he fled into the darkness with yells, much more unnerved than he would have been by the arrival of any number of Spaniards. The eagle was let loose and not only walked at will up and down the company streets, but also at times flew wherever he wished. He was a young bird, having been taken out of his nest when a fledgling. Josephine hated him and was always trying to make a meal of him, especially when we endeavored to take their photographs together. The eagle, though good-natured, was an entirely competent individual and ready at any moment to beat Josephine off. Cuba was also oppressed at times by Josephine, and was of course no match for her, but was frequently able to overawe by simple decision of character.

In addition to the animal mascots, we had two or three small boys who had also been adopted by the regiment. One, from Tennessee, was named Dabney Royster. When we embarked at Tampa he smuggled himself on board the transport with a 22-calibre rifle and three boxes of cartridges, and wept bitterly when sent ashore. The squadron which remained behind adopted him, got him a little Rough Rider's uniform, and made him practically one of the regiment. The men who had remained at Tampa, like ourselves, had suffered much from fever, and the horses were in bad shape. So many of the men were sick that none of the regiments began to drill for some time after reaching Montauk. There was a great deal of paper-work to be done; but as I still had charge of the brigade only a little of it fell on my shoulders. Of this I was sincerely glad, for I knew as little of the paper-work as my men had originally known of drill. We had all of us learned how to fight and march; but the exact limits of our rights and duties in other respects were not very clearly defined in our minds; and as for myself, as I had not had the time to learn exactly what they were, I had assumed a large authority in giving rewards and punishments. In particular I had looked on court-martials much as Peter Bell looked on primroses—they were court-martials and nothing more, whether resting on the authority of a lieutenant-colonel or of a major-general. The mustering-out officer, a thorough soldier, found to his horror that I had used the widest discretion both in imposing heavy sentences which I had no power to impose on men who shirked their duties, and, where men atoned for misconduct by marked gallantry, in blandly remitting sentences approved by my chief of division. However, I had done substantial, even though somewhat rude and irregular, justice—and no harm could result, as we were just about to be mustered out.

My chief duties were to see that the camps of the three regiments were thoroughly policed and kept in first-class sanitary condition. This took up some time, of course, and there were other matters in connection with the mustering out which had to be attended to; but I could always get two or three hours a day free from work. Then I would summon a number of the officers, Kane, Greenway, Goodrich, Church, Ferguson, McIlhenny, Frantz, Ballard and others, and we would gallop down to the beach and bathe in the surf, or else go for long rides over the beautiful rolling plains, thickly studded with pools which were white with water-lilies. Sometimes I went off alone with my orderly, young Gordon John-

ston, one of the best men in the regiment; he was a nephew of the
Governor of Alabama, and when at Princeton had played on the
eleven. We had plenty of horses, and these rides were most enjoyable. Galloping over the open, rolling country, through the cool fall
evenings, made us feel as if we were out on the great Western
plains and might at any moment start deer from the brush, or see
antelope stand and gaze, far away, or rouse a band of mighty elk
and hear their horns clatter as they fled.

An old friend, Baron von Sternberg, of the German Embassy,
spent a week in camp with me. He had served, when only seventeen, in the Franco-Prussian War as a hussar, and was a noted
sharp-shooter—being "the little baron" who is the hero of Archibald Forbes's true story of "The Pig-dog." He and I had for years
talked over the possibilities of just such a regiment as the one I was
commanding, and he was greatly interested in it. Indeed I had
vainly sought permission from the German ambassador to take him
with the regiment to Santiago.

One Sunday before the regiment disbanded I supplemented
Chaplain Brown's address to the men by a short sermon of a rather
hortatory character. I told them how proud I was of them, but
warned them not to think that they could now go back and rest on
their laurels, bidding them remember that though for ten days or so
the world would be willing to treat them as heroes, yet after that
time they would find they had to get down to hard work just like
everyone else, unless they were willing to be regarded as worthless
do-nothings. They took the sermon in good part, and I hope that
some of them profited by it. At any rate, they repaid me by a very
much more tangible expression of affection. One afternoon, to
my genuine surprise, I was asked out of my tent by Lieutenant-
Colonel Brodie (the gallant old boy had rejoined us), and found the
whole regiment formed in hollow square, with the officers and
color-sergeant in the middle. When I went in, one of the troopers
came forward and on behalf of the regiment presented me with
Remington's fine bronze, "The Bronco-buster." There could have
been no more appropriate gift from such a regiment, and I was not
only pleased with it, but very deeply touched with the feeling

which made them join in giving it. Afterward they all filed past and I shook the hands of each to say good-by.

Most of them looked upon the bronze with the critical eyes of professionals. I doubt if there was any regiment in the world which contained so large a number of men able to ride the wildest and most dangerous horses. One day while at Montauk Point some of the troopers of the Third Cavalry were getting ready for mounted drill when one of their horses escaped, having thrown his rider. This attracted the attention of some of our men and they strolled around to see the trooper remount. He was instantly thrown again, the horse, a huge, vicious sorrel, being one of the worst buckers I ever saw; and none of his comrades were willing to ride the animal. Our men, of course, jeered and mocked at them, and in response were dared to ride the horse themselves. The challenge was instantly accepted, the only question being as to which of a dozen noted bronco-busters who were in the ranks should undertake the task. They finally settled on a man named Darnell. It was agreed that the experiment should take place next day when the horse would be fresh, and accordingly next day the majority of both regiments turned out on a big open flat in front of my tent—brigade head-quarters. The result was that, after as fine a bit of rough riding as one would care to see, in which one scarcely knew whether most to wonder at the extraordinary viciousness and agile strength of the horse or at the horsemanship and courage of the rider, Darnell came off victorious, his seat never having been shaken. After this almost every day we had exhibitions of bronco-busting, in which all the crack riders of the regiment vied with one another, riding not only all of our own bad horses but any horse which was deemed bad in any of the other regiments.

Darnell, McGinty, Wood, Smoky Moore, and a score of others took part in these exhibitions, which included not merely feats in mastering vicious horses, but also feats of broken horses which the riders had trained to lie down at command, and upon which they could mount while at full speed.

Toward the end of the time we also had mounted drill on two or three occasions; and when the President visited the camp we turned out mounted to receive him as did the rest of the cavalry. The last night before we were mustered out was spent in noisy, but entirely harmless hilarity, which I ignored. Every form of celebration took place in the ranks. A former Populist candidate for Attorney-General in Colorado delivered a fervent oration in favor of free silver; a number of the college boys sang; but most of the men gave vent to their feelings by improvised dances. In these the Indians took the lead, pure bloods and half-breeds alike, the cowboys and miners cheerfully joining in and forming part of the howling, grunting rings, that went bounding around the great fires they had kindled.

Next morning Sergeant Wright took down the colors, and Sergeant Guitilias the standard, for the last time; the horses, the rifles, and the rest of the regimental property had been turned in; officers and men shook hands and said good-by to one another, and then they scattered to their homes in the North and the South, the few going back to the great cities of the East, the many turning again toward the plains, the mountains, and the deserts of the West and the strange Southwest. This was on September 15th, the day which marked the close of the four months' life of a regiment of as gallant fighters as ever wore the United States uniform.

The regiment was a wholly exceptional volunteer organization, and its career cannot be taken as in any way a justification for the belief that the average volunteer regiment approaches the average regular regiment in point of efficiency until it has had many months of active service. In the first place, though the regular regiments may differ markedly among themselves, yet the range of variation among them is nothing like so wide as that among volunteer regiments, where at first there is no common standard at all; the very best being, perhaps, up to the level of the regulars (as has recently been shown at Manila), while the very worst are no better than mobs, and the great bulk come in between.* The average reg-

---

* For sound common-sense about the volunteers see Parker's excellent little book, "The Gatlings at Santiago."

ular regiment is superior to the average volunteer regiment in the physique of the enlisted men, who have been very carefully selected, who have been trained to life in the open, and who know how to cook and take care of themselves generally.

Now, in all these respects, and in others like them, the Rough Riders were the equals of the regulars. They were hardy, self-reliant, accustomed to shift for themselves in the open under very adverse circumstances. The two all-important qualifications for a cavalryman, are riding and shooting—the modern cavalryman being so often used dismounted, as an infantryman. The average recruit requires a couple of years before he becomes proficient in horsemanship and marksmanship; but my men were already good shots and first-class riders when they came into the regiment. The difference as regards officers and non-commissioned officers, between regulars and volunteers, is usually very great; but in my regiment (keeping in view the material we had to handle), it was easy to develop non-commissioned officers out of men who had been round-up foremen, ranch foremen, mining bosses, and the like. These men were intelligent and resolute; they knew they had a great deal to learn, and they set to work to learn it; while they were already accustomed to managing considerable interests, to obeying orders, and to taking care of others as well as themselves.

As for the officers, the great point in our favor was the anxiety they showed to learn from those among their number who, like Capron, had already served in the regular army; and the fact that we had chosen a regular army man as Colonel. If a volunteer organization consists of good material, and is eager to learn, it can readily do so if it has one or two first-class regular officers to teach it. Moreover, most of our captains and lieutenants were men who had seen much of wild life, who were accustomed to handling and commanding other men, and who had usually already been under fire as sheriffs, marshals, and the like. As for the second in command, myself, I had served three years as captain in the National Guard; I had been deputy sheriff in the cow country, where the position was not a sinecure; I was accustomed to big game hunting and to work on a cow ranch, so that I was thoroughly familiar with the use both of horse and rifle, and knew how to handle cowboys, hunters, and miners; finally, I had studied much in the literature of war, and especially the literature of the great modern wars, like our own Civil War, the Franco-German War, the Turco-Russian War; and I was especially familiar with the deeds, the successes and failures alike, of the frontier horse riflemen who had fought at King's Mountain and the Thames, and on the Mexican border. Finally, and most important of all, officers and men alike were eager for fighting, and resolute to do well and behave properly, to encounter hardship and privation, and the irksome monotony of camp routine, without grumbling or complaining; they had counted the cost before they went in, and were delighted to pay the penalties inevitably attendant upon the career of a fighting regiment; and from the moment when the regiment began to gather, the higher officers kept instilling into those under them the spirit of eagerness for action and of stern determination to grasp at death rather than forfeit honor.

The self-reliant spirit of the men was well shown after they left the regiment. Of course, there were a few weaklings among them; and there were others, entirely brave and normally self-sufficient, who, from wounds or fevers, were so reduced that they had to apply for aid—or at least, who deserved aid, even though they often could only be persuaded with the greatest difficulty to accept it. The widows and orphans had to be taken care of. There were a few light-hearted individuals, who were entirely ready to fight in time of war, but in time of peace felt that somebody ought to take care of them; and there were others who, never having seen any aggregation of buildings larger than an ordinary cowtown, fell a victim to the fascinations of New York. But, as a whole, they scattered out to their homes on the disbandment of the regiment; gaunter than when they had enlisted, sometimes weakened by fever or wounds, but just as full as ever of sullen, sturdy capacity for self-help; scorning to ask for aid, save what was entirely legitimate in the way of one comrade giving help to another. A number of the examining surgeons, at the muster-out, spoke to me with admiration of the contrast offered by our regiment to so many others, in the fact that our men always belittled their own bodily injuries and sufferings; so that whereas the surgeons ordinarily had to be on the look-out lest a man who was not really disabled should claim to be so, in our case they had to adopt exactly the opposite attitude and guard the future interests of the men, by insisting upon putting upon their certificates of discharge whatever disease they had contracted or wound they had received in line of duty. Major J. H. Calef, who had more than any other one man to do with seeing to the proper discharge papers of our men, and who took a most generous interest in them, wrote me as follows: "I also wish to bring to your notice the fortitude displayed by the men of your regiment, who have come before me to be mustered out of service, in making their personal declarations as to their physical conditions. Men who bore on their faces and in their forms the traces of long days of illness, indicating wrecked constitutions, declared that nothing was the matter with them, at the same time disclaiming any intention of applying for a pension. It was exceptionally heroic."

When we were mustered out, many of the men had lost their jobs, and were too weak to go to work at once, while there were helpless dependents of the dead to care for. Certain of my friends, August Belmont, Stanley and Richard Mortimer, Major Austin Wadsworth—himself fresh from the Manila campaign—Belmont Tiffany, and others, gave me sums of money to be used for helping these men. In some instances, by the exercise of a good deal of tact and by treating the gift as a memorial of poor young Lieutenant Tiffany, we got the men to accept something; and, of course, there were a number who, quite rightly, made no difficulty about accepting. But most of the men would accept no help whatever. In the first chapter, I spoke of a lady, a teacher in an academy in the Indian Territory, three or four of whose pupils had come into my regiment, and who had sent with them a letter of introduction to me. When the regiment disbanded, I wrote to her to ask if she could not use a little money among the Rough Riders, white, Indian, and half-breed, that she might personally know. I did not hear from her for some time, and then she wrote as follows:

"Muscogee, Ind. Ter.,
"December 19, 1898.

"MY DEAR COLONEL ROOSEVELT:

I did not at once reply to your letter of September 23d, because I waited for a time to see if there should be need among any of our Rough Riders, of the money you so kindly offered. Some of the boys are poor, and in one or two cases they seemed to me really needy, but they all said no. More than once I saw the tears come to their eyes, at thought of your care for them, as I told them of your letter. Did you hear any echoes of our Indian war-whoops over your election? They were pretty loud. I was particularly exultant, because my father was a New Yorker and I was educated in New York, even if I was born here. So far as I can learn, the boys are taking up the dropped threads of their lives, as though they had never been away. Our two Rough Rider students, Meagher and Gilmore, are doing well in their college work.

"I am sorry to tell you of the death of one of your most devoted troopers, Bert Holderman, who was here serving on the Grand Jury. He was stricken with meningitis in the jury-room, and died after three days of delirium. His father, who was twice wounded, four times taken prisoner, and fought in thirty-two battles of the civil war, now old and feeble, survives him, and it was indeed pathetic to see his grief. Bert's mother, who is a Cherokee, was raised in my grandfather's family. The words of commendation which you wrote upon Bert's discharge are the greatest comfort to his friends. They wanted you to know of his death, because he loved you so.

"I am planning to entertain all the Rough Riders in this vicinity some evening during my holiday vacation. I mean to have no other guests, but only give them an opportunity for reminiscences. I regret that Bert's death makes one less. I had hoped to have them sooner, but our struggling young college salaries are necessarily small and duties arduous. I make a home for my widowed mother and an adopted Indian daughter, who is in school; and as I do the cooking for a family of five, I have found it impossible to do many things I would like to.

"Pardon me for burdening you with these details, but I suppose I am like your boys, who say, 'The Colonel was always as ready to listen to a private as to a major-general.'

"Wishing you and yours the very best gifts the season can bring, I am,

"VERY TRULY YOURS,

"ALICE M. ROBERTSON."

—

Is it any wonder that I loved my regiment?

MUSTER – OUT ROLL

[Owing to the circumstances of the regiment's service, the paper-work was very difficult to perform. This muster-out roll is very defective in certain points, notably in the enumeration of the wounded who had been able to return to duty. Some of the dead are also undoubtedly passed over. Thus I have put in Race Smith, Sanders, and Tiffany as dead, correcting the rolls; but there are doubtless a number of similar corrections which should be made but have not been, as the regiment is now scattered far and wide. I have also corrected the record for the wounded men in one or two places where I happen to remember it; but there are a number of the wounded, especially the slightly wounded, who are not down at all.]

FIELD, STAFF, AND BAND

Theodore Roosevelt	Colonel	New York, N. Y.
Alexander O. Brodie	Lieut. Colonel	Prescott, Ariz.
Henry B. Hersey	Major	Santa Fé, N. M.
George M. Dunn	Major	Denver, Col.
Micah J. Jenkins	Major	Youngs Is., S. C.
Henry A. Brown	Chaplain	Prescott, Ariz.
Maxwell Keyes	1st Lt. & Adjt.	San Antonio, Tex.

Sherrard Coleman	1st Lt. & Q. M.	Santa Fé, N. M.
Ernest Secker	Sergt. Major	Los Angeles, Cal.
Matthew Douthett	Q. M. Sergeant	Denver, Col.
Clay Platt	Cf. Trumpeter	San Antonio, Tex.
Joseph F. Kansky	Sad. Sergeant	Tacoma, Wash.
Leonard Wood	Colonel	Cape Cod, Mass.

Promoted, July 9, 1898, to Brig.-Gen. of U. S. Vols.

Thomas W. Hall	1st Lieut. & Adjt.	

Tendered his resignation as 1st Lieut. and Adjt.,
which took effect Aug. 1, 1898, in compliance with S. O. No. 175,
O. G. O., dated July 29, 1898.

Jacob Schwaizer	1st Lt. & Q. M.	El Reno, O. T.

Resigned his commission as 1st Lieut., Aug. 4, 1898.
Resignation took effect Sept. 7, 1898.

Joseph A. Carr	Sergt. Major	Washington, D. C.

Discharged at San Antonio, Texas, by way of favor to enable him to
accept a commission as 1st Lieut. in the Regiment, May 19, 1898.

Christian Madsen	R. Q. M. Sergt.	El Reno, O. T.

Discharged on Surgeon's certificate of disability at
Camp Wikoff, L. I., Aug. 26, 1898.

Alfred E. Lewis	R. Q. M. Sergt.	

Deserted from Camp at San Antonio, Tex., on or about May 5, 1898.

Ernest Haskell	Cadet	West Point

Acted with regiment as second lieutenant.
Dangerously wounded by Mauser bullet, July 1st.

THE HOSPITAL CORPS

Henry La Motte	Major	Williamsburg, Mass.
James A. Massie	1st Lieutenant	Santa Fé, N. M.
*James R. Church	1st Lieutenant	Washington, D. C.
James B. Brady	Steward	Santa Fé, N. M.
Herbert J. Rankin	Steward	Las Vegas, N. M.
Charles A. Wilson	Steward	Colorado Springs, Col.
John R. Rawdin	Private.	

---

* Acted as Regimental Surgeon during most of the campaign.

TROOP A

CAPTAIN FRANK FRANTZ

Frank Frantz	Captain	Prescott, Ariz.
John C. Greenway	1st Lieutenant	Hot Springs, Ark.
Joshua D. Carter	2d Lieutenant	Prescott, Ariz.
William W. Greenwood	1st Sergeant	Prescott, Ariz.

Shot in left foot and leg in battle, July 1, 1898.
Engaged in battles of Las Guasimas, June 24th; San Juan, July 1st.

James T. Greenley	Sergeant	Prescott, Ariz.

Wounded in leg, July 1, 1898. Engaged in battles of Las Guasimas,
June 24th; San Juan, July 1st; and siege of Santiago following.

King C. Henley	Q. M. Sergeant	Winslow, Ariz.
Henry W. Nash	Sergeant	Young, Ariz.
Samuel H. Rhodes	Sergeant	Tonto Basin, Ariz.
Robert Brown	Sergeant	Prescott, Ariz.
Charles E. McGarr	Sergeant	Prescott, Ariz.
Carl Holtzschue	Sergeant	Prescott, Ariz.
George L. Bugbee	Corporal	Lordsburg, N. M.
Harry G. White	Corporal	Richenbar, Ariz.

Absent from July 2, 1898, in Governor's Island, N. Y., Hospital,
on account of wound in leg, received on July 2, 1898. Engaged in
battles of Las Guasimas, June 24, 1898; San Juan, July 1, 1898.

Cade C. Jackson	Corporal	Flagstaff, Ariz.
Harry B. Fox	Corporal	Jerome, Ariz.
William Cranfurd	Corporal	San Antonio, Tex.
George A. McCarter	Corporal	Safford, Ariz.
Rufus H. Marine	Corporal	Flagstaff, Ariz.
John D. Honeyman	Corporal	San Antonio, Tex.
Emilio Cassi	Trumpeter	Jerome, Ariz.

Wounded in hand on July 2, 1898.

Frank Harner	Trumpeter	Preston, Ariz.
Thomas Hamilton	Blacksmith	Jerome, Ariz.
Wallace B. Willard	Farrier	Cottonwood, Ariz.
Forest Whitney	Saddler	Richenbar, Ariz.
John H. Waller	Wagoner	Prescott, Ariz.

Wounded in left arm in battle of July 1, 1898.
Engaged in Las Guasimas, June 24, 1898; San Juan, July 1, 1898;
and siege of Santiago following.

TROOPERS

Adams, Ralph R., Yonkers, N. Y.
Allen, George L., Prescott, Ariz.
Azbill, John, St. John's, Ariz.
Azbill, William, St. John's, Ariz.
Arnold, Henry N., New York City
Barnard, John C., New York City
Bartoo, Nelson E., Winslow, Ariz.
Belknap, Prescott H. Boston,
Brookline, Mass.
Brauer, Lee W., Richmond, Va.
Bugbee, Fred. W., Lordsburg,
N. M.
Wounded in head in battle of
San Juan, July 1, 1898. Slight.
Mauser rifle.
Bull, Charles C., San Francisco,
Cal.
Bulzing, William, Santa Fé, N. M.
Burke, Edward F., Orange, N. J.
Bardshar, Henry P., Prescott, Ariz.
Church, Leroy B., Ithaca, Mich.
Curtis, Harry A., Boston, Mass.
Freeman, Thomas L., Thurber,
Tex.
Griffen, Walter W., Globe, Ariz.
Glover, William H., Liberty, Tex.
Hawes, George P., Jr., Richmond,
Va.
Haymon, Edward G. B., Chicago,
Ill.
Huffman, Lawrence E., Las
Cruces, Mex.
Hoffman, Fred., Pueblo, Col.
Hodgdon, Charles E., Prescott,
Ariz.
Hogan, Daniel L., Flagstaff, Ariz.
Howard, John L., St. Louis, Mo.

Hubbell, John D., Boston, Mass.
Jackson, Charles B., Prescott, Ariz.
Wounded in neck at battle of
San Juan, July 1, 1898. Nature
of injury slight. Mauser rifle.
Johnson, John W., Kingman, Ariz.
Lefors, Jefferson D., Prescott, Ariz.
Lewis, William F., Congress, Ariz.
Larned, William A., Summit, N. J.
Le Roy, Arthur M., Prescott,
Ariz.
May, James A., Safford, Ariz.
McCarty, Frank, Flagstaff, Ariz.
Mills, Charles E., Cedar Rapids, Ia.
Murchie, Guy, Calais, Me.
Osborne, George, Bungendera,
N. S. W., Australia
O'Brien, Edward, Jerome, Ariz.
Wounded in head, by shrapnel,
morning of July 2, 1898.
Page, William, Richenbar, Ariz.
Perry, Charles B., Perry's Landing,
Tex.
Shot in head, July 2, 1898.
Severe.
Paxton, Frank, Safford, Ariz.
Pearsall, Paul S., New York, N. Y.
Pettit, Louis P., Flagstaff, Ariz.
Philip, Hoffman, Washington,
D. C.
Pierce, Harry B., Central City,
N. M.
Raudebaugh, James D., Flagstaff,
Ariz.
Rapp, Adolph, San Antonio, Tex.
Sells, Henry, Flagstaff, Ariz.
Sellers, Henry J., Williams, Ariz.

Sewall, Henry F., New York, N. Y.
Shaw, James A., Prescott, Ariz.
Shanks, Lee P., Paducah, Ky.
Stark, Wallace J., Safford, Ariz.
Sullivan, Patrick J., Prescott, Ariz.
Thomas, Rufus K., Boston, Mass.
Thomson, Joseph F., Jr.,
   Washington, D. C.
Tuttle, Arthur L., Safford, Ariz.
Van Siclen, Frank, Safford, Ariz.
Wager, Oscar G., Jerome, Ariz.

Wallace, Walter D., Flagstaff, Ariz.
Wallace, William F., Flagstaff, Ariz.
   Wounded in neck in battle of
   San Juan, July 1, 1898.
Wayland, Thomas J., Williams,
   Ariz.
Webb, Adelbert B., Safford, Ariz.
Weil, Henry J., Kingman, Ariz.
Wilson, Jerome, Chloride, Ariz.
Wrenn, Robert D., Chicago, Ill.

DISCHARGED

Garret, Samuel H. Prescott, Ariz.
   Honorably discharged the service by order of A. G. O.
   Special Order No. 14, Aug. 24, 1898.
Greenwald, Sam Prescott, Ariz.
   Discharged by authority of Secretary of War, at Camp Wikoff,
   Aug. 31, 1898.
McCormick, Willis Salt Lake City, Utah.
   Honorably discharged the service, Aug. 23, 1898.
   By order Secretary of War.

KILLED IN ACTION

O'Neill, William O. Captain Prescott, Ariz.
   Engaged and killed in battle of San Juan, July 1, 1898,
   by gunshot wound in the head.
Doherty, George H. Corporal Jerome, Ariz.
   Engaged and killed in battle of Las Guasimas, June 24, 1898,
   by bullet wound in the head.
Boyle, James Private Prescott, Ariz.
   Engaged in and mortally wounded at battle of San Juan, July 1, 1898;
   shot through neck and body; died July 2, 1898.
Champlin, Fred E. Private Flagstaff, Ariz.
   Engaged in battle of Las Guasimas, June 24, 1898, and battle of
   San Juan, July 1, 1898, where he was mortally wounded.
   Died, July 2, 1898; shot in leg and foot by shrapnel and arm
   torn off by shell. Left thigh and hand.

Liggett, Edward   Private   Jerome, Ariz.
Engaged and killed in battle of Las Guasimas, June 24, 1898;
shot through the body.
Reynolds, Lewis   Private   Kingman, Ariz.
Engaged in battle of Las Guasimas, June 24, 1898, and San Juan,
July 1, 1898. Killed on July 1, 1898; shot through the stomach.

DIED OF DISEASE

Hollister, Stanley   Private   Santa Barbara, Cal.
Wounded in left thigh in battle, July 2, 1898; severe.
Died of typhoid fever in general U. S. Hospital, Fortress Monroe, Va.,
Aug. 17, 1898.
Wallace, Alexander H.   Private   Pasadena, Cal.
Died of typhoid fever at St. Peter's Hospital, Brooklyn, Aug. 31, 1898.
Walsh, George   Private   San Francisco, Cal.
Died at sea, aboard S. S. Miami, Aug. 11, 1898, of chronic dysentery;
buried at sea, Aug. 12, 1898.

SUICIDE

De Vol, Harry P.   San Antonio, Tex.
While in Guard-House, Camp Wikoff, died of self-inflicted wound
in the head.

DESERTER

Jackson, John W.   Private   Jerome, Ariz.
Deserted the service at Tampa, Fla., July 7, 1898.

TROOP B

CAPTAIN JAMES H. MCCLINTOCK

James H. McClintock   Captain   Phœnix, Ariz.
Wounded at battle of Las Guasimas, June 24, 1898.
Wounded in left ankle.
George B. Wilcox   1st Lieutenant   Prescott, Ariz.
Thomas H. Rymning   2d Lieutenant   Tucson, Ariz.
William A. Davidson   1st Sergeant   Phœnix, Ariz.
Stephen A. Pate   Q. M. Sergeant   Tucson, Ariz.
Wounded in right lung before Santiago de Cuba, July 1, 1898.
Elmer Hawley   Sergeant   Phœnix, Ariz.

John E. Campbell	Sergeant	Phœnix, Ariz.
Charles H. Utling	Sergeant	Phœnix, Ariz.
Edward G. Norton	Sergeant	Phœnix, Ariz.
David L. Hughes	Sergeant	Tucson, Ariz.

Wounded in head, July 1, 1898, at battle before Santiago de Cuba.

Jerry F. Lee	Sergeant	Globe, Ariz.

Shot in head before Santiago de Cuba, July 1, 1898.

Eugene W. Waterbury	Corporal	Tucson, Ariz.
Walter T. Gregory	Corporal	Phœnix, Ariz.
Thomas W. Pemberton, Jr.	Corporal	Phœnix, Ariz.
George J. McCabe	Corporal	Bisbee, Ariz.
Calvin McCarthy	Corporal	Phœnix, Ariz.
Charles E. Heitman	Corporal	Phœnix, Ariz.
Frank Ward	Corporal	Globe, Ariz.
Dudly S. Dean	Corporal	Boston, Mass.
John Foster	Bugler	Bisbee, Ariz.
Jesse Walters	Bugler	Phœnix, Ariz.
Frank W. Harmson	Farrier	Tucson, Ariz.
Fred A. Pomeroy	Blacksmith	Kingman, Ariz.
Joseph E. McGinty	Wagoner	Tucson, Ariz.
Richard E. Goodwin	Saddler	Phœnix, Ariz.

TROOPERS

Boggs, Looney L., Phœnix, Ariz.
Buckholdt, Chas., Kickapoo Springs, Tex.
Beebe, Walter S., Prescott, Ariz.
Brady, Fred L., New York, N. Y.
Butler, James A., Albuquerque, N.M.
Barrowe, Beekman K., Tampa, Fla.
Colwell, Grant, Phœnix, Ariz.
Collier, Edward G., Globe, Ariz.
Chester, Will M., Oakwell, Tex.
Christian, Benjamin, Norfolk, Va.
Chamberlin, Lowell A., Washington, D. C.
Day, Robert, Santa Fé, N. M.
Drachman, Sol. B., Tucson, Ariz.

Draper, Durward D., Phœnix, Ariz.
Eakin, Alva L., Globe, Ariz.
Eads, Wade Q., San Antonio, Tex.
Fitzgerald, Frank T., Tucson, Ariz.
Goss, Conrad F., Tampa, Fla.
Gurney, Frank W., Tampa, Fla.
Hall, John M., Phœnix, Ariz.
Wounded in shoulder by shrapnel, July 1, 1898, before Santiago de Cuba. Piece of shell not removed.
Hammer, John S., San Antonio, Tex.
Slightly wounded by shell, July 1, 1898, before Santiago de Cuba. Wounded in leg.

Hildreth, Fenn S., Tucson, Ariz.
Hartzell, Ira C., Phœnix, Ariz.
Haydon, Roy F., Prescott, Ariz.
Henderson, Sibird, Globe, Ariz.
Hildebrand, Louis T., Prescott,
Ariz.
Heywood, John P., Tampa, Fla.
James, William T., Jerome, Ariz.
Johnson, Anton E., Prescott, Ariz.
King, Geo. C., Prescott, Ariz.
Keir, Alex. S., Bisbee, Ariz.
Laird, Thomas J., Prescott, Ariz.
Merritt, Fred M., Tucson, Ariz.
Merritt, William W., Red Oak, Ia.
McCann, Walter J., Phœnix, Ariz.
Iron stanchion fell upon right
side of head, right arm and
shoulder, while asleep in quar-
ters on transport Yucatan, en
route for Cuba, June 21, 1898.
Middleton, Clifton C., Globe,
Ariz.
Misner, Jackson H., Bisbee, Ariz.
McMillen, Albert C., New York,
N. Y.
Norton, Gould G., Tampa, Fla.
Orme, Norman L., Phœnix, Ariz.
Shot in left arm and side,
June 24, 1898, at Las Guasimas.
G. S. left shoulder.
Owens, William A., Jerome, Ariz.
Proffitt, William B., Prescott, Ariz.
Peck, John C., Santa Fé, N. M.
Pollock, Horatio C., Phœnix, Ariz.
Patterson, Hal. A., Selma, Ala.
Roberts, Frank S., San Antonio, Tex.

Rinehart, Robert, Phœnix, Ariz.
Stanton, Richard H., Phœnix, Ariz.
Saunders, Wellman H., Salem,
Mass.
Snodderly, William L., Bisbee,
Ariz.
Smith, Race H., San Antonio, Tex.
Shot in stomach, breast, and
arms by shrapnel, July 2, 1898,
before Santiago.
Schenck, Frank W., Phœnix, Ariz.
Stewart, W. Walton, Selma, Ala.
Toland, Jesse T., Bisbee, Ariz.
Truman, George E., San Antonio,
Tex.
Townsend, Albert B., Prescott,
Ariz.
Tilkie, Charles M., Chicago, Ill.
Van Treese, Louis H., Tucson,
Ariz.
Warford, David E., Globe, Ariz.
Shot in both thighs, July 1,
1898, before Santiago de Cuba.
Webb, William W., Prescott, Ariz.
Wiggins, Thomas W., Bisbee, Ariz.
Shot in right hip at Las Guasi-
mas, June 24, 1898. G. S. left
hip.
Whittaker, George C., Silver City,
N. M.
Wilkerson, Wallace W., Santa Fé,
N. M.
Woodward, Sidney H., Kingman,
Ariz.
Young, Thomas H., Phœnix,
Ariz.

DISCHARGED

Bird, Marshall M. California.
Discharged on Surgeon's certificate of disability. Fracture of skull
and concussion of brain incurred in line of duty, Aug. 8, 1898.
Cronin, Cornelius P. Yuma, Ariz.
Discharged, June 13, 1898, on Surgeon's certificate.
Crimmins, Martin L. New York, N. Y.
Mustered out to accept commission, July 29, 1898.
Goodrich, David M. Akron, O.
Discharged, May 19, 1898, to accept commission.
Murphy, James E. Delrio, Ariz.
Discharged, Sept. 10th, by order of Secretary of War.
Shot in head, July 1, 1898, before Santiago de Cuba.

DIED

Hall, Joel R.   Corporal   Seattle, Wash.
Killed, July 1, 1898, before Santiago de Cuba;
buried on field of battle.
Logue, David Globe, Ariz.
Killed, July 1, 1898, before Santiago de Cuba;
buried on field of battle.
Norton, Oliver B.
Killed, July 1, 1898, before Santiago de Cuba;
buried on field of battle.
Saunders, W. H. Salem, Mass.
Died of fever at Santiago.
Smith, Race W. San Antonio, Tex.
Died of wounds received July 2, 1898.
Swetman, John W. Globe, Ariz.
Killed, July 1, 1898, before Santiago de Cuba;
buried on field of battle.
Tomlinson, Leroy E.
Sent to hospital boat, June 19, 1898, en route to Cuba; fever.
Certificate of death dated June 23, 1898. Body and effects sent
ashore, care Capt. Stephens, Signal Corps, U. S. A.
Typhoid fever contracted in line of duty.

TROOP C

CAPTAIN JOSEPH L. B. ALEXANDER

Joseph L. B. Alexander	Captain	Phœnix, Ariz.
Robert S. Patterson	1st Lieutenant	Safford, Ariz.
Hal Sayre, Jr.	2d Lieutenant	Denver, Col.
Willis O. Huson	1st Sergeant	Yuma, Ariz.
James H. Maxey	Q. M. Sergeant	Yuma, Ariz.
Sam W. Noyes	Sergeant	Tucson, Ariz.
Adam H. Klingham	Sergeant	Flagstaff, Ariz.
Sumner H. Gerard	Sergeant	New York, N. Y.
John McAndrew	Sergeant	Congress Junction, Ariz.
Eldridge E. Jordan	Sergeant	Phœnix, Ariz.
Wilbur D. French	Corporal	Safford, Ariz.
Hedrick M. Warren	Corporal	Phœnix, Ariz.
Bruce C. Weathers	Corporal	Safford, Ariz.
Frank A. Woodin	Corporal	Phœnix, Ariz.
Charles A. Armstrong	Corporal	San José, Cal.
Elisha E. Garrison	Corporal	New York, N. Y.
William T. Atkins	Corporal	Selma, Ala.
Oscar J. Mullen	Corporal	Tempe, Ariz.
Frank Marti	Trumpeter	Jerome, Ariz.
John A. W. Stelzriede	Trumpeter	Tempe, Ariz.
James G. Yost	Blacksmith	Prescott, Ariz.
Frank Vans Agnew	Farrier	Kissimee, Fla.
Francis L. Morgan	Saddler	White Hills, Ariz.
Jerome W. Lankford	Wagoner	White Hills, Ariz.

TROOPERS

Asay, William, Safford, Ariz.
Anderson, Thomas A., San Antonio, Tex.
Barthell, Peter K., Kingman, Ariz.
Bradley, Peter, Jerome, Ariz.
Burks, Robert E., Prescott, Ariz.
Byrns, Orlando C., Prescott, Ariz.
Bowler, George P., New York, N. Y.

Carleton, William C., Tempe, Ariz.
Carlson, Carl, Tempe, Ariz.
Cartledge, Crantz, Tempe, Ariz.
Coleman, Lockhart G., St. Louis, Mo.
Danforth, Clyde L., Flagstaff, Ariz.
Danforth, Wm. H., Flagstaff, Ariz.
Dewees, John L., San Antonio, Tex.

Duncan, Arthur G., New York.
Engel, Edwin P., Phœnix, Ariz.
Force, Peter, Selma, Ala.
Gaughan, James, Phœnix, Ariz.
Gibbins, Floyd J., Prescott, Ariz.
Goodwin, James C., Tempe, Ariz.
Gardiner, John P., Boston, Mass.
Gavin, Anthony, Buffalo, N. Y.
Hanson, Ivan M., Phœnix, Ariz.
Hanson, William, Prescott, Ariz.
Herold, Philip M., Phœnix, Ariz.
Howland, Harry, Flagstaff, Ariz.
Hubbell, William C., Nogales, Ariz.
Hall, Edward C., New Haven, Conn.
Kastens, Harry E., Winslow, Ariz.
Marvin, William E., Yuma, Ariz.
Mason, David P., Brownsville, Tex.
Moffett, Edward B., Yuma, Ariz.
Neville, George A., Yuma, Ariz.
Norton, John W., Lockport, Ill.
O'Leary, Daniel, Tempe, Ariz.
Parker, John W., Safford, Ariz.

Payne, Forest B., Phœnix, Ariz.
Pond, Ashley, Detroit, Mich.
Perry, Arthur R., Phœnix, Ariz.
Ricketts, William L., Phœnix, Ariz.
Roederer, John, Prescott, Ariz.
Rupert, Charles W., Prescott, Ariz.
Reed, George W., Tucson, Ariz.
Sayers, Samuel E., Yuma, Ariz.
Scharf, Charles A., Flagstaff, Ariz.
Sexsmith, William, Yuma, Ariz.
Shackelford, Marcus L., Jerome, Ariz.
Shoemaker, John, Phœnix, Ariz.
Skogsburg, Charles G., Safford, Ariz.
Scull, Guy H., Boston, Mass.
Sloan, Thomas H., Phœnix, Ariz.
Somers, Fred B., Flagstaff, Ariz.
Trowbridge, Lafayette, Prescott, Ariz.
Vines, Jesse G., Phœnix, Ariz.
Vance, William E., Austin, Tex.
Wormell, John A., Phœnix, Ariz.
Younger, Charles, Winslow, Ariz.

Wright, Albert P.   Color Sergeant*   Yuma, Ariz.

DISCHARGED   DISABILITY

Alamia, John B.   Private   Port Isabel, Tex.
Discharged, account epileptic fits, per order O. A. G. O.
Pearson, Rufus W.   Sergeant   Phœnix, Ariz.
Discharged, Aug. 26, 1898, on certificate of discharge signed by
Secretary of War General Alger.

DISCHARGED BY ORDER

Grindell, Thomas F.   Sergeant   Tempe, Ariz.
Discharged by telegraph order A. G. O., Sept. 8, 1898.

* Color Sergeant of Regiment.

Hill, Wesley   Private   Tempe, Ariz.
   Discharged by telegraph order A. G. O., Sept. 8, 1898.
Scudder, William M.   Private   Chicago, Ill.
   Discharged per special order 204, par. 52,
   War Department, A. G. O., Washington, D. C., Aug. 30, 1898.
Wallack, Robt. R.   Private   Washington
   Discharged, July 19, 1898, per par. 27, S. O. 203.
   War Department, A. G. O., Washington, D. C., Aug. 29, 1898,
   being appointed 2d Lieutenant for Regular Army.

TRANSFERRED

Rowdin, John E.   Private   Phœnix, Ariz.
   Transferred, June 8, 1898, per R. O. No. 6, dated Tampa, Fla.,
   June 8, 1898.

DIED

Adsit, Nathaniel B.   Private   Buffalo, N. Y.
   Died, Aug. 1st, at Buffalo, of typhoid fever.
Clearwater, Frank H.   Private   Brownsville, Tex.
   Died at Corpus Christi, Sept. 2, 1898, of typhoid malaria.
Newnhone, Thomas M.   Private   Phœnix, Ariz.
   Died at hospital Fort McPherson, of typhoid fever, Aug. 4, 1898.

TROOP D

CAPTAIN R. B. HUSTON

Robert B. Huston	Captain	Guthrie, O. T.
David M. Goodrich	1st Lieutenant	Akron, Ohio.
Robert H. M. Ferguson	2d Lieutenant	New York City.
Orlando G. Palmer	1st Sergeant	Ponco City, O. T.
Gerald A. Webb	Sergeant	Guthrie, O. T.
Joseph A. Randolph	Sergeant	Waukomis, O. T.
Ira A. Hill	Sergeant	Newkirk, O. T.
Charles E. Hunter	Sergeant	Enid, O. T.
Scott Reay	Sergeant	Blackwell, O. T.
Paul W. Hunter	Sergeant	Chandler, O. T.
Thomas Moran	Sergeant	Fort Sill, O. T.
Calvin Hill	Corporal	Pawnee, O. T.

George Norris   Corporal   Kingfisher, O. T.
John D. Roades   Corporal   Hennessey, O. T.
Wounded in battle of Las Guasimas, June 24, 1898. G. S. leg.
Lyman F. Beard   Corporal   Shawnee, O. T.
Henry Meagher   Corporal   El Reno, O. T.
Wounded in the battle before Santiago, July 1, 1898. Both shoulders.
Alexander H. Denham   Corporal   Oklahoma City, O. T.
Wounded in battle of Las Guasimas, June 24, 1898. G. S. left thigh.
Henry K. Love   Corporal   Tecumseh, O. T.
Harrison J. Holt   Corporal   Denver, Col.
William D. Amrine   Saddler   Newkirk, O. T.
Starr W. Wetmore   Trumpeter   Newkirk, O. T.
Wounded in battle before Santiago, July 1, 1898. Right thigh, severe.
Missile or weapon, Mauser rifle.
James T. Brown   Trumpeter   Newkirk, O. T.
Lorrin D. Muxlow   Wagoner   Guthrie, O. T.

TROOPERS

Baily, William, Norman, O. T.
Wounded in battle before
Santiago, July 2, 1898. Right
foot. Missile or weapon,
Mauser rifle.
Beal, Fred N., Kingfisher, O. T.
Wounded in battle of Las
Guasimas, June 24, 1898.
G. S. leg.
Burgess, George, Shawnee, O. T.
Brandon, Perry H., Lancaster, O. T.
Byrne, Peter F., Guthrie, O. T.
Cease, Forrest L., Guthrie, O. T.
Chase, Leslie C., Kingfisher, O. T.
Cook, Walter M., Enid, O. T.
Crawford, William S., Enid, O. T.
Cross, William E., El Reno, O. T.
Crockett, Warren E., Marietta, Ga.
Wounded in battle before
Santiago, July 2, 1898. Leg.
Missile or weapon, Mauser rifle.

Cunningham, Solomon M., San
Antonio, Tex.
Carlow, Gerald, Boerne, Tex.
David, Icem J., Enid, O. T.
Emery, Elzie E., Shawnee, O. T.
Faulk, William A., Guthrie, O. T.
Hill, Edwin M., Tecumseh, O. T.
Honeycutt, James V., Shawnee,
O. T.
Eppley, Kurtz, Orange, N. J.
Green, Charles H., Albuquerque,
N. M.
Hatch, Charles P., Newport, R. I.
Holmes, Thomas M., Newkirk,
O. T.
Wounded in battle before
Santiago, July 1, 1898. Left leg,
severe. Missile or weapon,
Mauser rifle.
Haynes, Jacob M., Newkirk, O. T.
Howard, John S., Boerne, Tex.

Ishler, Shelby F., Enid, O. T.
Wounded in battle of Las
Guasimas, June 24, 1898.
G. S. right forearm.
Ivy, Charles B., Waco, Tex.
Johnston, Edward W., Cushing,
O. T.
Wounded in battle before
Santiago, July 1, 1898.
Right thigh.
Joyce, Walter, Guthrie, O. T.
Knox, William F.
Laird, Emmett, Albuquerque, N. M.
Loughmiller, Edgar F., Oklahoma
City, O. T.
Lovelace, Carl, Waco, Tex.
Lush, Henry, El Reno, O. T.
McMillan, Robert L., Shawnee,
O. T.
Wounded in battle before San-
tiago, July 1, 1898. Left shoul-
der and arm.
McClure, David V., Oklahoma
City, O. T.
McMurtry, George G., Pittsburg,
Pa.
Miller, Roscoe B., Guthrie, O. T.
Miller, Volney D., Guthrie, O. T.
Munn, Edward, Elizabeth, N. J.

Newcomb, Marcellus L.,
Kingfisher, O. T.
Wounded in battle of Las
Guasimas, June 24, 1898.
G. S. right knee.
Norris, Warren, Kingfisher, O. T.
Palmer, William F., Shawnee, O. T.
Proctor, Joseph H., Pawnee, O. T.
Pollock, William, Pawnee, O. T.
Russell, Albert P., El Reno, O. T.
Sands, George H., Guthrie, O. T.
Schmutz, John C., Germantown,
Ohio.
Scott, Cliff D., Clifton, O. T.
Schupp, Eugene, Santa Fé, N. M.
Shanafelt, Dick, Perry, O. T.
Shipp, Edward M., Kingfisher, O. T.
Stewart, Clare H., Pawnee, O. T.
Stewart, Clyde H., Pawnee, O. T.
Tauer, William L., Ponca City,
O. T.
Thomas, Albert M., Guthrie, O. T.
Vanderslice, James E., Enid, O. T.
Van Valen, Alexander L.,
Poughkeepsie, N. Y.
Wolff, Frederick W., San Antonio,
Tex.
Wright, William O., Pawnee, O. T.
Wright, Edward L., Guthrie, O. T.

DISCHARGED

Shockey, James M.   Corporal   Perry, O. T.
Discharged, July 1, 1898, by order of Asst. Adjt. Gen'l.
Luther, Arthur A.   Farrier   Pawnee, O. T.
Discharged, July 1, 1898, by order of Asst. Adjt. Gen'l.
Page, John F.   Private   Alva, O. T.
Discharged by verbal order of Gen'l Wood, Aug. 6, 1898.
Wells, Joseph O.   Private   St. Joseph, Mich.
Discharged by order of Asst. Adjt. Gen'l., Aug. 27, 1898.

Simpson, William S.   Corporal   Dallas, Tex.
Discharged by reason of promotion into regular army,
as 2d Lieut., Sept. 3, 1898.

Schuyler, A. McGinnis   1st Lieutenant   Newkirk, O. T.
Promoted to Captain and transferred to Troop I 1st U. S. V. C., May
19, 1898.
Schweizer, Jacob   2d Lieutenant   El Reno, O. T.
Promoted to 1st Lieut. and assigned to duty as Q. M. 1st U. S. V. C.,
May 19, 1898.
Carr, Joseph A.   1st Lieutenant   Washington, D. C.
Transferred to Troop K 1st U. S. V. C., Sept. 5, 1898.
Wounded in battle before Santiago, July 2, 1898. Left testicle.
Missile or weapon, Mauser rifle.

Douthett, Matthew, Guthrie, O. T.
Appointed Q. M. Sergeant 1st
U. S. V. C., and assigned to duty,
Aug. 31, 1898.
Freeman, Elisha L., Ponca City,
O. T.
Transferred to Troop K 1st
U. S. V. C., May 11, 1898.
Folk, Theodore, Oklahoma City,
N. M.
Transferred to Troop K 1st
U. S. V. C., May 11, 1898.
Hulme, Robert A., El Reno, O. T.
Transferred to Troop K 1st
U. S. V. C., May 11, 1898.
Jordan, Andrew M., El Reno, O. T.
Transferred to Troop K 1st
U. S. V. C., May 11, 1898.
McGinty, William, Stillwater, O. T.
Transferred to Troop K 1st
U. S. V. C., May 11, 1898.

Mitchell, William H., Guthrie, O. T.
Transferred to Troop K 1st
U. S. V. C., May 11, 1898.
Staley, Francis M., Waukomis, O. T.
Transferred to Troop K 1st
U. S. V. C., May 11, 1898.
Smith, Fred, Guthrie, O. T.
Transferred to Troop K 1st
U. S. V. C., May 11, 1898.
Weitzel, John F., Newkirk, O. T.
Transferred to Troop K 1st
U. S. V. C., May 11, 1898.
Woodward, John A., El Reno, O. T.
Transferred to Troop K 1st
U. S. V. C., May 11, 1898.
Wilson, Frank M., Guthrie, O. T.
Transferred to Troop K 1st
U. S. V. C., May 11, 1898.
Burke, Edward F., Orange, N. J.
Transferred to Troop A 1st
U. S. V. C., July 13, 1898.

DIED

Cashion, Roy V.   Private   Hennessey, O. T.
Killed in battle before Santiago, July 1, 1898. Head.
Miller, Theodore W.   Private   Akron, Ohio.
Wounded in battle before Santiago, July 1, 1898.
Died from effects of wound, July 8, 1898. Penetrating neck; severe—
totally paralyzed from head down.

DESERTED

Crosley, Henry S.   Private   Guthrie, O. T.
Dropped from the rolls as deserted, July 8, 1898.

TROOP E

CAPTAIN FREDERICK MULLER

Frederick Muller   Captain   Santa Fé, N. M.
William E. Griffin   1st Lieutenant   Santa Fé, N. M.
John A. McIlhenny   2d Lieutenant   New Orleans, La.
John S. Langston   1st Sergeant   Cerrillos, N. M.
Royal A. Prentice   Q. M. Sergeant   Las Vegas, N. M.
Hugh B. Wright   Sergeant   Las Vegas, N. M.
Albert M. Jones   Sergeant   Santa Fé, N. M.
Timothy Breen   Sergeant   Santa Fé, N. M.
Wounded and sent to hospital, July 1, 1898. Arm.
Berry F. Taylor   Sergeant   Las Vegas, N. M.
Thomas P. Ledgwidge   Sergeant   Santa Fé, N. M.
John Mullen   Sergeant   Chicago, Ill.
Wounded and sent to hospital, July 1, 1898. Side and head; severe.
Harman H. Wynkoop   Corporal   Santa Fé, N. M.
Wounded in line of duty and sent to hospital, July 2, 1898.
Returned to duty, Sept. 4, 1898.
James M. Dean   Corporal   Santa Fé, N. M.
Wounded in line of duty and sent to hospital, June 24, 1898.
Returned to duty, Aug. 31, 1898. G. S left thigh.
Edward C. Waller   Corporal   Chicago, Ill.
Wounded in line of duty, July 2, 1898. Scalp, slight.
G. Roland Fortescue   Corporal   New York, N. Y.
Slight bullet wound in foot, July 1, 1898.

Edward Bennett	Corporal	Cripple Creek, Col.
Charles E. Knoblauch	Corporal	New York, N. Y.
Richard C. Conner	Corporal	Santa Fé, N. M.
Ralph E. McFie	Corporal	Las Cruces, N. M.
Arthur J. Griffin	Trumpeter	Santa Fé, N. M.
Edward S. Lewis	Trumpeter	Las Vegas, N. M.
Robert J. Parrish	Blacksmith	Clayton, N. M.
Grant Hill	Farrier	Santa Fé, N. M.
Joe T. Sandoval	Saddler	Santa Fé, N. M.
Guilford B. Chapin	Wagoner	Santa Fé, N. M.

TROOPERS

Ausburn, Charles G., New Orleans, La.

Almack, Roll, Santa Fé, N. M.

Brennan, John M., Santa Fé, N. M.

Baca, Jose M., Las Vegas, N. M.

Beard, William M., San Antonio, Tex.

Cooper, George B., Tampa, Fla.

Conway, James, San Antonio, Tex.

Dettamore, George W., Clayton, N. M. Wounded in line of duty and sent to hospital, July 1, 1898.

Davis, Harry A., Boston, Mass.

Dodge, George H., Denver, Col.

Debli, Joseph, Tampa, Fla.

Donavan, Freeman M., Santa Fé, N. M.

Douglas, James B., New York, N. Y.

Easley, William T., Clayton, N. M.

Edwards, Lawrence W.

Fries, Frank D., Santa Fé, N. M.

Francis, Mack, Maynesville, N. C.

Fettes, George, Antonito, Col.

Gisler, Joseph, Santa Fé, N. M.

Gibbs, James P., Santa Fé, N. M.

Gibbie, William R., Las Vegas, N. M.

Grigsby, Braxton, New York, N. Y.

Grigg, John G., San Antonio, Tex.

Gammel, Roy U., Jersey Co., Ill.

Harding, John D., Socoro, N. M.

Hood, John B., New York, N. Y.

Harkness, Daniel D., Las Vegas, N. M.

Hutchison, William M., Santa Fé, N. M.

Hall, John P., Williamson Co., Tex. Wounded in line of duty and sent to hospital, July 1, 1898. Returned to duty, Aug. 31, 1898.

Hogle, William H., Santa Fé, N. M.

Hudson, Arthur J., Santa Fé, N. M.

Hulskotter, John, Santa Fé, N. M.

Hutchason, Joseph M., Jimtown, Tenn.

Howell, William S. E., Cerrillos, N. M.

Hadden, David A., San Antonio, Tex.

Hixon, Thomas L., Las Vegas, N. M.

Heard, Judson, Pecos City, Tex.

Hamlin, Warden W., Chicago, Ill.
Jones, Thomas B., Santa Fé, N. M.
Johnston, Charles E., San Antonio,
Tex.
Jacobus, Charles W., Santa Fé,
N. M.
Knapp, Edgar A., Elizabeth, N. J.
Kingsley, Charles E., Las Vegas,
N. M.
Kissam, William A., New York,
N. Y.
Lowe, Frank, Santa Fé, N. M.
Ludy, Dan, Las Vegas, N. M.
Livingston, Thomas C., Hamilton
Co., Tex.
Lowitzki, Hyman S., Santa Fé,
N. M.
Lewis, James.
Merchant, James E., Cerrillos,
N. M.
Moran, William J., Cerrillos,
N. M.
McKinnon, Samuel, Madrid,
N. M.
McKinely, Charles E., Cerrillos,
N. M.
Wounded in line of duty, July
1, 1898. Head.
McKay, Charles F., Santa Fé, N. M.
McCabe, Frederick H., Santa Fé,
N. M.

McDowell, John C., Santa Fé, N. M.
Morrison, Amaziah B., Las Vegas,
N. M.
Mahan, Lloyd L., Cerrillos, N. M.
Martin, Henry D., Cerrillos, N. M.
Menger, Otto F., Clayton, N. M.
Wounded in line of duty, July
1, 1898. Sent to hospital. Left
side.
Mungor, William C., Santa Fé,
N. M.
Nettleblade, Adolph F., Cerrillos,
N. M.
Roberts, Thomas, Golden, N. M.
Ryan, John E., Santa Fé, N. M.
Wounded, July 1, 1898, in line
of duty.
Ramsey, Homer M., Pearsall, Tex.
Seaders, Ben. F., Las Vegas, N. M.
Skinner, Arthur V., Santa Fé, N. M.
Schnepple, William C., Santa Fé,
N. M.
Scanlon, Edward, Cerrillos, N. M.
Slevin, Edward, Tampa, Fla.
Taylor, William R., New York, N. Y.
Wagner, William W., Bland, N. M.
Wright, George, Madrid, N. M.
Wynkoop, Charles W., Santa Fé,
N. M.
Warren, George W., Santa Fé,
N. M.

DISCHARGED

Dame, William E.   1st Sergeant   Cerrillos, N. M.
    Discharged per O. reg. comds., Aug. 10, 1898.
Wesley, Frederick C.   Sergeant   Santa Fé, N. M.
    Discharged on account of disability, Aug. 26, 1898.
    Wounded forearm, slight, July 1, 2, or 3.

TRANSFERRED BY VERBAL ORDER REGIMENTAL
COMMANDER, MAY 12, 1898

Reber, William R.	Sergeant
Price, Stuart R.	Corporal
Bernard, William C.	Trooper
Brown, Hiram T.	Trooper
Bump, Arthur L.	Trooper
Cloud, William	Trooper
Davis, Henry Clay	Trooper
Duran, Jose L.	Trooper
Easton, Stephen	Trooper
Fennell, William A.	Trooper
Fleming, Clarence A.	Trooper
Holden, Prince A.	Trooper
Land, Oscar N.	Trooper
Martin, John	Trooper
Roberts, John P.	Trooper
Stephens, Orregon	Trooper
Torbett, John G.	Trooper
Williams, Thomas C.	Trooper
Zigler, Daniel J.	Trooper

DIED

Cochran, Irad, Jr.   Trooper
    Died, May 26, 1898, San Antonio, Tex. Spinal meningitis.
Miller, John S.   Trooper
    Died, July 16, 1898, of yellow fever, at Siboney, Cuba.
Judson, Alfred M.   Trooper
    Died Aug. 17, 1898, of typhoid fever, at Montauk Point, L. I.
O'Neill, John   Trooper
    Died, Aug. 3, 1898, of dysentery, at Edgmont Key, Fla.

KILLED

Green, Henry C.   Trooper
    Killed in action, July 1, 1898, near Santiago de Cuba.
Robinson, John F.   Trooper
    Killed in action, July 2, 1898, near Santiago de Cuba.

| Sherrard, Coleman | 1st Lieutenant | Santa Fé, N. M. |
| John A. McIlhenny | 2d Lieutenant | New Orleans, La. |

TROOP F

CAPTAIN MAXIMILIAN LUNA

Maximilian Luna	Captain	Santa Fé, N. M.
Horace W. Weakley	1st Lieutenant	Santa Fé, N. M.
William E. Dame	2d Lieutenant	Santa Fé, N. M.

Transferred from Troop E to F.

Horace E. Sherman	1st Sergeant	Santa Fé, N. M.
Garfield Hughes	Sergeant	Santa Fé, N. M.
Thomas D. Fennessy	Sergeant	Santa Fé, N. M.
William L. Mattocks	Sergeant	Santa Fé, N. M.
James Doyle	Sergeant	Santa Fé, N. M.
George W. Armijo	Sergeant	Santa Fé, N. M.

Wounded in action, June 24th. G. S. wrist.

Eugene Bohlinger	Sergeant	Santa Fé, N. M.
Herbert A. King	Sergeant	Santa Fé, N. M.
Edward Donnelly	Corporal	Santa Fé, N. M.
John Cullen	Corporal	Santa Fé, N. M.
Edward Hale	Corporal	Santa Fé, N. M.
Arthur P. Spenser	Corporal	Santa Fé, N. M.
John Boehnke	Corporal	Santa Fé, N. M.
Albert Powers	Corporal	Santa Fé, N. M.

Wounded in action, July 1, 1898.

| Wentworth S. Conduit | Corporal | Santa Fé, N. M. |
| Ray V. Clark | Farrier | Santa Fé, N. M. |

Contusion scalp, slight. Missile shrapnel.
Wounded near Santiago de Cuba, July 1, 2, or 3, 1898.

Charles R. Gee	Farrier	Santa Fé, N. M.
Jefferson Hill	Wagoner	Santa Fé, N. M.
J. Kirk McKurdy	Trumpeter	San Antonio, Tex.
Arthur L. Perry	Bugler	Santa Fé, N. M.

Shoulder. Mauser rifle. Wounded near Santiago de Cuba,
July 1, 2, or 3, 1898.

TROOPERS

Albers, H. L., Santa Fé, N. M.
Wounded in action, June 24,
1898. G. S. right wrist.
Albertson, Ed. J., Santa Fé, N. M.
Wounded in action, June 24.
G. S. wrist.
Alexander James, Santa Fé, N. M.
Abbott, Chas. G., Santa Fé, N. M.
Adams, Edgar S., San Antonio,
Tex.
Alexander, James F., Santa Fé, N. M.
Black, James S., Santa Fé, N. M.
Bailey, Rob't Z., Santa Fé, N. M.
Wounded in action, June 24th.
G. S. both legs.
Boschen, John, San Antonio, Tex.
Bell, Wm. A., Tampa, Fla.
Brennan, Jeremiah, Santa Fé,
N. M.
Burris, Walter C., Santa Fé, N. M.
Byrne, John, Muscogee, I. T.
Transferred from Troop L to F.
Bell, John H., Santa Fé, N. M.
Cochran, William O., Santa Fé,
N. M.
Clark, Frank J., San Antonio, Tex.
Colbert, Benjamin H.,
San Antonio, Tex.
Christian, Edward D., Tampa, Fla.
Clelland, Calvin G., Santa Fé,
N. M.
Conley, Edward C., Santa Fé, N. M.
Cochran, Willard M., Santa Fé,
N. M.
Cherry, Charles C., Santa Fé, N. M.
Dougherty, Louis, Santa Fé, N. M.
De Bohun, John C., Santa Fé, N. M.

Farley, William, Santa Fé, N. M.
Freeman, Will, Santa Fé, N. M.
Wounded by fragments of shell
in wrist, July 1, 1898. Left
wrist.
Gibbs, Henry M., Santa Fé, N. M.
Gunshot wound in foot, July 1,
1898.
Gallagher, Wm. D., Santa Fé,
N. M.
Goldberg, Samuel, Santa Fé, N. M.
Wounded in action, July 1,
1898. Hip. Mauser rifle.
Glessner, Otis, Santa Fé, N. M.
Green, John D., Santa Fé, N. M.
Hartle, Albert C., Santa Fé, N. M.
Gunshot wound in testicles,
June 24, 1898.
Hopping, Charles O., Santa Fé,
N. M.
Hammer, George, Santa Fé, N. M.
Kennedy, Stephan A., Santa Fé,
N. M.
Leffert, Charles E., Santa Fé, N. M.
Lisk, Guy M., Santa Fé, N. M.
Leach, John M., Santa Fé, N. M.
Le Stourgeon, E. Guy,
San Antonio, Tex.
Lavelle, Nolan Z., San Antonio,
Tex.
Martin, Thomas, Santa Fé, N. M.
Mills, John B., Santa Fé, N. M.
McGregor, Herbert P., Santa Fé,
N. M.
Wounded in action, July 1,
1898. Left shoulder. Mauser
rifle.

166 · Appendix A

McCurdy, F. Allen, San Antonio,
Tex.
Nickell, William E., Santa Fé, N. M.
Nesbit, Otto W., Santa Fé, N. M.
Newitt, George W., Santa Fé,
N. M.
Neal, John M., Santa Fé, N. M.
Parmele, Charles A., Santa Fé,
N. M.
Quier, Frank T., Santa Fé, N. M.
Raymond, Milliard L., Santa Fé,
N. M.
Reed, Harry B., Santa Fé, N. M.
Reed, Clifford L., Santa Fé, N. M.
Wounded in action, June 24,
1898. In arm.
Renner, Charles L., Santa Fé, N. M.
Reynolds, Edwin L., Santa Fé,
N. M.
Russell, Arthur L., Santa Fé, N. M.
Rebentisch, Adolph, San Antonio,
Tex.
Gunshot wound in shoulder,
June 24, 1898. Left shoulder.
Reyer, Adolph T., Santa Fé, N. M.
Rogers, Albert, Santa Fé, N. M.
Rice, Lee C., Santa Fé, N. M.
Staub, Louis E., Santa Fé, N. M.
Shields, William G., Santa Fé,
N. M.

Stockbridge, Arthur H., Santa Fé,
N. M.
Sharland, George H., Santa Fé,
N. M.
Skipwith, John G., Santa Fé, N. M.
Sinnett, James B., Santa Fé, N. M.
Tangen, Edward, Santa Fé, N. M.
Trump, Norman O., Santa Fé,
N. M.
Vinnedge, George E., Santa Fé,
N. M.
Wardwell, Louis C., Santa Fé,
N. M.
Warren, Paul, Santa Fé, N. M.
Watrous, Charles E., Santa Fé,
N. M.
Weber, Beauregard, Santa Fé,
N. M.
Weller, Samuel M., San Antonio,
Tex.
Winter, John G., San Antonio, Tex.
Gunshot wounds in shoulder,
arm and leg, July 1, 1898.
Winter, Otto R., San Antonio, Tex.
Wertheim, Adolph S.,
San Antonio, Tex.
Walsh, John, Santa Fé, N. M.
Wells, Thomas J., Santa Fé, N. M.
Wilson, Harry W., Tampa, Fla.

DISCHARGED

Douglass, James   Private   Santa Fé, N. M.
Discharged acct. Surgeon's certificate of disability.

TRANSFERRED

Keyes, Maxwell   2d Lieutenant   Santa Fé, N. M.
Promoted to Adjutant, August 1, 1898.

PRIVATES

Flynn, Joseph F., Santa Fé, N. M.
Transferred from Troop F to I, May, 12, 1898, San Antonio, Tex.
Goodrich, Hedrick Ben, Santa Fé, N. M.
Transferred from Troop F to I, May 12, 1898, San Antonio, Tex.
Hickey, Walter, Santa Fé, N. M.
Transferred from Troop F to I, May 12, 1898, San Antonio, Tex.
Hogan, Michael, Santa Fé, N. M.
Transferred from Troop F to I, May 12, 1898, San Antonio, Tex.
King, Harry Bruce, Santa Fé, N. M.
Transferred from Troop F to I, May 12, 1898, San Antonio, Tex.
Kerney, George M., Santa Fé, N. M.
Transferred from Troop F to I, May 12, 1898, San Antonio, Tex.
Larsen, Louis, Santa Fé, N. M.
Transferred from Troop F to I, May 12, 1898, San Antonio, Tex.
McCoy, John, Santa Fé, N. M.
Transferred from Troop F to I, May 12, 1898, San Antonio, Tex.
Nehmer, Charles A., Santa Fé, N. M.
Transferred from Troop F to I, May 12, 1898, San Antonio, Tex.
Rogers, Leo G., N. M.
Transferred from Troop F to I, May 12, 1898, San Antonio, Tex.
Rafalowitz, Hyman, Santa Fé, N. M.
Transferred from Troop F to I, May 12, 1898, San Antonio, Tex.
Spencer, Edwards John, Santa Fé, N. M.
Transferred from Troop F to I, May 12, 1898, San Antonio, Tex.
Schearnhorst, Jr., Carl J., Santa Fé, N. M.
Transferred from Troop F to I, May 12, 1898, San Antonio, Tex.
Temple, Frank, Santa Fé, N. M.
Transferred from Troop F to I, May 12, 1898, San Antonio, Tex.
Bawcom, Joseph L., Santa Fé, N. M.
Transferred from Troop F to I, May 12, 1898, at San Antonio, Tex.

DIED

Booth, Frank B.   Private   Madison, Wis.
Wounded in action at Las Guasimas, June 24, 1898;
died at Key West, August 30, 1898. G. S. right shoulder.
Erwin, William T.   Private   Austin, Tex.
Killed in action, June 24, 1898, Las Guasimas. G. S. head.

Endsley, Guy D. Private Somerfield, Pa.
Died in Cuba, July 18, 1898, of fever.

DESERTED

Thompson, Charles Private Mercer Co., W. Va.
Deserted at Tampa, Fla., July 27, 1898.

DISCHARGED

McIlhenny, John A. Corporal San Antonio, Tex.
Discharged to accept commission.

TROOP G

CAPTAIN WILLIAM H. H. LLEWELLEN

William H. H. Llewellen Captain Las Cruces, N. M.
John Wesley Green 1st Lieutenant Gallup, N. M.
David J. Leahy 2d Lieutenant Raton, N. M.
    On sick list from July 1st to Sept. 3d from wound received in
    San Juan battle.
Columbus H. McCaa 1st Sergeant Gallup, N. M.
Jacob S. Mohler Q. M. Sergeant Gallup, N. M.
Raymond Morse Sergeant
Rolla A. Fullenweider Sergeant Raton, N. M.
Matthew T. McGehee Sergeant Raton, N. M.
James Brown Sergeant Gallup, N. M.
Nicholas A. Vyne Sergeant Emporia, Kan.
Raleigh L. Miller Sergeant Pueblo, Col.
Henry Kirah Corporal Gallup, N. M.
James D. Ritchie Corporal Gallup, N. M.
Luther L. Stewart Corporal Raton, N. M.
    Wounded in battle, June 24th. Absent since on account of wound.
    G. S. left forearm.
John McSparron Corporal Gallup, N. M.
    Wounded, July 1st. Absent since on account of wound.
    Right thigh, severe. Missile, shrapnel.
Frank Briggs Corporal Raton, N. M.
Edward C. Armstrong Corporal Albuquerque, N. M.
William S. Reid Corporal Raton, N. M.

Hiram E. Williams	Corporal	Raton, N. M.
George V. Haefner	Farrier	Gallup, N. M.
Frank A. Hill	Saddler	Raton, N. M.
Thomas O'Neal	Wagoner	Springer, N. M.
Willis E. Somers	Trumpeter	Raton, N. M.
Edward G. Piper	Trumpeter	Silver City, N. M.
Alvin C. Ash	Trooper	Raton, N. M.

Absence from command since July 1st to Sept. 7th on account of wound received in battle. Wrist, slight. Missile, shrapnel.

TROOPERS

Arnold, Edward B., Prescott, Ariz.

Akin, James E., Dolores, Col.

Anderson, Arthur T., Albuquerque, N. M.

Andrews, William C., Sulphur Springs, Tex.

Beck, Joseph H., San Antonio, Tex.

Bishop, Louis B., San Antonio, Tex.

Brumley, Jr., William H., Dolores, Cal.

Brown, Robert, Gallup, N. M.

Brown, Edwin M., San Antonio, Tex.

Brazelton, William H., St. Louis, Mo.

Beissel, John J., Gallup, N. M.

Camp, Cloid, Raton, N. M.

Camp, Marion, Raton, N. M.

Covenaugh, Thomas F., Raton, N. M.
  Absent since June 24th on account of wound received in battle.

Cody, William E., St. Louis, Mo.

Chopetal, Frank W., Buffalo, N. Y.

Coyle, Michael H., Raton, N. M.
  Absent on sick leave since June

24th on account of wound in arm received in battle.

Clark, Winslow, Milton, Mass.
  Absent on sick leave since July 1st on account of gunshot wound through lung received in battle. Right lung, severe. Missile or weapon, Mauser rifle.

Cotton, Frank W., Jennings, La.

Conover, Alfred J., Chicasee, I. T.

Detwiler, Sherman, Muscatine, Ia.

Dunn, Alfred B., Calvert, Tex.

Edmunds, John H., Alleghany, Pa.

Faupel, Henry F., Martington, Ill.

Fornoff, Frederick, Albuquerque, N. M.

Fitch, Roger S., Buffalo, N. Y.

Gibson, William C., Gallup, N. M.

Gevers, Louis, Austin, Tex.
  Absent from July 1st till Aug. 2d on account of gunshot wound in hips received in battle.

Goodwin, John, Gallup, N. M.

Healey, Frank F., Brooklyn, N. Y.

Henderson, John, Gallup, N. M.

Absent from July 1st to Sept. 2d on account of wound in arm received in battle. Wrist. Missile or weapon, Mauser rifle.

Henshaw, Laten R., El Paso, Tex.

Johnson, Albert John, Raton, N. M.

Kline, John S., San Marcial, N. M.

Keeley, Bert T., Lamy, N. M.

King, Henry A., Massitee, Mich.

Littleton, Elias M., Springer, N. M.

Lincoln, Malcom D., Lucknow, I. T.

Larson, Anton, Silverton, Col.

Lyle, James C., Georgetown, Col.

Miller, Frank P., Los Angeles, Cal.

Meyers, Fred P., Gallup, N. M. Reduced from 1st Sergt. to Trooper on account of absence caused by wound received in battle, July 1, 1898. Head, severe.

Moran, Daniel, Gallup, N. M.

Mann, Eugene M., Omaha, Neb.

McCarthy, George H., Los Angeles, Cal.

McKinney, Frank G., Harrison, Ark.

McKinney, Oliver, Cannon City, Col.

McMullen, Samuel J., St. Louis, Mo.

Noish, John, Raton, N. M.

Phipps, T. W., Bland, N. M.

Petty, Archibald, Gallup, N. M.

Pennington, Elijah, San Antonio, Tex.

Preston, Robert A., Stiles, Tex.

Quigg, George H., Gallup, N. M.

Quinn, Walter D., San Marcial, N. M.

Radcliff, William, Gallup, N. M.

Richards, Richard, Albuquerque, N. M.

Rayburn, Harry C., Camden, Ia.

Reid, Robert W., Raton, N. M. Absent on sick leave from June 24th to Sept. 8th on account of wound in side received in battle. G. S. to right hip.

Ragland, Robert C., Guthrie, O. T.

Roland, George, Deming, N. M. G. S. right side, June 24, 1898.

Stillson, Earl, Topeka, Kan.

Simmons, Charles M., Raton, N. M.

Slaughter, Benjamin, San Antonio, Tex.

Shannon, Charles W., Raton, N. M.

Thomas, Neal, Aztec, N. M.

Travis, Grant, Aztec, N. M.

Van Horn, Eustace E., Halstead, Kan.

Welch, Toney, Durango, Col.

Whittington, Richard, Gallup, N. M.

Whited, Lyman E., Raton, N. M.

Wood, William D., Bland, N. M.

Wright, Clarence, Springer, N. M.

DISCHARGED

Swan, George D.   Gallup, N. M.
  Discharged on account of disability.
Thompson, Frank M.   Aztec, N. M.
  Discharged on account of disability.

DESERTED

McCulloch, Samuel T.   Springer, N. M.
  Deserted from camp at Tampa, Fla., Aug. 4, 1898.

DEATHS

Green, J. Knox   Rancho, Tex.
  Died at Montauk Point, N. Y., Camp U. S. Troops, Aug. 15,
  because of sickness which originated in line of duty.
Lutz, Eugene A.   Raton, N. M.
  Detained in yellow-fever hospital by medical authorities when
  regiment left Cuba. Died in same, Aug. 15, 1898.

KILLED IN ACTION

Haefner, Henry J.   Gallup, N. M.
  In battle, June 24, 1898.
Russell, Marcus D.   Troy, N. Y.
  Killed in action, June 24, 1898.

TRANSFERRED

Arendt, Henry J.   Sergeant   Gallup, N. M.
  Transferred to Troop I, May 12th.
Corbe, M. C.   Trumpeter
  Transferred to Troop K, May 11.

TROOPERS

Bailie, Henry C., Gallup, N. M.   Morgan, Schuyler C., Hazard, Ky.
  Transferred from Troop I to   Transferred to Troop I,
  Troop G, Aug. 31, 1898.   May 12th.
Love, William J., Raton, N. M.   Morgan, Ulysses G., Hazard, Ky.
  Transferred to Troop I,   Transferred to Troop I,
  May 12th.   May 12th.

Odell, William D., Parkersburg,
W. Va.
Transferred to Troop I,
May 12th.
Donnelly, Rutherford B. H.,
Jefferson, O. T.
Transferred to Troop I,
May 12th.
Evans, Evan, Gallup, N. M.
Transferred to Troop I,
May 12th.
Groves, Oscar W., Raton, N. M.
Transferred to Troop I,
May 12th.
Jones, William H., Raton, N. M.
Transferred to Troop I,
May 12th.
Kania, Frank, Jamestown, N. D.
Transferred to Troop K,
May 11th.
Pierce, Ed., Chicago, Ill.
Transferred to Troop I,
May 12th.

Saville, Michael, Chicago, Ill.
Transferred to Troop I,
May 12th.
Sinnett, Lee, Maizeville, W. Va.
Transferred to Troop I,
May 12th.
Tait, John H., Raton, N. M.
Transferred to Troop I,
May 12th.
Peabody, Harry, Raton, N. M.
Transferred to Troop I,
May 12th.
McGowan, Alexander, Gallup,
N. M.
Transferred to Troop I,
May 12th.
Brown, John, Gallup, N. M.
Transferred to Troop I,
May 12th.
Crockett, Joseph B., Raton, N. M.
Transferred to Troop I,
May 12th.

TROOP H

CAPTAIN GEORGE CURRY

George Curry	Captain	Tularosa, N. M.
William H. Kelly	1st Lieutenant	East Las Vagas, N. M.
Charles L. Ballard	2d Lieutenant	Roswell, N. M.
Green A. Settle	1st Sergeant	Jackson Co., Ky.
Nevin P. Gutilius	Sergeant	Tularosa, N. M.
William A. Mitchell	Sergeant	El Paso, Tex.
Oscar de Montell	Sergeant	Roswell, N. M.
Thomas Darnell	Sergeant	Denver, Col.
Willis J. Physioc	Sergeant	Columbia, S. C.
Michael C. Rose	Sergeant	Silver City, N. M.
Nova A. Johnson	Sergeant	Roswell, N. M.
Morton M. Morgan	Corporal	Silver City, N. M.

Arthur E. Williams	Corporal	Las Cruces, N. M.
Frank Murray	Corporal	Roswell, N. M.
Morgan O. B. Lewellyn	Corporal	Las Cruces, N. M.
James C. Hamilton	Corporal	Roswell, N. M.
George F. Jones	Corporal	El Paso, Tex.
Charles P. Cochran	Corporal	Eddy, N. M.
John M. Kelly	Corporal	El Paso, Tex.
Robert E. Ligon	Trumpeter	Beaumont, Tex.
Gaston R. Dehumy	Trumpeter	Santa Fé, N. M.
Uriah Sheard	Blacksmith	El Paso, Tex.
Robert L. Martin	Farrier	Santa Fé, N. M.
John Shaw	Saddler	Scott Co., Iowa.
Taylor B. Lewis	Wagoner	Las Cruces, N. M.

TROOPERS

Allison, Jovillo, Bentonville, Ark.

Amonette, Albert B., Roswell, N. M.

Bendy, Cecil C., El Paso, Tex.

Black, Columbus L., Las Cruces, N. M.

Bryan, John B., Las Cruces, N. M.

Bogardus, Frank, Las Cruces, N. M.

Brown, Percy, Spring Hill, Tenn.

Baker, Philip S., Clinton, Ia.

Bullard, John W., Guadaloupe, Tex.

Connell, Thomas J., Bennett, Tex.

Corbett, Thomas F., Roswell, N. M.

Cornish, Thomas J., Freestone, Tex.

Crawford, Clinton K., Cincinnati, O.

Cone, John S., Tularosa, N. M.

Duran, Abel B., Silver City, N. M.

Duran, Jose L., Santa Fé, N. M.

Dorsey, Lewis, Silver City, N. M.

Doty, George B., Santa Fé, N. M.

Dunkle, Frederick W., East Las Vegas, N. M.

Douglas, Arthur L., Eddy, N. M.

Eaton, Frank A., Silver City, N. M.

Fletcher, Augustus C., Silver City, N. M.

Frye, Obey B., Flagstaff, Ariz.

Gasser, Louis, El Paso, Tex.

George, Ira W., Quincy, Ill.

Grisby, James B., Deming, N. M.

Hamilton, James M., Deming, N. M.

Herring, Leary O., Silver City, N. M.

Hunt, Le Roy R., Cincinnati, O.

Houston, Robert C., Hillsboro, N. M.

James, Frank W., Marion Co., Ga.

Johnson, Charles, Lund, Sweden.

Johnson, Harry F., Beaumont, Tex.

Johnson, Lewis L., Beaumont, Tex.

Kehoe, Michael J., Ottawa, Canada.

Kehn, Amandus, Silver City, N. M.

Kinnebrugh, Ollie A., El Paso, Tex.
Kendall, Harry J., Coldsborg, Ky.
Lawson, Frank H., Las Cruces,
   N. M.
Lewis, Adelbert, Beaver Co., Utah.
Lannon, John, Hillsboro, N. M.
Mooney, Thomas A., Silver City,
   N. M.
Moneckton, William J.,
   San Antonio, Tex.
McAdams, Joel H., Mt. Pilia, Tenn.
McAdams, Richard P., Mt. Pilia,
   Tenn.
McCarty, Frederick J., Mentzville,
   Mo.
Murray, George F., Deming, N. M.
Nobles, William H., Silver City,
   N. M.
Neff, Nettleton, Cincinnati, O.
Owens, Clay T., El Paso, Tex.
Ott, Charles H., Silver City, N. M.
Pace, John, Bentonville, Ark.
Pipkins, Price.
Powell, Lory H., Roswell, N. M.
Pronger, Norman W., Silver City,
   N. M.
Pollock, John F., Tularosa, N. M.
Piersol, James M., Osborne, Mo.
Roberson, James R., Belle Co., Tex.

Rutherford, Bruce H., Pana, Ill.
Regan, John J., Beaumont, Tex.
Sharp, Emerson E., Wanamaker,
   Tenn.
Stewart, Newtown, El Paso, Tex.
Scroggins, Oscar, Logan Co., Ill.
St. Clair, Edward C., New Orleans,
   La.
Saucier, Harry S., New Orleans,
   La.
Schutt, Henry, Warren, Pa.
Sawyer, Benjamin, Hillsboro, Ill.
Thompson, Alexander M.,
   Deming, N. M.
Traynor, William S., Wilcox, Ariz.
Thomas, Theodore C.,
   Leavenworth, Kan.
Waggoner, Daniel G., Roswell,
   N. M.
Waggoner, Curtis C., Roswell, N. M.
Wilson, Charles E., Boulder, Col.
Wilkinson, Samuel I., Cincinnati,
   O.
Woodson, Pickens E., Honey
   Grove, Tex.
Wheeler, Frank G., Chautauqua
   Co., N. Y.
Wickham, Patrick A., Socorro,
   N. M.

DISCHARGED

Rynerson, William L.   Sergeant   Las Cruces, N. M.
   Discharged from service of U. S. Army by reason of special order
   No. 145 Hd. Qrs., U. S. Army, Washington, D. C.

TRANSFERRED

John B. Wiley   Sergeant
   Transferred to Troop I, May 12, 1898.

Joseph F. Kansky   Sergeant
John V. Morrison   Sergeant   Santa Fé, N. M.
Transferred to Troop I, May 12, 1898.

PRIVATES

Lee, Robert E., Donabua, N. M.
Transferred to Troop I,
May 12, 1898.
Bennett, Orton A., Jack Co., Tex.
Transferred to Troop I,
May 12, 1898.
Brito, Jose, El Paso, Tex.
Transferred to Troop I,
May 12, 1898.
Brito, Frank C., El Paso, Tex.
Transferred to Troop I,
May 12, 1898.
Cate, James S., Grape Vine, Tex.
Transferred to Troop I,
May 12, 1898.
Casad, C. Darwin, Las Cruces,
N. M.
Transferred to Troop I,
May 12, 1898.
Dolan, Thomas P., Ticonderoga,
N. Y.
Transferred to Troop I,
May 12, 1898.
Farrell, Frederick P., El Paso,
Tex.
Transferred to Troop I,
May 12, 1898.
Frenger, Muna C., Las Cruces,
N. M.
Transferred to Troop I,
May 12, 1898.
Hermeyer, Ernest H., Germany
Transferred to Troop I,
May 12, 1898.

Jopling, Cal., Hamilton Co., Tex.
Transferred to Troop I,
May 12, 1898.
Nehmer, William, Staten, Germany.
Transferred to Troop I,
May 12, 1898.
Roediger, August, Charlotte, N. C.
Transferred to Troop I,
May 12, 1898.
Schafer, George, Pinos Altos, N. M.
Transferred to Troop I,
May 12, 1898.
Storms, Morris J., Roswell, N. M.
Transferred to Troop I,
May 12, 1898.
Sullivan, William J., Manchester, Va.
Transferred to Troop I,
May 12, 1898.
Fritz, William H., Windsor, Conn.
Transferred to Troop I,
May 12, 1898.
Eberman, Henry J, Bremen,
Germany.
Transferred from Troop K to
Troop H, May 16, 1898. Re-
transferred to K, June 8, 1898.
Died.
Bucklin, E. W., Chautauqua Co.,
N. Y.
Transferred to Troop L,
June 8, 1898.
Wright, Grant, Cold Springs, N. Y.
Transferred to Troop L,
June 8, 1898.

DIED

Gosling, Frederick W.   Bedfordshire, Eng.
  Died in hospital at Camp Wikoff, N. Y., Aug. 19, 1898.
Casey, Edwin Eugene   Las Cruces, N. M.
  Died in hospital at Camp Wikoff, N. Y., Sept. 1, 1898.

DESERTED

Ewell, Edward A.   Adrian, Ill.
  Deserted, June 28, 1898, at Tampa, Fla.
Miller, Samuel   Roswell, N. M.
  Deserted, June 28, 1898, at Tampa, Fla.

TROOP I

CAPTAIN SCHUYLER A. MCGINNIS

Schuyler A. McGinnis	Captain	Newkirk, O. T.
Frederick W. Wintge	1st Lieutenant	Santa Fé, Mex.
Samuel Grenwald	2d Lieutenant	Prescott, Ariz.
John B. Wylie	1st Sergeant	Fort Bayard, N. Mex.
Schuyler C. Morgan	Q. M. Sergeant	Durango, Col.
John V. Morrison	Sergeant	Springerville, Ariz.
William R. Reber	Sergeant	
Basil M. Ricketts	Sergeant	Lambs' Club, N. Y.
Percival Gassett	Sergeant	Dedham, Mass.
James S. Cate	Sergeant	Grape Vine, Tex.
William H. Waffensmith	Sergeant	Raton, N. M.
August Roediger	Corporal	Charlotte, N. C.
Numa C. Freuger	Corporal	Las Cruces, N. Mex.
William J. Sullivan	Corporal	Silver City, N. M.
William J. Nehmer	Corporal	Silver City, N. M.
Abraham L. Bainter	Corporal	Colorado Springs, Col.
Hiram T. Brown	Corporal	Albuquerque, N. M.
Errickson M. Nichols	Corporal	52 E. 78th St., New York City
George M. Kerney	Corporal	Globe, Ariz.
Robert E. Lea	Trumpeter	Dona Ana, N. M.
Clarence H. Underwood	Trumpeter	Colorado Springs, Col.

Charles A. Nehmer	Blacksmith	Chicago, Ill.
Hayes Donnelly	Farrier	Jefferson, O. T.
Leo G. Rogers	Saddler	Bogart, Mo.
Everett E. Holt	Wagoner	Coffeyville, Kan.

TROOPERS

Alexis, George D., New Orleans, La.
Arendt, Henry J., Hoboken, N. J.
Armstrong, Charles M.
Adkins, Joseph R.
Bates, William H.
Barrowe, Hallett A.
Bawcom, Joseph L., Bisbee, Ariz.
Bennett, Horton A., Tularosa, N. M.
Brito, Frank C., Pinos Altos, N. M.
Brito, Jose, Los Angeles, Cal.
Brush, Charles A., Hanford, Cal.
Bassage, Albert C., Corning, N. Y.
Casad, Charles D., Mesilla, N. M.
Cloud, William.
Crockett, Joseph B., Topeka, Kan.
Coe, George M., Albuquerque, N. M.
Clark, Frank M., Hiawatha, Kan.
Davis, Henry C., Santa Fé, N. M.
Dolan, Thomas P., Pinos Altos, N. M.
Denny, Robert W., Raton, Mex.
Duke, Henry K., Lipscomb, Tex.
Evans, Evan, Gallup, N. M.
Fennel, William A., Reunion, Md.
Flynn, Joseph F., Albuquerque, N. M.
Geiger, Percy A., Durango, Col.
Gooch, John R., Santa Fé, N. M.
Groves, Oscar W., Raton, N. M.

Goodrich, Ben Hedric.
Giller, Alfred C. Topeka, Kan.
Hermeyer, Ernest H., Roswell, N. M.
Hickey, Walter, Wishua, N. H.
Hogan, Michael.
Jones, William H., Raton, N. M.
Jopling, Cal, La Luz, N. M.
King, Harry B., Raton, N. M.
Larsen, Louis.
Love, William J., Jersey City, N. J.
McCoy, John, Monrovia, Cal.
McGowan, Alexander, Gallup, N. M.
Martin, John, Decanter, Ill.
Miller, Edwin H., Junction City, Kan.
Miller, David R.
Miller, Jacob H., Needles, Cal.
Morgan, U. S. Grant, Durango, Col.
Morris, Ben F. T., Raton, N. M.
Moore, Roscoe E., Raton, N. M.
North, Franklin H., 2 W. 35th St., New York City
O'Dell, William W., Parkersburg, W. Va.
Peabody, Harry, Raton, N. M.
Pierce, Edward, Chicago, Ill.
Price, Stewart R., Plattsburg, Mo.
Rafalowitz, Hyman, Philadelphia, Pa.

Roberts, John P., Clayton, N. M.
Reisig, Max, Y. M. C. A., St. Louis,
  Mo.
Raulett, Charles, New Orleans,
  La.
Reidy, John, Ottawa, Kan.
Shornhorst, Carl J. Jr.
Schafer, George, Pinos Altos, N. M.
Sennett, Lee, Marysville, W. Va.
Storms, Morris J., Centerpoint,
  Tex.
Spencer, Edward John, Clay
  County, Tex.
Tait, John H.

Temple, Frank, Lafayette, Ind.
Torbett, John T., Yale, Kan.
Tritz, William H., Windsor,
  Conn.
Townsend, Charles M., Faribault,
  Minn.
Twyman, John L., Raton, N. M.
Thompson, George.
Williams, Thomas C.
Wiley, Harry B., Santa Fé, N. M.
Wisenberg, Roy O., Raton,
  N. M.
Zeigler, Daniel J., Como, Mont.

DISCHARGED

Brown, Harry R.   Private   Tampa, Fla.
  Discharged at Tampa, Fla., Aug. 5, 1898, per S. O. 153 A. G. O.,
  dated June 30, 1898, and final statements forwarded to A. G. O.,
  Washington, D. C., Aug. 3, 1898.
Young, Howard G.   Private
  Discharge to date from Aug. 23, 1898.

TRANSFERRED

Girard, Alfred O.   1st Sergeant
  Transferred, July 18, 1898, to 2d Army Corps, Camp Alger,
  per telegraphic instructions A. G. O., Washington, D. C.
Cowdin, Elliot C.   Corporal
  Transferred to Troop L 1st U. S. Vol. Cav., to date June 7, 1898,
  per verbal order Reg. Commander.
Fish, Hamilton Jr.   Sergeant
  Transferred to Troop L 1st U. S. Vol. Cav., June 7, 1898,
  per verbal order Reg. Commander. Killed in battle, June 24, 1898.
Wilson, Charles A.   Private
  Transferred to Hosp. Corps 1st U. S. Vol. Cav., June 7, 1898,
  verbal order Reg. Commander.
Greenway, John C.   2d Lieutenant
  Promoted 1st Lieut. Troop A 1st U. S. Vol. Cav.
Bailey, Harry C.   Private

Transferred back to Troop G, Sept. 1, 1898, per verbal order Reg. Commander.

DIED

Tiffany, William   2d Lieutenant
Died Aug. 26, 1898.

DESERTED

Saville, Michael   Private
Deserted from Camp Wikoff, L. I., Aug. 20, 1898.
Brown, John   Private
Deserted while en route from Camp Wood, San Antonio, Tex.,
to camp at Tampa, Fla., June 3, 1898.
Farrell, Fred. P.   Private
Deserted while en route from Camp Wood, San Antonio, Tex.,
to camp at Tampa, Fla., June 3, 1898.

TROOP K

CAPTAIN WOODBURY KANE

Woodbury Kane	Captain	319 Fifth Ave., New York City
Joseph A. Carr	1st Lieutenant	2127 R. St., Washington, D. C.
Horace K. Devereux	2d Lieutenant	Colorado Springs, Col.

Wounded at San Juan, July 1, 1898; forearm and arm; Mauser rifle.

Frederik K. Lie	1st Sergeant	Orgun P. O., N. M.
Thaddeus Higgins	Sergeant	210 W. 104th St., New York City.
Reginald Ronalds	Sergeant	Knickerbocker Club, N. Y. City.
Samuel G. Devore	Sergeant	Wheeling, W. Va.

Wounded at El Poso, July 1st; left forearm; shrapnel.

Philip K. Sweet	Sergeant	226 W. 121st St., New York City.
William J. Breen	Sergeant	510 E. 144th St., New York City.
Craig W. Wadsworth	Sergeant	Geneseo, N. Y.

Henry W. Buel	Sergeant	319 Fifth Ave., New York City.
James B. Tailor	Corporal	Ardsley on Hudson, N. Y.
Joseph S. Stevens	Corporal	Narragansett Ave., Newport, R. I.
Maxwell Norman	Corporal	Newport, R. I.
Edwin Coakley	Corporal	Prescott, Ariz.
George Kerr, Jr.	Corporal	East Downington, Pa.
Henry S. Van Schaick	Corporal	100 Broadway, New York City.
Frederick Herrig	Corporal	Pleasant Valley, Kalispel, Flat Head Co., Mont.
Oscar Land	Trumpeter	720 S. 8th St., Denver, Col.
George W. Knoblauch	Trumpeter	205 W. 57th St., New York City.
Benjamin A. Long	Saddler	New York City.

Wounded at El Poso, July 1st; left thigh.

Thomas G. Bradley	Farrier	Potomac, Montgomery Co., Md.
George T. Crucius	Blacksmith	50 Amanda St., Montgomery, Ala.
Lee Burdwell	Wagoner	Langtry, Tex.

TROOPERS

Armstrong, James T.

Adams, John H., Selma, Ala. Wounded, July 1st.

Bell, Sherman, Colorado Springs, Col.

Bernard, William C., Las Vegas, N. M.

Batchelder, Wallace N., Chester, Pa.

Bump, Arthur L., New London, O. Slightly wounded, July 1st.

Cameron, Charles H., McDonald, Pa.

Campbell, Douglass.

Cash, Walter S., Colorado Springs, Col. Wounded, July 1st; arm, slight; Mauser rifle.

Cooke, Henry B.

Carroll, John F., Hillsboro, Tex.

Cartmell, Nathaniel M., Lexington, Va.

Clagett, Jesse C., Moters Station, Frederick Co., Md.

Corbe, Max C., El Paso, Tex.

Coville, Allen M., Topeka, Kan.

Crowninshield, Francis B., Marblehead, Mass.

Channing, Roscoe A., 34 Park Place, New York City.

Daniels, Benjamin F., Colorado Springs, Col.

Davis, John, care W. S. Dickinson, Tarpon Springs, Fla.

Easton, Stephen, Santa Fé, N. M.

Eberman, Edwin.

Emerson, Edwin, Collier's Weekly, New York City.

Flemming, Clarence A.

Fletcher, Henry, Green Point, Cumberland Co., Pa.

Folk, Theodore, Oklahoma City, O. T.

Freeman, Elisha L., Burden, Kan.

Holden, Prince A., Grayson Co., Tex.

Hulme, Robert A., El Reno, O. T.

James, William F., San Antonio, Tex.

Jordan, Andrew M., Rossa, Tex.

Kania, Frank, Jamestown, N. D.

Langdon, Jesse D., Fargo, N. D.

Marshall, Creighton, 1807 G St., N. W., Washington, D. C.

Maverick, Lewis, San Antonio, Tex.

McGinty, William, Stillwater, O. T.

McKoy, William J., Oshkosh, Wis.

Mitchell, Mason, Lambs' Club, New York City.
Wounded at El Poso, July 1st; left arm, slight; shrapnel.

Mitchell, William H., Salem, Mass.

Montgomery, Lawrence N., Hempstead, Tex.

Nicholson, Charles P., 1617 John St., Baltimore, Md.

Norris, Edmund S., Guthrie, O. T.

Poey, Alfred.

Pollak, Albin J.

Quaid, William, Newberg, N. Y.

Robinson, Kenneth D., 55 Liberty St., New York City.
Wounded on July 1st; right side, severe; Mauser rifle.

Reed, Colton, San Antonio, Tex.

Smith, Frederick, Guthrie, O. T.

Smith, George L., Frankfort, Mich.

Smith, Joseph S., 1322 Brown St., Philadelphia, Pa.

Smith, Clarke T., 2008 Wallace St., Philadelphia, Pa.

Stockton, Richard, 218 W. Jersey St., Elizabeth, N. J.

Stephens, Oregon, Purdy, I. T.

Thorp, Henry, Southampton, L. I.

Test, Clarence L., Austin, Tex.
Transferred from 3d Penn. Inf. and reported for duty with troop at Montauk Point, Aug. 25th.

Toy, J. Frederick, 602 S. 42d St., Philadelphia, Pa.
Transferred from 3d Penn. Inf. and reported for duty with troops at Montauk Point, Aug. 25th.

Tudor, William, 37 Brimer St., Boston, Mass.

Venable, Warner M., Stephenville, Tex.

Wiberg, Axel E.

Weitzel, John F., care Windsor Hotel, Newkirk, O. T.

Wilson, Frank M., Guthrie, O. T.   Young, James E., 628 W. 37th St.,
Woodward, John A., Taylor, Tex.   Los Angeles, Cal.
Wright, Grant, Cold Springs, N. Y.

DISCHARGED

Maloon, Winthrop L.   Private
    Discharged per S. O. No. 141, A. G. O. Dated June 6th.
McMasters, Frederick D.   Private
    Discharged per S. O. No. 178, A. G. O.
    Dated July 30th, Washington, D. C.
Ferguson, Robert M.   Sergeant   55 Liberty St.,
                                        New York City.
    Discharged, Aug. 10th, 1898.
Worden, John L.   Private   27 W. 43d St.,
                                        New York City.
    Discharged by way of favor per telegraphic order from
    Assistant Secretary of War. Dated Aug. 15th, Washington, D. C.
Cosby, Arthur F.   Private
    Discharged per S. O. No. 103, A. G. O., Aug. 17th, Washington, D. C.,
    to enable the soldier to accept a commission. Wounded, July 1st;
    right hand.
Babcock, Campbell E.   Private   The Plaza, Chicago, Ill.
    Discharged, Sept. 5th, to accept commission.
Lee, Joseph J.   Private   Knoxville, Md.
    Discharged per S. O. No. 205, A. G. O., Washington, D. C., Aug. 31st.

TRANSFERRED

Duran, Joseph L.   Private   Santa Fé, N. M.
    Transferred to Troop H, this regiment, July 15th.
Brandon, Perry H.   Private   Douglass, Kan.
    Transferred to Troop D, this regiment, July 29th.
David M. Goodrich   1st Lieutenant.   Akron, O.
    Transferred from Troop D, this regiment, Aug. 11th.
    Transferred to Troop D, this regiment, Sept. 5th.

DIED

Haywood, Henry   Sergeant   Police Department,
                                        New York City.
    Abdomen; Mauser rifle; killed, July 2d. Wounded, July 1st;

died in Division Hospital, Cuba, July 2, 1898, from bullet wound received July 1st.

Ives, Gerard M.   Private   New York
Died at his home, 338 W. 71st St., New York City (date not known), from typhoid fever.

Tiffany, William   Lieutenant   New York City.
Died of fever.

DESERTED

Staley, Frank   Private
Deserted from troop at San Antonio, Tex., May 1st.

Curzon   Private
Deserted from detachment at Tampa, Fla., June 13th.

PROMOTED

Jenkins, Micah J.   Major   Youngs Island, S. C.
Promoted to Major, Aug. 11, 1898.

TROOP L

CAPTAIN RICHARD C. DAY

Richard C. Day   Captain   Vinita, I. T.
Shot through left shoulder on line of duty at San Juan.
Left shoulder and arm, severe; Mauser rifle.

John R. Thomas   1st Lieutenant   Muscogee, I. T.
G. S. wound in right lower leg at Las Guasimas, June 24th.
G. S. right leg.

Frank P. Hayes   2d Lieutenant   San Antonio, Tex.
Elhanan W. Bucklin   1st Sergeant   Jamestown, N. Y.
Jerome W. Henderlider   Sergeant   Saranac, Mich.
William M. Simms   Sergeant   Vinita, I. T.
Wounded at San Juan, July 1, 1898, in line of duty. Leg; Mauser rifle.

Joe A. Kline   Sergeant   Vinita, I. T.
Wounded at San Juan, July 1st, in line of duty. Leg; Mauser rifle.

William W. Carpenter   Sergeant   Vinita, I. T.
Wounded at San Juan, July 1st, in line of duty. Left thigh; Mauser rifle.

James McKay   Sergeant   Vinita, I. T.

Dillwyn M. Bell	Sergeant	Guthrie, O. T.

Hurt in back by fragment of shell at El Paso, July 1st.
Contusion: back, slight; shrapnel.

James E. McGuire	Sergeant	Chelsea, I. T.
George H. Seaver	Corporal	Muscogee, I. T.

Wounded at El Poso, July 2, 1898, in line of duty. Right foot, slight;
Mauser rifle.

John W. Davis	Corporal	Vinita, I. T.

Wounded at San Juan, July 1, 1898. Right leg and arm; Mauser rifle.

Samuel G. Davis	Corporal	Sardis, Ark.

Wounded at San Juan, July 1, 1898.

Bud Parnell	Corporal	Muscogee, I. T.
Joseph J. Roger	Corporal	Tillou, Ark.

Wounded at San Juan, July 1, 1898. Abdomen and arm; Mauser rifle.

George B. Dunnigan	Corporal	Vinita, I. T.
Maynard R. Williams	Corporal	Fairland, I. T.
Elliot C. Cowdin	Corporal	New York City.
Mike Kinney	Blacksmith	Imlay, Mich.
John R. Kean	Farrier	Maxwell, Ont.

Wounded at Las Guasimas, June 24th. G. S. left shoulder and lungs.

Nicholas H. Cochran	Wagoner	Vinita, I. T.
Guy M. Babcock	Saddler	Cherryville, Kan.
Thomas F. Meagher	Trumpeter	Muscogee, I. T.

Wounded at Las Guasimas, June 24th. G. S. left forearm.

Frank R. McDonald	Trumpeter	Oolagah, I. T.

Wounded at San Juan, July 1, 1898. Head; Mauser rifle.

TROOPERS

Adair, John M., Claremore, I. T.
Benson, Victor H.
Carey, Oren E., Clonau, Ia.
Chilcoot, Frederick, Howels,
   Neb.
Cook, James, Cherokee City, Ark.
Cruse, James, St. Joe, Ark.
Culver, Ed., Muscogee, I. T.
   Wounded at Las Guasimas,
   June 24th. G. S. breast.
Davis, James C., Waggone, I. T.

Damet, John P., Alexander, S. D.
   Wounded at Las Guasimas,
   June 24th. G. S. left shoulder.
Dennis, David C., Nelson, Mo.
Dobson, William H., Muscogee,
   I. T.
Ennis, Richard L., Cornell, Ill.
Evans, James R., Baldwin, Ark.
Gilmore, Maurice E., Muscogee,
   I. T.
Haley, Robert M., Wagoner, I. T.

Hawkins, Charles D., Vinita, I. T.
Heagert, Rudolph, Vinita, I. T.
Holderman, Bert. T., Artopa, Kan.
Hughes, Frank, Vinita, I. T.
Hughes, William E., Vinita, I. T.
Isbell, Thomas J., Vinita, I. T.
Wounded at Las Guasimas,
June 25th. G. S. neck, hip, and
thumb.
Jones, Levi, Vinita, I. T.
Johns, William S., Hemasville, Mo.
Kinkade, Elyah S., Muscogee, I. T.
Knox, Robert G., Clinton, La.
Lawrence, Richard, La Porte, Ind.
Lane, Edward K., Chetopa, Kan.
Lane, Sanford J., Saupulpa, I. T.
Lentz, Edward, Bowling Green, O.
Lewis, Frank A., Newark, N. J.
Little, Rollie L., West Fork, Ark.
McDonald, Asa W., Bearing Cross,
Ark.
McCamish, Andrew L., Bethel,
Kan.
Miller, John S., Garrison, Neb.
Miller, Boot, Chelsea, I. T.
Moore, John J., Vinita, I. T.
Oskison, Richard L., Vinita, I. T.
Wounded at San Juan, July 1st.
Left leg; Mauser rifle.
Owens, Edward L., Vinita, I. T.
Parker, Ora E., Dickins, Ia.
Wounded near Santiago de
Cuba, July 1, 2, or 3, 1898. Right
thigh, severe; shrapnel.
Pulley, William O., Marion, Ill.
Philpot, Leigh T., Bryson, Ky.
Poe, Nathaniel M., Adair, I. T.
Wounded at Las Guasimas,
June 24th. G. S. foot.

Price, Benjamin W., Eufaula,
I. T.
Rich, Allen K., Fort Gibson, I. T.
Robertson, George W., Muscogee,
I. T.
Robinson, Frank P., Borbora, Kan.
Russell, Daniel, Goodland, I. T.
Scobey, Arthur E., Willis Point,
Tex.
Wounded at San Juan Hill,
June 1, 1898. Right hand;
Mauser rifle.
Sharp, Walter L., Chicago, Ill.
Skelton, James W., Trinity Mills,
Tex.
Smith, Bert., Vinita, I. T.
Smith, Sylvester S., Vinita, I. T.
Stefens, Luke B., Rio Vista, I. T.
Stidham, Theodore E., Eufaula,
I. T.
Swearinger, George, Maysville,
Mo.
Taylor, Warren P., Hillsboro,
Tex.
Thompson, Sylvester V.
Wounded at San Juan, July 1,
1898. Left leg and arm; Mauser
rifle.
Wetmore, Robert C., Montclair,
N. J.
Whitney, Schuyler C., Pryor
Creek, I. T.
Wounded at Las Guasimas,
June 24th. G. S. neck.
Wilkins, George W., Vinita, I. T.
Wilson, James E., Madrid, Mo.
Winn, Arthur N., Muscogee,
I. T.

DISCHARGED

Hutchinson, Charles A.   Private
Price, Walter W.   Private
Hayes, Frank P.   1st Sergeant
    Discharged, June 24, 1898, to enable him to accept commission
    as 2d Lieut. in 1st U. S. Vol. Cav.

TRANSFERRED

Robert, William J.   Private
    Transferred to Troop M, June 7, 1898, by order Col. Wood.
Byrne, John   Sergeant   Vinita, I. T.
    Transferred to Troop F, July 10, 1898, by order Col. Wood.

DIED

Capron, Allyn K.   Captain   Fort Sill, Okla.
    Killed at battle of Las Guasimas, June 24, 1898. G. S. lungs.
Fish, Hamilton   Sergeant   New York City.
    Killed at battle of Las Guasimas, June 24, 1898. G. S. heart.
Dawson, Tilden W.   Private   Vinita, I. T.
    Killed at battle of Las Guasimas, June 24, 1898. G. S. head.
Santo, William T.   Private   Chouteau, I. T.
    Killed at battle of San Juan, July 1, 1898. Mauser rifle.
Hendricks, Milo A.   Private   Muscogee, I. T.
    Mortally wounded at battle of San Juan, July 1st; died in hospital,
    July 6, 1898. Mauser rifle.
Enyart, Silas R.   Private   Sapulpa, I. T.
    Mortally wounded at San Juan, July 1st; died in hospital, July 6, 1898.

TROOP M

CAPTAIN ROBERT H. BRUCE

Robert H. Bruce   Captain   Mineola, Tex.
Ode C. Nichols   1st Lieutenant   Durant, I. T.
Albert S. Johnson   2d Lieutenant   Oklahoma City, O. T.
Harry E. Berner   1st Sergeant   Durant, I. T.
Joseph L. Smith   Q. M. Sergeant   Caddo, I. T.
William E. Lloyd   Sergeant   Durant, I. T.

Frederick E. Nichols	Sergeant	Purcell, I. T.
Morency A. Hawkins	Sergeant	Tioga, Tex.
Wilbert L. Poole	Sergeant	Durant, I. T.
Otis B. Weaver	Sergeant	Mt. Vernon, Tex.
Henry C. Foley	Sergeant	Muscogee, I. T.
Samuel Downing	Corporal	Atoka, I. T.
Charles S. Lynch	Corporal	Caddo, I. T.
John N. Jackson	Corporal	Caddo, I. T.
Frank U. Talman	Corporal	So. McAlester, I. T.
Hiram S. Creech	Corporal	Durant, I. T.
Charles J. Fandru	Corporal	Caddo, I. T.
Theodore E. Schulz	Corporal	Tampa, Fla.
William G. Jones	Corporal	Ardmore, I. T.
Frank Marion	Trumpeter	Muscogee, I. T.
Charles J. Hokey	Trumpeter	Krebs, I. T.
John McMullen	Wagoner	Ardmore, I. T.
John Hall	Farrier	Durant, I. T.
Cragg Parsons	Blacksmith	Ardmore, I. T.
Luther M. Kiethly	Saddler	Hartshorn, I. T.
Samuel Young	Chief Cook	Caddo, I. T.

TROOPERS

Allaun, Jacob, Sapulpa, I. T.
Byrd, Samuel J. W., Muscogee, I. T.
Boydstun, John F., Caddo, I. T.
Barlow, John W., Caddo, I. T.
Barrington, John P., Ardmore, I. T.
Baird, Thompson M., Thurber, Tex.
Brierty, Thomas, Tampa, Fla.
Butler, Peter L., Kiowa, I. T.
Beal, Andy R., Durant, I. T.
Bruce, Peter R., Wagoner, I. T.
Brown, Leon, Ardmore, I. T.
Barney, Leland, Ardmore, I. T.
Burks, Jesse S., Ardmore, I. T.
Case, George, Durant, I. T.
Calhoun, Wesley, Durant, I. T.
Carter, Arthur E., Ardmore, I. T.

Carden, Horace W., Ardmore, I. T.
Cox, Walter, Durant, I. T.
Cooper, Bud G., Muscogee, I. T.
Dorell, Charles, Vinita, I. T.
Duping, Joseph, Muscogee, I. T.
Flying, Crawford D., Muscogee, I. T.
Fairman, Charles E., Ardmore, I. T.
Griffith, Ezra E., Sapulpa, I. T.
Gárland, George W., Ardmore, I. T.
Hall, James T., Wagoner, I. T.
Hawes, Frederick W., Dennison, Tex.
Houchin, Willis C., Durant, I. T.
Hamilton, Troy, Hartshorne, I. T.

Howell, William, Muscogee, I. T.
Harris, Chester, Muscogee, I. T.
Hoffman, George B., Somerville,
   N. J.
Johnson, Bankston, Caddo, I. T.
Johnson, Charles L., Ardmore, I. T.
Johnson, Gordon, Birmingham,
   Ala.
Jones, Charles L., McAlester, I. T.
Keithly, Ora E., Hartshorn, I. T.
Kings, John, McAlester, I. T.
Kearns, Edward L., Tampa, Fla.
Mitchell, William, Wagoner, I. T.
Madden, Charles E., Brooken, I. T.
Murphy, William S., Caddo, I. T.
McPherren, Charles E., Caddo,
   I. T.
Maytubby, Bud, Caddo, I. T.
McDaniel, Thomas E., Muscogee,
   I. T.
McPherson, Charles E., Caddo,
   I. T.
Morrell, Robert W., Elizabeth, N. J.
Owens, John M., Oologah, I. T.
Pipkins, Virgil A., Brooken, I. T.
Rouse, John L., Durant, I. T.
Rose, Lewis W., Los Angeles, Cal.

Russell, Walter L., Caddo, I. T.
Rynerson, Benjamin A., Durant,
   I. T.
Reynolds, Benjamin F., Ardmore,
   I. T.
Ross, William E., Ardmore, I. T.
Roberts, William J., Vinita, I. T.
Sloane, Samuel P., So. McAlester,
   I. T.
Sykes, Marion, Muscogee, I. T.
Stewart, Henry J., Caddo, I. T.
Thomas, Jesse C., Caddo, I. T.
Tyler, Edwin, Ardmore, I. T.
Vickers, John W., So. McAlester,
   I. T.
Williams, Benjamin H., So.
   McAlester, I. T.
Williams, George W., Ardmore,
   I. T.
Wolfe, John W., Ardmore, I. T.
Webster, David, Durant, I. T.
Wagner, John D., Caddo, I. T.
Woog, Benjamin B., Washington,
   D. C.
de Zychlinski, William T.,
   Bismarck, N. D.

TRANSFERRED

Lane, Sanford G.   Trooper   Sapulpa, I. T.
   Transferred to Troop L 1st U. S. V. C., June 8, 1898,
   per verbal order Reg. Com.

DIED OF DISEASE

Kyle, Yancy   Trooper   McAlester, I. T.
   Died of typhoid fever at Tampa, July 15, 1898.
   Final statements rendered and settled per Capt. Bruce.

As said above, this is not a complete list of the wounded, or even of the dead, among the troopers. Moreover, a number of officers and men died from fever soon after the regiment was mustered out. Twenty-eight field and line officers landed in Cuba on June 22d; ten of them were killed or wounded during the nine days following. Of the five regiments of regular cavalry in the division, one, the Tenth, lost eleven officers; none of the others lost more than six. The loss of the Rough Riders in enlisted men was heavier than that of any other regiment in the cavalry division. Of the nine infantry regiments in Kent's division, one, the Sixth, lost eleven officers; none of the others as many as we did. None of the nine suffered as heavy a loss in enlisted men, as they were not engaged at Las Guasimas.

No other regiment in the Spanish-American War suffered as heavy a loss as the First United States Volunteer Cavalry.

COLONEL ROOSEVELT'S REPORT
TO THE SECRETARY OF WAR
OF SEPTEMBER 10TH

[Before it was sent, this letter was read to and approved by every officer of the regiment who had served through the Santiago campaign.]

[Copy.]

Camp Wikoff, September 10, 1898.

TO THE SECRETARY OF WAR.

SIR: In answer to the circular issued by command of Major-General Shafter under date of September 8, 1898, containing a request for information by the Adjutant-General of September 7th, I have the honor to report as follows:

I am a little in doubt whether the fact that on certain occasions my regiment suffered for food, etc., should be put down to an actual shortage of supplies or to general defects in the system of administration. Thus, when the regiment arrived in Tampa after a four days' journey by cars from its camp at San Antonio, it received no food whatever for twenty-four hours, and as the travel rations had been completely exhausted, food for several of the troops was purchased by their officers, who, of course, have not been reimbursed by the Government. In the same way we were short one or two meals at the time of embarking at Port Tampa on the transport; but this I think was due, not to a failure in the quantity of supplies, but to the lack of system in embarkation.

As with the other regiments, no information was given in advance what transports we should take, or how we should proceed to get aboard, nor did anyone exercise any supervision over the embarkation. Each regimental commander, so far as I know, was left to find out as best he could, after he was down at the dock, what transport had not been taken, and then to get his regiment aboard it, if he was able, before some other regiment got it. Our regiment was told to go to a certain switch, and take a train for Port Tampa at twelve o'clock, midnight. The train never came. After three hours of waiting we were sent to another switch, and finally at six o'clock in the morning got possession of some coal-cars and came down in them. When we reached the quay where the embarkation was proceeding, everything was in utter confusion. The quay was piled with stores and swarming with thousands of men of different regiments, besides onlookers, etc. The commanding General, when we at last found him, told Colonel Wood and myself that he did not know what ship we were to embark on, and that we must find Colonel Humphrey, the Quartermaster-General. Colonel Humphrey was not in his office, and nobody knew where he was. The commanders of the different regiments were busy trying to find him, while their troops waited in the trains, so as to discover the ships to which they were allotted—some of these ships being at the dock and some in mid-stream. After a couple of hours' search, Colonel Wood found Colonel Humphrey and was allotted a ship. Immediately afterward I found that it had already been allotted to two other regiments. It was then coming to the dock. Colonel Wood boarded it in midstream to keep possession, while I double-quicked the men down from the cars and got there just ahead of the other two regiments. One of these regiments, I was afterward informed, spent the next thirty-six hours in cars in consequence. We suffered nothing beyond the loss of a couple of meals, which, it seems to me, can hardly be put down to any failure in the quantity of supplies furnished to the troops.

We were two weeks on the troop-ship Yucatan, and as we were given twelve days' travel rations, we of course fell short toward the end of the trip, but eked things out with some of our field rations and troop stuff. The quality of the travel rations given to us was good, except in the important item of meat. The canned roast beef is worse than a failure as part of the rations, for in effect it amounts to reducing the rations by just so much, as a great majority of the men find it un-eatable. It was coarse, stringy, tasteless, and very disagreeable in ap-pearance, and so unpalatable that the effort to eat it made some of the men sick. Most of the men preferred to be hungry rather than eat it. If cooked in a stew with plenty of onions and potatoes—i.e., if only one ingredient in a dish with other more savory ingredients—it could be eaten, especially if well salted and peppered; but, as usual (what I re-gard as a great mistake), no salt was issued with the travel rations, and of course no potatoes and onions. There were no cooking facilities on the transport. When the men obtained any, it was by bribing the cook. Toward the last, when they began to draw on the field rations, they had to eat the bacon raw. On the return trip the same difficulty in rations obtained—i.e., the rations were short because the men could not eat the canned roast beef, and had no salt. We purchased of the ship's sup-plies some flour and pork and a little rice for the men, so as to relieve the shortage as much as possible, and individual sick men were helped from private sources by officers, who themselves ate what they had purchased in Santiago. As nine-tenths of the men were more or less sick, the unattractiveness of the travel rations was doubly unfortunate. It would have been an excellent thing for their health if we could have had onions and potatoes, and means for cooking them. Moreover, the water was very bad, and sometimes a cask was struck that was positively undrinkable. The lack of ice for the weak and sickly men was very much felt. Fortunately there was no epidemic, for there was not a place on the ship where patients could have been isolated.

During the month following the landing of the army in Cuba the food-supplies were generally short in quantity, and in quality were never such as were best suited to men undergoing severe hardships and great exposure in an unhealthy tropical climate. The rations were, I understand, the same as those used in the Klondike. In this connection, I call especial attention to the report of Captain Brown, made by my orders when I was Brigade-Commander, and herewith appended. I also call attention to the report of my own Quartermaster. Usually we re-ceived full rations of bacon and hardtack. The hardtack, however, was often mouldy, so that parts of cases, and even whole cases, could not be used. The bacon was usually good. But bacon and hardtack make poor food for men toiling and fighting in trenches under the mid-summer sun of the tropics. The ration of coffee was often short, and that of sugar generally so; we rarely got any vegetables. Under these circumstances the men lost strength steadily, and as the fever speedily attacked them, they suffered from being reduced to a bacon and hardtack diet. So much did the shortage of proper food tell upon their health that again and again officers were compelled to draw upon their private purses, or upon the Red Cross Society, to make good the deficiency of the Government supply. Again and again we sent down improvised pack-trains composed of officers' horses, of captured Spanish cavalry ponies, or of mules which had been shot or abandoned but were cured by our men. These expeditions—sometimes under the Chaplain, sometimes under the Quartermaster, sometimes under myself, and occasionally under a trooper—would go to the sea-coast or to the Red Cross head-quarters, or, after the surrender, into the city of Santiago, to get food both for the well and the sick. The Red Cross Society rendered invaluable aid. For example, on one of these expeditions I personally brought up 600 pounds of beans; on another occasion I personally brought up 500 pounds of rice, 800 pounds of cornmeal, 200 pounds of sugar, 100 pounds of tea, 100 pounds of oatmeal, 5 barrels of potatoes, and two of onions, with cases of canned soup and condensed milk for the sick in hospitals. Every scrap of the food thus brought up was eaten with avidity by the soldiers, and put new heart and strength into them. It was only our constant care of the men in this way that enabled us to keep them in any trim at all. As for the sick in the hospital, unless we were able from outside sources to get them such simple delicacies as rice and condensed milk, they usually had the alternative of eating salt pork and hardtack or going without. After each fight we got a good deal of food from the Spanish camps in the way of beans, peas, and rice, together with green coffee, all of which the men used and relished greatly. In some respects the Spanish rations were preferable to ours, notably in the use of rice. After we had been ashore a month the supplies began to come in in abundance, and we then fared very well. Up to that time the men were under-fed, during the very weeks when the heaviest drain was being made upon their vitality, and the deficiency was only partially supplied through the aid of the Red Cross, and out of the officers' pockets and the pockets of various New York friends who sent us money. Before, during, and immediately after the fights of June 24th and July 1st, we were very short of even the bacon and hardtack. About July 14th, when the heavy rains interrupted communication, we were threatened with famine, as we were informed that there was not a day's supply of provisions in advance nearer than the sea-coast; and another twenty-four hours' rain would have resulted in a complete break-down of communications, so that for several days we should have been reduced to a diet of mule-meat and mangos. At this time, in anticipation of such a contingency, by foraging and hoarding we got a little ahead, so that when our supplies were cut down for a day or two we did not suffer much, and were even able to furnish a little aid to the less fortunate First Illinois Regiment, which was camped next to us. Members of the Illinois Regiment were offering our men $1 apiece for hardtacks.

I wish to bear testimony to the energy and capacity of Colonel Weston, the Commissary-General with the expedition. If it had not been for his active aid, we should have fared worse than we did. All that he could do for us, he most cheerfully did.

As regards the clothing, I have to say: As to the first issue, the blue shirts were excellent of their kind, but altogether too hot for Cuba. They are just what I used to wear in Montana. The leggings were good; the shoes were very good; the undershirts not very good, and the drawers bad—being of heavy, thick canton flannel, difficult to wash, and entirely unfit for a tropical climate. The trousers were poor, wearing badly. We did not get any other clothing until we were just about to leave Cuba, by which time most of the men were in tatters; some being actually barefooted, while others were in rags, or dressed partly in clothes captured from the Spaniards, who were much more suitably clothed for the climate and place than we were. The ponchos were poor, being inferior to the Spanish rain-coats which we captured.

As to the medical matters, I invite your attention, not only to the report of Dr. Church accompanying this letter, but to the letters of Captain Llewellen, Captain Day, and Lieutenant McIlhenny. I could readily produce a hundred letters on the lines of the last three. In actual medical supplies, we had plenty of quinine and cathartics. We were apt to be short on other medicines, and we had nothing whatever in the way of proper nourishing food for our sick and wounded men during most of the time, except what we were able to get from the Red Cross or purchase with our own money. We had no hospital tent at all until I was able to get a couple of tarpaulins. During much of the time my own fly was used for the purpose. We had no cots until by individual effort we obtained a few, only three or four days before we left Cuba. During most of the time the sick men lay on the muddy ground in blankets, if they had any; if not, they lay without them until some of the well men cut their own blankets in half. Our regimental surgeon very soon left us, and Dr. Church, who was repeatedly taken down with the fever, was left alone—save as he was helped by men detailed from among the troopers. Both he and the men thus detailed, together with the regular hospital attendants, did work of incalculable service. We had no ambulance with the regiment. On the battlefield our wounded were generally sent to the rear in mule-wagons, or on litters which were improvised. At other times we would hire the little springless Cuban carts. But of course the wounded suffered greatly in such conveyances, and more-over, often we could not get a wheeled vehicle of any kind to transport even the most serious cases. On the day of the big fight, July 1st, as far as we could find out, there were but two ambulances with the army in condition to work—neither of which did we ever see. Later there were, as we were informed, thirteen all told; and occasionally after the sur-render, by vigorous representations and requests, we would get one as-signed to take some peculiarly bad cases to the hospital. Ordinarily, however, we had to do with one of the makeshifts enumerated above. On several occasions I visited the big hospitals in the rear. Their condi-tion was frightful beyond description from lack of supplies, lack of medicine, lack of doctors, nurses, and attendants, and especially from lack of transportation. The wounded and sick who were sent back suf-fered so much that, whenever possible, they returned to the front. Fi-nally my brigade commander, General Wood, ordered, with my hearty acquiescence, that only in the direst need should any men be sent to the rear—no matter what our hospital accommodations at the front might be. The men themselves preferred to suffer almost anything lying alone in their little shelter-tents, rather than go back to the hospitals in the rear. I invite attention to the accompanying letter of Captain Llewellen in relation to the dreadful condition of the wounded on some of the transports taking them North.

The greatest trouble we had was with the lack of transportation. Under the order issued by direction of General Miles through the Ad-jutant-General on or about May 8th, a regiment serving as infantry in the field was entitled to twenty-five wagons. We often had one, often none, sometimes two, and never as many as three. We had a regimental pack-train, but it was left behind at Tampa. During most of the time our means of transportation were chiefly the improvised pack-trains spoken of above; but as the mules got well they were taken away from us, and so were the captured Spanish cavalry horses. Whenever we shifted camp, we had to leave most of our things behind, so that the night before each fight was marked by our sleeping without tentage and with very little food, so far as officers were concerned, as everything had to be sacrificed to getting up what ammunition and medical supplies we had. Colonel Wood seized some mules, and in this manner got up the medical supplies before the fight of June 24th, when for three days the officers had nothing but what they wore. There was a repetition of this, only in worse form, before and after the fight of July 1st. Of course much of this was simply a natural incident of war, but a great deal could readily have been avoided if we had had enough transportation; and I was sorry not to let my men be as comfortable as possible and rest as much as possible just before going into a fight when, as on July 1st and 2d, they might have to be forty-eight hours with the minimum quantity of food and sleep. The fever began to make heavy ravages among our men just before the surrender, and from that time on it became a most serious matter to shift camp, with sick and ailing soldiers, hardly able to walk—not to speak of carrying heavy burdens—when we had no transportation. Not more than half of the men could carry their rolls, and yet these, with the officers' baggage and provisions, the entire hospital and its appurtenances, etc., had to be transported somehow. It was usually about three days after we reached a new camp before the necessaries which had been left behind could be brought up, and during these three days we had to get along as best we could. The entire lack of transportation at first resulted in leaving most of the troop mess-kits on the beach, and we were never able to get them. The men cooked in the few utensils they could themselves carry. This rendered it impossible to boil the drinking water. Closely allied to the lack of transportation was the lack of means to land supplies from the transports.

In my opinion, the deficiency in transportation was the worst evil with which we had to contend, serious though some of the others were. I have never served before, so have no means of comparing this with previous campaigns. I was often told by officers who had seen service against the Indians that, relatively to the size of the army, and the character of the country, we had only a small fraction of the transportation always used in the Indian campaigns. As far as my regiment was concerned, we certainly did not have one-third of the amount absolutely necessary, if it was to be kept in fair condition, and we had to partially make good the deficiency by the most energetic resort to all kinds of makeshifts and expedients.

YOURS RESPECTFULLY,
(Signed) THEODORE ROOSEVELT,
COLONEL FIRST UNITED STATES CAVALRY.

Forwarded through military channels.
(5 enclosures.)

First Endorsement.
Head-quarters Fifth Army Corps.
Camp Wikoff, September 18, 1898.

Respectfully forwarded to the Adjutant-General of the Army.

(Signed) WILLIAM R. SHAFTER,
MAJOR-GENERAL COMMANDING.

THE "ROUND ROBIN" LETTER

[The following is the report of the Associated Press correspondent of the "round-robin" incident. It is literally true in every detail. I was present when he was handed both letters; he was present while they were being written.]

SANTIAGO DE CUBA, August 3d (delayed in transmission).—Summoned by Major-General Shafter, a meeting was held here this morning at head-quarters, and in the presence of every commanding and medical officer of the Fifth Army Corps, General Shafter read a cable message from Secretary Alger, ordering him, on the recommendation of Surgeon-General Sternberg, to move the army into the interior, to San Luis, where it is healthier.

As a result of the conference General Shafter will insist upon the immediate withdrawal of the army North.

As an explanation of the situation the following letter from Colonel Theodore Roosevelt, commanding the First Cavalry, to General Shafter, was handed by the latter to the correspondent of The Associated Press for publication:

MAJOR-GENERAL SHAFTER.

SIR: In a meeting of the general and medical officers called by you at the Palace this morning we were all, as you know, unanimous in our views of what should be done with the army. To keep us here, in the opinion of every officer commanding a division or a brigade, will simply involve the destruction of thousands. There is no possible reason for not shipping practically the entire command North at once.

Yellow-fever cases are very few in the cavalry division, where I command one of the two brigades, and not one true case of yellow fever has occurred in this division, except among the men sent to the hospital at Siboney, where they have, I believe, contracted it.

But in this division there have been 1,500 cases of malarial fever. Hardly a man has yet died from it, but the whole command is so weakened and shattered as to be ripe for dying like rotten sheep, when a real yellow-fever epidemic instead of a fake epidemic, like the present one, strikes us, as it is bound to do if we stay here at the height of the sickness season, August and the beginning of September. Quarantine against malarial fever is much like quarantining against the toothache.

All of us are certain that as soon as the authorities at Washington fully appreciate the condition of the army, we shall be sent home. If we are kept here it will in all human possibility mean an appalling disaster, for the surgeons here estimate that over half the army, if kept here during the sickly season, will die.

This is not only terrible from the stand-point of the individual lives lost, but it means ruin from the standpoint of military efficiency of the flower of the American army, for the great bulk of the regulars are here with you. The sick list, large though it is, exceeding four thousand, affords but a faint index of the debilitation of the army. Not twenty per cent. are fit for active work.

Six weeks on the North Maine coast, for instance, or elsewhere where the yellow-fever germ cannot possibly propagate, would make us all as fit as fighting-cocks, as able as we are eager to take a leading part in the great campaign against Havana in the fall, even if we are not allowed to try Porto Rico.

We can be moved North, if moved at once, with absolute safety to the country, although, of course, it would have been infinitely better if we had been moved North or to Porto Rico two weeks ago. If there were any object in keeping us here, we would face yellow fever with as much indifference as we faced bullets. But there is no object.

The four immune regiments ordered here are sufficient to garrison the city and surrounding towns, and there is absolutely nothing for us to do here, and there has not been since the city surrendered. It is impossible to move into the interior. Every shifting of camp doubles the sick-rate in our present weakened condition, and, anyhow, the interior is rather worse than the coast, as I have found by actual reconnoissance. Our present camps are as healthy as any camps at this end of the island can be.

I write only because I cannot see our men, who have fought so bravely and who have endured extreme hardship and danger so uncomplainingly, go to destruction without striving so far as lies in me to avert a doom as fearful as it is unnecessary and undeserved.

YOURS RESPECTFULLY,
THEODORE ROOSEVELT,
COLONEL COMMANDING SECOND CAVALRY BRIGADE.

———

After Colonel Roosevelt had taken the initiative, all the American general officers united in a "round robin" addressed to General Shafter. It reads:

We, the undersigned officers commanding the various brigades, divisions, etc., of the Army of Occupation in Cuba, are of the unanimous opinion that this army should be at once taken out of the island of Cuba and sent to some point on the Northern sea-coast of the United States; that can be done without danger to the people of the United States; that yellow fever in the army at present is not epidemic; that there are only a few sporadic cases; but that the army is disabled by malarial fever to the extent that its efficiency is destroyed, and that it is in a condition to be practically entirely destroyed by an epidemic of yellow fever, which is sure to come in the near future.

We know from the reports of competent officers and from personal observations that the army is unable to move into the interior, and that there are no facilities for such a move if attempted, and that it could not be attempted until too late. Moreover, the best medical authorities of the island say that with our present equipment we could not live in the interior during the rainy season without losses from malarial fever, which is almost as deadly as yellow fever.

This army must be moved at once, or perish. As the army can be safely moved now, the persons responsible for preventing such a move will be responsible for the unnecessary loss of many thousands of lives.

Our opinions are the result of careful personal observation, and they are also based on the unanimous opinion of our medical officers with the army, who understand the situation absolutely.

J. FORD KENT,
MAJOR-GENERAL VOLUNTEERS COMMANDING
FIRST DIVISION, FIFTH CORPS.

J. C. BATES,
MAJOR-GENERAL VOLUNTEERS COMMANDING
PROVISIONAL DIVISION.

ADNAH R. CHAFFEE,
MAJOR-GENERAL COMMANDING THIRD BRIGADE, SECOND DIVISION.

SAMUEL S. SUMMER,
BRIGADIER-GENERAL VOLUNTEERS COMMANDING
FIRST BRIGADE, CAVALRY.

WILL LUDLOW,
BRIGADIER-GENERAL VOLUNTEERS COMMANDING
FIRST BRIGADE, SECOND DIVISION.

ADELBERT AMES,
BRIGADIER-GENERAL VOLUNTEERS COMMANDING
THIRD BRIGADE, FIRST DIVISION

LEONARD WOOD,
BRIGADIER-GENERAL VOLUNTEERS COMMANDING
THE CITY OF SANTIAGO.

THEODORE ROOSEVELT,
COLONEL COMMANDING SECOND CAVALRY BRIGADE.

———

Major M. W. Wood, the chief Surgeon of the First Division, said: "The army must be moved North," adding, with emphasis, "or it will be unable to move itself."

General Ames has sent the following cable message to Washington:

CHARLES H. ALLEN,
ASSISTANT SECRETARY OF THE NAVY:

This army is incapable, because of sickness, of marching anywhere except to the transports. If it is ever to return to the United States it must do so at once.

APPENDIX D

CORRECTIONS

It has been suggested to me that when Bucky O'Neill spoke of the vultures tearing our dead, he was thinking of no modern poet, but of the words of the prophet Ezekiel: "Speak unto every feathered fowl...ye shall eat the flesh of the mighty and drink the blood of the princes of the earth."

At San Juan the Sixth Cavalry was under Major Lebo, a tried and gallant officer. I learn from a letter of Lieutenant McNamee that it was he, and not Lieutenant Hartwick, by whose orders the troopers of the Ninth cast down the fence to enable me to ride my horse into the lane. But one of the two lieutenants of B troop was overcome by the heat that day; Lieutenant Rynning was with his troop until dark.

One night during the siege, when we were digging trenches, a curious stampede occurred (not in my own regiment) which it may be necessary some time to relate.

Lieutenants W. E. Shipp and W. H. Smith were killed, not far from each other, while gallantly leading their troops on the slope of Kettle Hill. Each left a widow and young children.

Captain (now Colonel) A. L. Mills, the Brigade Adjutant-General, has written me some comments on my account of the fight on July

1st. It was he himself who first brought me word to advance. I then met Colonel Dorst—who bore the same message—as I was getting the regiment forward. Captain Mills was one of the officers I had sent back to get orders that would permit me to advance; he met General Sumner, who gave him the orders, and he then returned to me. In a letter to me Colonel Mills says in part:

> I reached the head of the regiment as you came out of the lane and gave you the orders to enter the action. These were that you were to move, with your right resting along the wire fence of the lane, to the support of the regular cavalry then attacking the hill we were facing. "The red-roofed house yonder is your objective," I said to you. You moved out at once and quickly forged to the front of your regiment. I rode in rear, keeping the soldiers and troops closed and in line as well as the circumstances and conditions permitted. We had covered, I judge, from one-half to two-thirds the distance to Kettle Hill when Lieutenant-Colonel Garlington, from our left flank, called to me that troops were needed in the meadow across the lane. I put one troop (not three, as stated in your account*) across the lane and went with it. Advancing with the troop, I began immediately to pick up troopers of the Ninth Cavalry who had drifted from their commands, and soon had so many they demanded nearly all my attention. With a line thus made up, the colored troopers on the left and yours on the right, the portion of Kettle Hill on the right of the red-roofed house was first carried. I very shortly thereafter had a strong firing-line established on the crest nearest the enemy, from the corner of the fence around the house to the low ground on the right of the hill, which fired into the strong line of conical straw hats, whose brims showed just above the edge of the Spanish trench directly west of that part of the hill.[†] These hats made a fine target! I had placed a young officer of your regiment in charge of the portion of the line on top of the hill, and was about to go to the left to keep the connection of the brigade—Captain McBlain, Ninth Cavalry, just then came up on the hill from the left and rear—when the shot struck that put me out of the fight.

---

* The other two must have followed on their own initiative.
[†] These were the Spaniards in the trenches we carried when we charged from Kettle Hill, after the infantry had taken the San Juan block-house.

There were many wholly erroneous accounts of the Guasimas fight published at the time, for the most part written by newspapermen who were in the rear and utterly ignorant of what really occurred. Most of these accounts possess a value so purely ephemeral as to need no notice. Mr. Stephen Bonsal, however, in his book, "The Fight for Santiago," has cast one of them in a more permanent form; and I shall discuss one or two of his statements.

Mr. Bonsal was not present at the fight, and, indeed, so far as I know, he never at any time was with the cavalry in action. He puts in his book a map of the supposed skirmish ground; but it bears to the actual scene of the fight only the well-known likeness borne by Monmouth to Macedon. There was a brook on the battle-ground, and there is a brook in Mr. Bonsal's map. The real brook, flowing down from the mountains, crossed the valley road and ran down between it and the hill-trail, going nowhere near the latter. The Bonsal brook flows at right angles to the course of the real brook and crosses both trails—that is, it runs up hill. It is difficult to believe that the Bonsal map could have been made by any man who had gone over the hill-trail followed by the Rough Riders and who knew where the fighting had taken place. The position of the Spanish line on the Bonsal map is inverted compared to what it really was.

On page 90 Mr. Bonsal says that in making the "precipitate advance" there was a rivalry between the regulars and Rough Riders, which resulted in each hurrying recklessly forward to strike the Spaniards first. On the contrary. The official reports show that General Young's column waited for some time after it got to the Spanish position, so as to allow the Rough Riders (who had the more difficult trail) to come up. Colonel Wood kept his column walking at a smart pace, merely so that the regulars might not be left unsupported when the fight began; and as a matter of fact, it began almost simultaneously on both wings.

On page 91 Mr. Bonsal speaks of "The foolhardy formation of a solid column along a narrow trail, which brought them (the Rough Riders)...within point-blank range of the Spanish rifles and within the unobstructed sweep of their machine-guns." He also speaks as if the advance should have been made with the regiment deployed through the jungle. Of course, the only possible way by which the Rough Riders could have been brought into action in time to support the regulars was by advancing in column along the trail at a good smart gait. As soon as our advance-guard came into contact with the enemy's outpost we deployed. No firing began for at least five minutes after Captain Capron sent back word that he had come upon the Spanish outpost. At the particular point where this occurred there was a dip in the road, which probably rendered it, in Capron's opinion, better to keep part of his men in it. In any event, Captain Capron, who was as skilful as he was gallant, had ample time between discovering the Spanish outpost and the outbreak of the firing to arrange his troop in the formation he deemed best. His troop was not in solid formation; his men were about ten yards apart. Of course, to have walked forward deployed through the jungle, prior to reaching the ground where we were to fight, would have been a course of procedure so foolish as to warrant the summary court-martial of any man directing it. We could not have made half a mile an hour in such a formation, and would have been at least four hours too late for the fighting.

On page 92 Mr. Bonsal says that Captain Capron's troop was ambushed, and that it received the enemy's fire a quarter of an hour before it was expected. This is simply not so. Before the column stopped we had passed a dead Cuban, killed in the preceding day's skirmish, and General Wood had notified me on information he had received from Capron that we might come into contact with the Spaniards at any moment, and, as I have already said, Captain Capron discovered the Spanish outpost, and we halted and partially deployed the column before the firing began. We were at the time exactly where we had expected to come across the Spaniards. Mr. Bonsal, after speaking of L Troop, adds: "The remaining troops of the regiment had travelled more leisurely, and more than half an hour elapsed before they came up to Capron's support." As a matter of fact, all the troops travelled at exactly the same rate of speed, although there were stragglers from each, and when Capron halted and sent back word that he had come upon the Spanish out-post, the entire regiment closed up, halted, and most of the men sat down. We then, some minutes after the first word had been re-ceived, and before any firing had begun, received instructions to deploy. I had my right wing partially deployed before the first shots between the outposts took place. Within less than three minutes I had G Troop, with Llewellen, Greenway, and Leahy, and one pla-toon of K Troop under Kane, on the firing-line, and it was not until after we reached the firing-line that the heavy volley-firing from the Spaniards began.

On page 94 Mr. Bonsal says: "A vexatious delay occurred before the two independent columns could communicate and advance with concerted action.... When the two columns were brought into communication it was immediately decided to make a general at-tack upon the Spanish position.... With this purpose in view, the following disposition of the troops was made before the advance of the brigade all along the line was ordered." There was no commu-nication between the two columns prior to the general attack, nor was any order issued for the advance of the brigade all along the line. The attacks were made wholly independently, and the first communication between the columns was when the right wing of the Rough Riders in the course of their advance by their firing dis-lodged the Spaniards from the hill across the ravine to the right, and then saw the regulars come up that hill.

Mr. Bonsal's account of what occurred among the regulars par-allels his account of what occurred among the Rough Riders. He states that the squadron of the Tenth Cavalry delivered the main attack upon the hill, which was the strongest point of the Spanish position; and he says of the troopers of the Tenth Cavalry that "their better training enabled them to render more valuable service than the other troops engaged." In reality, the Tenth Cavalrymen were deployed in support of the First, though they mingled with them in the assault proper; and so far as there was any difference at all in the amount of work done, it was in favor of the First. The statement that the Tenth Cavalry was better trained than the First, and rendered more valuable service, has not the slightest basis

whatsoever of any kind, sort, or description, in fact. The Tenth
Cavalry did well what it was required to do; as an organization, in
this fight, it was rather less heavily engaged, and suffered less loss,
actually and relatively, than either the First Cavalry or the Rough
Riders. It took about the same part that was taken by the left wing
of the Rough Riders, which wing was similarly rather less heavily
engaged than the right and centre of the regiment. Of course, this
is a reflection neither on the Tenth Cavalry nor on the left wing of
the Rough Riders. Each body simply did what it was ordered to do,
and did it well. But to claim that the Tenth Cavalry did better than
the First, or bore the most prominent part in the fight, is like making the same claim for the left wing of the Rough Riders. All the
troops engaged did well, and all alike are entitled to share in the
honor of the day.

Mr. Bonsal out-Spaniards the Spaniards themselves as regards
both their numbers and their loss. These points are discussed elsewhere. He develops for the Spanish side, to account for their retreat, a wholly new explanation—viz., that they retreated because
they saw reinforcements arriving for the Americans. The Spaniards
themselves make no such claim. Lieutenant Tejeiro asserts that
they retreated because news had come of a (wholly mythical)
American advance on Morro Castle. The Spanish official report
simply says that the Americans were repulsed; which is about as ac-
curate a statement as the other two. All three explanations, those by
General Rubin, by Lieutenant Tejeiro, and by Mr. Bonsal alike, are
precisely on a par with the first Spanish official report of the battle of Manila Bay, in which Admiral Dewey was described as having been repulsed and forced to retire.

There are one or two minor mistakes made by Mr. Bonsal. He
states that on the roster of the officers of the Rough Riders there
were ten West Pointers. There were three, one of whom resigned.
Only two were in the fighting. He also states that after Las Guasimas Brigadier-General Young was made a Major-General and
Colonel Wood a Brigadier-General, while the commanding officers of the First and Tenth Cavalry were ignored in this "shower
of promotions." In the first place, the commanding officers of the

First and Tenth Cavalry were not in the fight—only one squadron of each having been present. In the next place, there was no "shower of promotions" at all. Nobody was promoted except General Young, save to fill the vacancies caused by death or by the promotion of General Young. Wood was not promoted because of this fight. General Young most deservedly was promoted. Soon after the fight he fell sick. The command of the brigade then fell upon Wood, simply because he had higher rank than the other two regimental commanders of the brigade; and I then took command of the regiment exactly as Lieutenant-Colonels Viele and Baldwin had already taken command of the First and Tenth Cavalry when their superior officers were put in charge of brigades. After the San Juan fighting, in which Wood commanded a brigade, he was made a Brigadier-General and I was then promoted to the nominal command of the regiment, which I was already commanding in reality.

Mr. Bonsal's claim of superior efficiency for the colored regular regiments as compared with the white regular regiments does not merit discussion. He asserts that General Wheeler brought on the Guasimas fight in defiance of orders. Lieutenant Miley, in his book, "In Cuba with Shafter," on page 83, shows that General Wheeler made his fight before receiving the order which it is claimed he disobeyed. General Wheeler was in command ashore; he was told to get in touch with the enemy, and, being a man with the "fighting edge," this meant that he was certain to fight. No general who was worth his salt would have failed to fight under such conditions; the only question would be as to how the fight was to be made. War means fighting; and the soldier's cardinal sin is timidity.

General Wheeler remained throughout steadfast against any retreat from before Santiago. But the merit of keeping the army before Santiago, without withdrawal, until the city fell, belongs to the authorities at Washington, who at this all-important stage of the operations showed to marked advantage in overruling the proposals made by the highest generals in the field looking toward partial retreat or toward the abandonment of the effort to take the city.

The following note, written by Sergeant E. G. Norton, of B Troop, refers to the death of his brother, Oliver B. Norton, one of the most gallant and soldierly men in the regiment:

> On July 1st I, together with Sergeant Campbell and Troopers Bardshar and Dudley Dean and my brother who was killed and some others, was at the front of the column right behind you. We moved forward, following you as you rode, to where we came upon the troopers of the Ninth Cavalry and a part of the First lying down. I heard the conversation between you and one or two of the officers of the Ninth Cavalry. You ordered a charge, and the regular officers answered that they had no orders to move ahead; whereupon you said: "Then let us through," and marched forward through the lines, our regiment following. The men of the Ninth and First Cavalry then jumped up and came forward with us. Then you waved your hat and gave the command to charge and we went up the hill. On the top of Kettle Hill my brother, Oliver B. Norton, was shot through the head and in the right wrist. It was just as you started to lead the charge on the San Juan hills ahead of us; we saw that the regiment did not know you had gone and were not following, and my brother said, "For God's sake follow the Colonel," and as he rose the bullet went through his head.

In reference to Mr. Bonsal's account of the Guasimas fight, Mr. Richard Harding Davis writes me as follows:

> We had already halted several times to give the men a chance to rest, and when we halted for the last time I thought it was for this same purpose, and began taking photographs of the men of L Troop, who were so near that they asked me to be sure and save them a photograph. Wood had twice disappeared down the trail beyond them and returned. As he came back for the second time I remember that you walked up to him (we were all dismounted then), and saluted and said: "Colonel, Doctor La Motte reports that the pace is too fast for the men, and that over fifty have fallen out from exhaustion." Wood replied sharply: "I have no time to bother with sick men now." You replied, more in answer, I suppose, to his tone than to his words: "I merely repeated what

the Surgeon reported to me." Wood then turned and said in explanation: "I have no time for them now; I mean that we are in sight of the enemy."

This was the only information we received that the men of L Troop had been ambushed by the Spaniards, and, if they were, they were very calm about it, and I certainly was taking photographs of them at the time, and the rest of the regiment, instead of being half an hour's march away, was seated comfortably along the trail not twenty feet distant from the men of L Troop. You deployed G Troop under Captain Llewellen into the jungle at the right and sent K Troop after it, and Wood ordered Troops E and F into the field on our left. It must have been from ten to fifteen minutes after Capron and Wood had located the Spaniards before either side fired a shot. When the firing did come I went over to you and joined G Troop and a detachment of K Troop under Woodbury Kane, and we located more of the enemy on a ridge.

If it is to be ambushed when you find the enemy exactly where you went to find him, and your scouts see him soon enough to give you sufficient time to spread five troops in skirmish order to attack him, and you then drive him back out of three positions for a mile and a half, then most certainly, as Bonsal says, "L Troop of the Rough Riders was ambushed by the Spaniards on the morning of June 24th."

———

General Wood also writes me at length about Mr. Bonsal's book, stating that his account of the Guasimas fight is without foundation in fact. He says: "We had five troops completely deployed before the first shot was fired. Captain Capron was not wounded until the fight had been going on fully thirty-five minutes. The statement that Captain Capron's troop was ambushed is absolutely untrue. We had been informed, as you know, by Castillo's people that we should find the dead guerilla a few hundred yards on the Siboney side of the Spanish lines."

He then alludes to the waving of the guidon by K Troop as "the only means of communication with the regulars." He mentions that his orders did not come from General Wheeler, and that he had no instructions from General Wheeler directly or indirectly at any time previous to the fight.

212 · Appendix D

General Wood does not think that I give quite enough credit to the Rough Riders as compared to the regulars in this Guasimas fight, and believes that I greatly underestimate the Spanish force and loss, and that Lieutenant Tejeiro is not to be trusted at all on these points. He states that we began the fight ten minutes before the regulars, and that the main attack was made and decided by us. This was the view that I and all the rest of us in the regiment took at the time; but as I had found since that the members of the First and Tenth Regular Regiments held with equal sincerity the view that the main part was taken by their own commands, I have come to the conclusion that the way I have described the action is substantially correct. Owing to the fact that the Tenth Cavalry, which was originally in support, moved forward until it got mixed with the First, it is very difficult to get the exact relative position of the different troops of the First and Tenth in making the advance. Beck and Galbraith were on the left; apparently Wainwright was farthest over on the right. General Wood states that Leonardo Ros, the Civil Governor of Santiago at the time of the surrender, told him that the Spanish force at Guasimas consisted of not less than 2,600 men, and that there were nearly 300 of them killed and wounded. I do not myself see how it was possible for us, as we were the attacking party and were advancing against superior numbers well sheltered, to inflict five times as much damage as we received; but as we buried eleven dead Spaniards, and as they carried off some of their dead, I believe the loss to have been very much heavier than Lieutenant Tejeiro reports.

General Wood believes that in following Lieutenant Tejeiro I have greatly underestimated the number of Spanish troops who were defending Santiago on July 1st, and here I think he completely makes out his case, he taking the view that Lieutenant Tejeiro's statements were made for the purpose of saving Spanish honor. On this point his letter runs as follows:

A word in regard to the number of troops in Santiago. I have had, during my long association here, a good many opportunities to get information which you have not got and probably never will get; that is, information from parties who were actually in the fight, who are now residents of the city; also information which came to me as commanding officer of the city directly after the surrender.

To sum up briefly as follows: The Spanish surrendered in Santiago 12,000 men. We shipped from Santiago something over 14,000 men. The 2,000 additional were troops that came in from San Luis, Songo, and small up-country posts. The 12,000 in the city, minus the force of General Iscario, 3,300 infantry and 680 cavalry, or in round numbers 4,000 men (who entered the city just after the battles of San Juan and El Caney), leaves 8,000 regulars, plus the dead, plus Cervera's marines and blue-jackets, which he himself admits landing in the neighborhood of 1,200 (and reports here are that he landed 1,380), and plus the Spanish Volunteer Battalion, which was between 800 and 900 men (this statement I have from the lieutenant-colonel of this very battalion), gives us in round numbers, present for duty on the morning of July 1st, not less than 10,500 men. These men were distributed 890 at Caney, two companies of artillery at Morro, one at Socapa, and half a company at Puenta Gorda; in all, not over 500 or 600 men, but for the sake of argument we can say a thousand. In round numbers, then, we had immediately about the city 8,500 troops. These were scattered from the cemetery around to Aguadores. In front of us, actually in the trenches, there could not by any possible method of figuring have been less than 6,000 men. You can twist it any way you want to; the figures I have given you are absolutely correct, at least they are absolutely on the side of safety.

———

It is difficult for me to withstand the temptation to tell what has befallen some of my men since the regiment disbanded; how McGinty, after spending some weeks in Roosevelt Hospital in New York with an attack of fever, determined to call upon his captain, Woodbury Kane, when he got out, and procuring a horse rode until he found Kane's house, when he hitched the horse to a lamp-post and strolled in; how Cherokee Bill married a wife in Hoboken, and as that pleasant city ultimately proved an uncongenial field for his activities, how I had to send both himself and his wife out to the Territory; how Happy Jack, haunted by visions of the social methods obtaining in the best saloons of Arizona, applied for the position of "bouncer out" at the Executive Chamber when I was elected Governor, and how I got him a job at railroading instead, and finally had to ship him back to his own Territory also; how a valued friend from a cow ranch in the remote West accepted a pressing invitation to spend a few days at the home of another ex-trooper, a New Yorker of fastidious instincts, and arrived with an umbrella as his only baggage; how poor Holderman and Pollock both died and were buried with military honors, all of Pollock's tribesmen coming to the burial; how Tom Isbell joined Buffalo Bill's Wild West Show, and how, on the other hand, George Row-land scornfully refused to remain in the East at all, writing to a gallant young New Yorker who had been his bunkie: "Well, old boy, I am glad I didnt go home with you for them people to look at, because I aint a Buffalo or a rhinoceros or a giraffe, and I dont like to be Stared at, and you know we didnt do no hard fighting down there. I have been in closer places than that right here in Yunited States, that is Better men to fight than them dam Spaniards." In another letter Rowland tells of the fate of Tom Darnell, the rider, he who rode the sorrel horse of the Third Cavalry: "There aint much news to write of except poor old Tom Darnell got killed about a month ago. Tom and another fellow had a fight and he shot Tom through the heart and Tom was dead when he hit the floor. Tom was sure a good old boy, and I sure hated to hear of him going, and he had plenty of grit too. No man ever called on him for a fight that he didn't get it."

———

My men were children of the dragon's blood, and if they had no outland foe to fight and no outlet for their vigorous and daring energy, there was always the chance of their fighting one another: but the great majority, if given the chance to do hard or dangerous work, availed themselves of it with the utmost eagerness, and though fever sickened and weakened them so that many died from it during the few months following their return, yet, as a whole, they are now doing fairly well. A few have shot other men or been shot themselves; a few ran for office and got elected, like Llewellen and Luna in New Mexico, or defeated, like Brodie and Wilcox in Arizona; some have been trying hard to get to the Philippines; some have returned to college, or to the law, or the factory, or the counting-room; most of them have gone back to the mine, the ranch, and the hunting camp; and the great majority have taken up the threads of their lives where they dropped them when the Maine was blown up and the country called to arms.

INDEX

A NOTE ON THE TYPE

The principal text of this Modern Library edition
was set in a digitized version of Janson,
a typeface that dates from about 1690 and was cut by Nicholas Kis,
a Hungarian working in Amsterdam. The original matrices have
survived and are held by the Stempel foundry in Germany.
Hermann Zapf redesigned some of the weights and sizes for Stempel,
basing his revisions on the original design.